Conferences & Conversations

Conferences & Conversations

LISTENING TO THE LITERATE CLASSROOM

Douglas Kaufman

AFTERWORD BY LINDA RIEF

HEINEMANN   Portsmouth, NH

Heinemann
A division of Reed Elsevier Inc.
361 Hanover Street
Portsmouth, NH 03801–3912
www.heinemann.com

Offices and agents throughout the world

Library of Congress Cataloging-in-Publication Data
Kaufman, Douglas, 1963–
    Conferences and conversations : listening to the literate classroom / Douglas Kaufman.
        p. cm.
    Includes bibliographical references.
    ISBN 0-325-00271-1 (alk. paper)
    1. Language arts.   2. English language—Composition and exercises—Study and teaching.
3. Teacher-student relationships.   4. Communication in education.   I. Title.
    LB1575 .K28   2000
    371.102′2—dc21

                                                                                      00-033503

Editor: Lois Bridges
Production: Sonja S. Chapman
Cover design: Cathy Hawkes, Cat & Mouse Design
Manufacturing: Deanna Richardson
Cover and interior photos: Andrew Edgar

Printed in the United States of America on acid-free paper
04   03   02   01   00   DA   1   2   3   4   5

To Jennifer, Rebecca, and Emily—my most loving conversationalists

Contents

PART 4   VERY DIFFERENT STUDENTS

PART 5   REFLECTIONS

Acknowledgments

To those who don't believe writing is a social event, try writing a book. The support, encouragement, and advice I received from colleagues, friends, and family helped grow and shape this book from its tiny conceptual seeds. I honor you all.

Jane Hansen guided me from the beginning, modeling the response we all should give.

Tom Newkirk offered his inquisitiveness and joy of pondering new perspectives. His courses on talk and pragmatism planted the seeds for this book.

When the act of writing seemed mean and forbidding, Don Graves got me unstuck with just the right comments.

My editor, Lois Bridges, always makes me wonder, "Can she be this encouraging, perceptive, and responsive to all her writers?" After reading the acknowledgements in *their* books, I know that she can. I thank her and all the people at Heinemann who create books we need to read. I'm grateful that they believe this is one of them.

Ann Diller, Tom Schram, and M. Cyrene Wells all read an early version of my manuscript, and Mary Anne Doyle and Judith Irwin read parts of a later draft. They pushed me to examine my writing critically without ever destroying my confidence.

Peter Johnston gave me insight into Linda Rief's previous incarnation as John Dewey.

Many students at Cleveland State University and the University of Connecticut read portions of this book and let me know what was important to new language arts teachers.

Lisa Lenz-Bianchi, Pat Wilson, Carol Hawkins, JoAnn Portalupi, Eleanor Abrams, Elizabeth Lane, Amy Smith, John Carney, Barbara Houston, Connie Israel, Paula Salvio, Kim Boothroyd, Kathy Staley, Andrea Luna, Cindy Cohen, Pat Sullivan, Terry Moher, Dale Wright, Julie Brooks-Pantano, Jane Kearns, Pam Mueller, Pat Bloem, Jerry Kelly, John Settlage, Kate Salvati, Bill Wansart, Dan Rothermel, Francisco Calvacante, and Carol Wilcox all shaped my knowledge and thinking. They are a special group of people, diverse in thinking but unified in their love of teaching and commitment to improving education.

For their friendship and support I thank the faculty and staff with whom I worked (and work) at the University of New Hampshire, Cleveland State University, and the University of Connecticut.

Thanks to my family, immediate and extended, who have been supportive, loving, and tolerant throughout. My wife, Jennifer, and my daughters, Rebecca and Emily, provide emotional sustenance always.

Thanks to the caring professionals at the Oyster River Middle School in Durham, New Hampshire, including Marcia Ross, Chris Pollett, Michelle McInnes, Susan Bissell, Mark Nichols, Beth Doran Healey, David Ervin, Donna DiPerri, Kip Deese-Laurent, Alice Hawkins, Jean Henry, and Mary Nazarro.

Special thanks to the students of Linda Rief's language arts classes, an insightful, reflective, passionate group of people. They were wonderful teachers.

And, finally, my gratitude to Linda Rief, an extraordinary and gracious teacher and learner. Her self-reflection, willingness to share, energy, and respect for the voices of her students honor all those with whom she works. Cheers to you, Linda.

1
—

Why Listen?

As a first year teacher I suffered a lot, trying to figure out just what it meant to *be* a teacher. Here is part of an entry from the journal I kept that year:

> JANUARY 14: So many ideas tear through my head, but to grasp one and exploit it and develop it before another obligation presents itself is almost impossible. I feel it will take years before I get everything right, and I'm so damn impatient! Now I just have to see enough inspiration in each day's events—through me, a student, or a piece of work—to keep me going and keep me proud.

It wasn't until later that I learned how valuable these written reflections were to my professional growth. By writing down my triumphs and (more often) my failures, I was able to go back and scrutinize my teaching and learning. Then I could capture some of those ideas tearing through my head and implement change.

Linda Rief

But it takes courage to open up our professional lives to scrutiny. Whether or not this scrutiny comes from an outside observer or from within, through self-reflection, we run the danger of exposing the warts of our classrooms along with the beauty. But it is exactly our willingness to lay out our instruction for others to see, to think carefully about what is happening in our classrooms, and to reflect on our own practice that helps us all to grow into better teachers.

Linda Rief, a language arts teacher at the Oyster River Middle School in Durham, New Hampshire, is one of those who take the risk. By sharing her teaching life with others and carefully evaluating her practices, triumphs, and failures on a daily basis, she has shown other teachers what it means to be a successful professional. She is acknowledged by many to be one of the best in her field (Johnston 1997; Graves 1990, 1994). Her first book, *Seeking Diversity: Language Arts with Adolescents* (1992), is one of the books (along with Nancie Atwell's *In the Middle*) that teachers most widely cite when they work to create their own language arts workshops.

I first became familiar with Linda and her work when I read *Seeking Diversity,* a book that highlights her conscious attempts to learn about her students, which was something I was trying hard to do with my own sixth-grade language arts students. A couple of years later I took her course on reading and writing instruction, which she teaches at the University of New Hampshire Summer Reading and Writing Program. Since *Seeking Diversity,* Linda has written another wonderful book, *Vision and Voice: Extending the Literacy Spectrum* (1999) and published articles in many professional journals. She has coedited *Workshop 6: The Teacher as Writer* (1994), *All that Matters: What Is It We Value in School and Beyond?* (1995), and the National Council of Teachers of English journal, *Voices from the Middle* (1994–1999).

In all her work rides the theme of learning and growing personally and professionally in ways that allow her to model the life of a learner for her students, provide them with outlets for expression, and respond effectively after learning their needs:

> [One] year my focus was on conferences. A professor taught me what not to do. "This is garbage," he said, throwing my master's thesis across the desk. With this comment all the constructive positive responses from the other four readers went right out of my head. I couldn't revise the paper for months. I carry that lesson with me every time I kneel down to talk with kids about their writing. What response helps the student learn best? Who gives that response? How can I best model constructive response? My first question to students has become, "How can I help you?" (1992, p. 3)

> We show our students we value them as individuals when we value their voices. And we hear their voices when we invite them to show us what they know and how they know that through their reading and writing. . . . We will hear the unique, honest, courageous voices of our students when they are allowed to show us what they think and know and feel. It is the kind of learning that matters. Listen to the voices that emerge when our students are reading and writing for life. (1994, p. 87)

I am an observer in my own classroom, jotting down what students say and do that intrigues me. (1994, p. 94)

The craft of teaching is inextricably tied to the craft of listening to our kids and acting on what they tell us. (1995, p. 9)

Indeed, while participating in her summer course, my colleagues and I were struck by the fact that we somehow spoke much more in class than did Linda. She *did* listen. When she spoke, she relayed back what she had learned about each of us in such a way that we could hear ourselves more clearly. Her careful listening and learning stance gave me new perspective on what it meant to be a teacher. "Why," I began to ask, "must the teacher always be in charge of the classroom's words?" This question gave rise to new concerns, not the least of which was, "But how does one create a classroom where students can share control of the talk and begin to use it to their advantage?"

In the Act of Learning

So, a few years later, when I decided to conduct research into what specific things a successful language arts teacher does that sets her apart from others—particularly in regard to how she converses with students and promotes their conversations with one another—my choice of a research participant was simple. I contacted Linda and she immediately welcomed me into her classroom for a year so that I could learn how she taught and talked. Her stated motive for inviting me highlights her learning stance and typifies the qualities that have led to her success: she did not think that she listened to her students well enough and she wanted to learn how she might become better. Linda Rief bravely welcomed the scrutiny.

I entered Linda's classroom as a participant observer, attending on the average of three to four days per week for a full school year. Watching and working with her and her students, I took extensive field notes, conducted surveys, collected thousands of pages of student writing and other documents, audiotaped and videotaped discussions and writing conferences, and interviewed Linda and her students countless times.

I believe my work in her class is valuable in that it shows parts of Linda's teaching world that she may not be able to show in her own books. Through her writing, Linda shows her readers her teaching vision, how she sets up her classes, and her success as evidenced by her students' consistently wonderful work. Now that I teach at a university, it has been interesting to listen to my students often ask about her books (and books by other practitioners), "This looks great, but what does she do to actually get there? More importantly, how can *I* get there? What are the obstacles?" They are worried that the success looks easy, and they are already learning that classroom teaching never is. They want to see a teacher in action, working through the same challenges they know they will inevitably face. They want to see struggles, along with triumphs, to reassure themselves that they are not alone in their confusion and trepidation. This book shows Linda and her students in the *acts* of talking, writing, reading, and learning—something hard for her to write about, immersed in these moments as she is. I felt validated when Linda read this manuscript. She commented that I had written, from my perspective as an observer, about interactions that offered her new, real insight into her own teaching—things she hadn't seen.

So, in the same way, I hope this book offers you new insight, standing as a testament to the complex nature of good teaching. As you read, I urge you to consider Linda's philosophy and practices in relation to your own. This book is a portrait of one master teacher, but I hope that it is also more than that. I certainly want to show how Linda Rief "does" teaching, so that we may use it as material for evolving our own work. But perhaps more importantly, I want to show the nature of Linda's learning stance—the practice of, and commitment to, carefully examining her beliefs and evaluating her activities in order to create a classroom that fits her and her students as individuals. After reading this book I hope that you will better be able to examine your *own* beliefs and activities, creating a classroom that is not formulaic—*not* a carbon copy of Linda Rief's—but that fits you and your newly clarified values. It takes a special teacher to open up his or her professional life to scrutiny. I hope this book offers you a sense of the real value in doing so.

2

Value Students' Voices

This book portrays an excellent teacher in action. Ultimately, it is about restructuring our language arts classrooms so that we all can communicate better, using meaningful conversations as the driving force behind the curriculum. It is for those of us who recognize the new challenges we face when we provide students with more time, choice, and response. We intellectually as well as intuitively understand the value of opening up the curriculum to a wider array of possibilities, offering more freedom and responsibility to our students. But in practice many of us have also encountered unexpected obstacles. While we champion giving students more voice in the classroom, we often have not considered the difficulty students may have in *finding* their voices or using their voices to grow academically. Our greater acceptance of students' voices might, in fact, undermine their learning if we do not determine how our roles as teachers shift to complement those voices. My own experience as a first year teacher illustrates the point.

My Experience

I entered my first sixth-grade language arts classroom with very little background. I envisioned a classroom where students wrote joyfully about their own topics, learned through experience in authentic situations, used one another as valuable resources, and took responsibility for their work. I wanted a classroom where students' voices were heard.

But I had little idea of how to create one. During the first tumultuous weeks of that first tumultuous year thoughts of my dream class evaporated as I desperately swam upstream to maintain a modicum of control. My journal

5

entries from the beginning of the year are a sad litany of self-pity, confusion, and blame:

> OCTOBER 1: Woe, woe, woe, I'm feeling sorry for myself. My classes were *shitty*. I wasn't prepared. I was very tired and short-fused. I bored the kids. I let them get to me. I'm falling behind and that worries me. I've got to prepare, but I've been so concerned with group dynamics that I've been slacking the academics. It just means more work for me. . . . Do more *activity-related* stuff with the kids!

But I had no idea how to do "activity-related stuff with the kids": how to establish safe boundaries for exploring, set up the physical classroom for easy student flow, or listen to what they said. My methodology was a hodgepodge of lesson plans borrowed from other teachers, many of whom had opposing educational philosophies. As my struggle for control intensified, my practices became more autocratic. By that October, my typical language arts class consisted of (*a*) a ten-question quiz to determine who had done the previous night's reading; (*b*) a discussion (i.e., a lecture by me) about the previous night's reading; (*c*) a whole-class read of the next chapter: "Student one, read the first paragraph please. Student two, read the next paragraph, please." To my credit, I felt humiliated and incompetent.

About halfway through the year, with an acute notion of what *didn't* work in my teaching, I began anew. A colleague lent me his copy of *In the Middle* by Nancie Atwell (1987). I gushed in my journal, "What a book! It touches on so many things that I want to do!" Over the next few days, I abandoned the busy work I had been assigning and began a writing workshop.

However, that beautifully efficient classroom and profound student writing in Atwell's book did not occur spontaneously, as I had hoped, or maybe even expected.

> DECEMBER 16: I started the new writing process today. Atwell says in her book that on the first day there has never been a student who didn't write.
> Trina didn't write.
> I knew she wouldn't. Thus beginneth the long, painful process. I must persist and stick to the program.

Students were wary, confused by the completely new approach thrust upon them. This new style also meant they would have to work harder, communicate better, and think more deeply. I, too, had trouble finding my new role. I alternated between ensuring chaos when I simply said to students, "Write or read what you want" without offering any modeling guidance and stifling my students' work as I compulsively monopolized the conversation during our writing conferences together. Most students resisted my earnest attempts at reform, and I received a lot of weak, diluted writing. But it *was* writing, and a far sight better than anything I had seen previously. As the year progressed I chalked my failures up to experience, consoling myself with my administrator's words: "Your first year of teaching you do not teach, you learn. Now get in there and learn."

I spent the following summer reading voraciously and learning more about teaching language arts. I planned out my classroom and ordered vast quantities of writing supplies, paper, and trade books. Much of the time I just sat and thought, visualizing how I wanted my classroom to run, dealing with imaginary problems that were sure to arise, trying to justify why I believed the things that I did.

Conditions, Not Formulas

The next year my classes ran more smoothly. My students, beginning the year with a coherent, consistent theme, felt comfortable in this literate world and produced some wonderful work. They were enthusiastic and inquisitive.

But I knew I still had not completely succeeded. Problems still nagged at me. For instance, as I sat down each day to confer with students about their writing, I found myself asking the same limited number of questions over and over again. "Why did you use the lead you did?" is one I remember. In response, students gave me stock answers that revealed little about their processes or interests. In essence, I had ritualized my instruction. I took what I had read and treated it as a formula, a step-by-step procedure for teaching reading and writing. It was easy to do. In fact, the commonly used term "process writing" unintentionally lends itself to the idea that there is indeed a single process by which students write and by which we can teach (Graves 1997). Today, several activity books for teachers depict writing as a set of step-by-step procedures.

However, the basis for this approach to literacy instruction is a philosophical stance that precedes and influences methodology (Bergeron 1990; Edelsky, Altwerger, and Flores 1991; Weaver 1994). This stance promotes students who learn through active experience, read and write through the context of meaningful language, focus on the process of creation as well as on the created product, interact socially, self-evaluate, and bring prior knowledge to their learning processes. But it does not promote any specific methodological formula. Donald Graves certainly did not conceive of Nancie Atwell's *In the Middle* as a book about formula:

> Readers looking for methods or step-by-step approaches to a sure-fire literacy program will be disappointed. Atwell has no method. Rather, she provides a full-immersion approach to reading and writing, an immersion not unlike the acquisition of a new language, where only the new language can

be spoken. There is relevant, literate talk in this room; there are no canned lessons, assigned topics, workbooks, language arts textbooks, or the following of prescribed curriculum guides. (Atwell 1987, Foreword)

Yet I, and I suspect others, found ways to turn the ideas into "methods." I relied too heavily at the beginning of the year on what I saw as a prescribed writing formula of "rehearse, draft, confer, re-draft, confer, edit." I also fell into formula when my repertoire of questions became finite. Even Nancie Atwell was at first taken aback to discover she had no "method." She had to rethink what her book was all about, and she concluded that her focus did, indeed, lay elsewhere: "When I wrote, read, and discovered what I and others did as writers and readers, I began to recognize the *conditions* [my emphasis] that fostered engagement and excellence" (Atwell 1991, xv).

When we focus on the *conditions* within which the student grows and excels, our priorities shift away from formula. In order to create those conditions, I realized, the first step I had to take was to stop *telling* students what I thought they needed and listen to them to truly find out. I began to ask, what conditions are necessary for a teacher to become a better listener and responder? What conditions are necessary for students to talk about their ideas and needs articulately? How do we better converse, confer . . . *communicate?*

Students Talk, We Listen

Students in many of today's language arts classroom choose their own reading material and writing topics, present their ideas and work through journals and portfolios, and confer extensively with others about their knowledge, work, wants, and needs. Their role has fundamentally changed from that of mere receivers of information to those of *communicators.* This new role means one important change for the teacher: a corresponding role shift to that of listener (Brown et al. 1996; Harris 1986). Classroom communication becomes more conversational and less didactic.

When children talk honestly about their work they hear themselves and are often able to solve their own problems. They learn, perhaps for the first time, what they know. When teachers listen they also learn what students know and care about, what their desires are, and what they need *specifically* in order to grow. It is essential, then, that we create classroom conditions where students are *willing and able* to talk about those things that are actually important to them. At the same time, we must recognize that the quality of our listening can only be judged by our active responses. Good listening is a process of engrossment (Noddings 1992) and reflection in which the teacher learns from the student and then acts according to what she has learned. A teacher who has listened well may discover that a student needs direct instruction in a specific skill or that the student simply needs to hear his or her words back. She may use what she learns to create long-term plans or immediate lessons. She may give a conscious *non*response or take elaborate action. All depends upon the student's situational need. Effective listening, then, is a deep receptivity of another, which leads the listener to create a conscious response that satisfies the other's immediate and long-term needs.

We know that our students' needs have been met if they can use our responses to move their thinking and work forward. John Dewey (1963) viewed education as a series of experiences. Experiences are only educative if they promote further, richer experiences. If an experience halts a student's further experience by creating confusion or decreasing desire, the experience is miseducative. This means we can define an effective response as one that helps students toward new, progressively expanding experiences, each experience building on previous ones and influencing subsequent ones. They help students to begin to direct their own development, making connections with their current conceptions of the world and arousing them to search out new experiences and evolved conceptions.

The Struggle for Richer Conversations

This kind of communication, of course, initially makes our jobs more complex. The mitigating difficulties of richer conversation—of helping students express themselves and then listening to provide educative response—are things we all can understand. Don Graves writes, "Listening to children is a more deliberate act than a natural one. It isn't easy to put aside personal preferences, anxieties about helping more children, or the glaring mechanical errors that stare from the page" (1983, 100). Don Murray notes, "But I thought a teacher had to talk. I feel guilty when I do nothing but listen" (1982, 160).

Indeed, we often take the path of least resistance, communicating through an Initiation-Reply-Evaluation (IRE) format (Cazden 1988; Mehan 1979): we ask a student a question or give a directive, the student replies according to what he or she thinks we expect, and we then evaluate the response as "right" or "wrong." Usually, students give one-word or short-sentence answers. Students who want to be recognized only speak at appropriate junctures in the pattern. I can remember well some of the exchanges I had with my students the first month of my first year teaching:

Me: Okay, next question. Shara, in *My Side of the Mountain,* what type of tree did Sam choose to live in?

Shara: Umm . . . a hemlock?

Me: Very good. Okay, next question. . . .

I gravitated toward this type of communication naturally, for comfort's sake. First, it provided me order: students focused on me and remained quiet when not answering my question. Second, it offered evidence that students had *learned:* they gave correct answers to specific questions. Third, it gave me control of the curriculum: I determined what was presented, how it was presented, and who responded to it. Fourth, it relieved me of my need to listen carefully: students' replies correlated with answers I already *expected.*

But by imposing this highly structured sequence of question and response, I effectively prohibited students from searching out new information, reasoning out answers through extended thought and conversation, and hypothesizing alternative answers (Johnson 1993). Therefore, the evidence of their learning was exaggerated. The students' short answers were discrete and recognizable, which made them appear powerful, but they offered little evidence that the students could carry on effective dialogues, analyze complex problems, access information independently, set goals and make plans, think metacognitively, and exploit their natural curiosity. The more complex evidence of learning, which reveals itself when students are in the *process* of learning, was superseded by the specific evidence of a very narrow band of factual knowledge.

Further, since my students rarely got to "initiate" topics or questions, and my sense of what was important dominated, many began to feel disenfranchised. Some resorted to apathetic acceptance of my view of the world, some deliberately rebelled, and some simply failed because they did not understand my expectations (Delpit 1995; Gilmore 1983, 1985; Heath 1983; Sadker and Sadker 1994; Taylor 1991).

All these difficulties were exacerbated because I had created no avenue to learn the *student's* educational expectations. Teachers and students each bring different sets of information, skills, and values to the classroom, which may cause each to misread the other's comments and responses (Sperling and Freedman 1987). Students, many argue, belong to a unique culture or social world within the classroom, with fundamentally different tastes, needs, rituals, and agendas from the teacher (Dyson 1993; Newkirk and McLure 1992). Being less familiar with the customs of a student's world, we do not necessarily know which student-given cues are significant, and therefore cannot always respond most effectively. Our natural tendency to dominate and simplify classroom conversation actually makes our teaching more difficult.

However, if we promote honest student talk and adopt a listening stance, we can attend better to their now clearer needs, attempting to bridge our different perspectives so that we may become knowledgeable about, and articulate in, each other's worlds. It is not a new idea, but it is still revolutionary. If we shift from "giver of knowledge" to "listener and responder," we create richer conversations that engender growth.

Vital Conferences and Conversations

I observed and participated in Linda Rief's classroom to learn more about how we might better make this shift. I discovered the profound importance of the teacher creating specific conditions that promote this rich and extensive student conversation about topics that are *worth* listening to. Linda determines worth by the value students place on the subjects about which they talk and write. Her first motivation, then, becomes to help students to discuss and write about topics that have real significance to them. This notion is quite foreign to some students, whose discussion and writing topics in previous years have been chosen by others. Many initially struggle to break down barriers between what is personally important and what is school-important.

In order for Linda to help her students most effectively talk and write about significant issues, she has to create two preliminary conditions:

Organization

The first condition is a deep attention to organization and procedures specifically designed to begin a chain of activity that creates a strong conversational community. Organization promotes more effective and efficient presentation of work and ideas, which in turn leads to the students' willingness to converse in richer, more meaningful ways. Organization creates time, space, and comfort for extended talk, reading, writing, listening, and response. It also teaches students how to manage new freedoms of time and choice.

In class, Linda is the center of attention for only brief periods of the day. She rarely guides students' work by rigid assignments. But the class functions smoothly and efficiently because students have internalized classroom organization and procedures and no longer need as much outside direction. Resultantly, the control Linda relinquishes by promoting student choice and freedom of movement is not lost. Instead, it shifts to another part of the classroom dynamic. Rather than inhibiting students' ideas and movements, organization serves as a map that offers direction, guides motion, and increases efficiency. Direction offers confidence, and efficiency offers time. Linda doesn't simply give students more freedom, she first teaches them how to organize freedom. As students become more responsible with freedom, Linda has more time to listen.

Relationships

The second condition is that of healthy relationships between the teacher and her students. Rapport—a mutual sense of comfort, trust, and affinity—engenders more open, effective communication. The teacher cannot always simply focus upon the student's work—either product *or* process—and expect growth and success. More often than not, interpersonal relationships have a profound effect on the student's motivation and work (McLeod 1995; Tobin 1993). Linda has to attend to her relationships with the students much more carefully than if she taught through lectures or textbooks. To encourage them to discuss personally important topics, often for the first time in their school careers, she has to attend to the emotional as well as the intellectual aspects of most of their lives—has to recognize and embrace social as well as academic concerns. Linda's listening becomes an activity that feeds itself. When she opens herself to what is truly significant to students and returns responses that satisfy their needs, their relationships grow. Talking to the teacher becomes easier. Listening helps to erase the line between personal and academic.

Building relationships forces Linda to abandon formula or a strict agenda. In a classroom of twenty-seven students, there are twenty-seven unique personalities and sets of needs. Pat questions don't work. Linda has to identify individual needs in individual situations, sometimes groping to find which words are truly important to the student and which are not.

But what a complex world! How tremendously difficult authentic conversation and relationship-building are, even for this most successful teacher. First, it is virtually impossible for Linda to give each student the individual time she wants to give. Instead, her actions have to serve as a *model* for effective talk and learning. Students in this class do not rely on the teacher alone for appropriate feedback. They learn to rely on one another.

Difficult, too, are the inevitable clashes of personalities and agendas. While Linda can quickly empathize and build rapport with many students, she struggles to relate to those students who have vastly different concepts about what is important. Linda's challenge is to discover what is important to them rather than immediately trying to save them from their own perspectives. This book reveals her successes and struggles as she implements a literacy program where untraditional responsibilities muddy—and enrich—the pedagogical waters.

3

A Teacher's Values

Linda Rief's teaching philosophy reveals itself in what she wants from her students, her classroom, and herself. She says, "I would like kids to be life-long learners and to love reading and writing and take great pleasure in it." She wants reading and writing to matter to her students. "I want students to find something that has meaning for *them*." She expects students to work thoughtfully and says she gets most upset when she perceives they don't care about their work. Once they do care, she wants them to use reading and writing to challenge themselves intellectually.

In addition, Linda wants students to:

- Have strategies for learning: "If they don't know something, they know where to go for help or they know what to do to help themselves."
- Become independent and work for personally relevant reasons. "I love it when I see an editorial in the paper written by a kid . . . and then find out that nobody solicited it; it wasn't an assignment, but they did it *totally* on their own because they felt strongly about something."
- Leave her class "better at reading and writing than when they came in."

Linda's emphasis on developing a love of literacy, an ability to find information, a life-long practice of reading and writing, and a sense of intellectual independence sets her in a philosophical camp that shifts away from a focus on specific subject matter and toward a focus on the *process* of learning for personally relevant purposes. Her approach values the completed product—a student's newspaper editorial, for instance—but her focus is to

13

nurture a process of creation where one learns how to proceed and produce continually in the future. Ultimately, she says, "I want these kids to be the most articulate readers, writers, and speakers they can be."

Throughout the year, Linda's remarks suggest several roles she and her students assume in order to accomplish these goals.

Students' Roles

Experience and Do

In the introduction to her book *Seeking Diversity: Language Arts with Adolescents* Linda writes,

> Like Aunt Addie Norton (Wigginton 1985) I want my students to learn by doing: "I tell you one thing, if you learn it by yourself, if you have to get down and dig for it, it never leaves you. It stays there as long as you live because you had to dig it out of the mud before you learned what it was." I want the same for me. (p. 4)

Her belief stems from personal experience. She says, "The things I learned in school were the things I actually participated in. I could take wonderful notes, but I couldn't fit them into anything, just a little box for quizzes and tests. I couldn't apply them."

Use Personal Knowledge to Make Meaning

Self-awareness of personal knowledge (metacognition) offers students a context within which to position new ideas that arise from their work. They use their prior knowledge to analyze their new experiences as they write, read, and converse. Commenting on a book students were reading, Linda said, "I'm looking for them to connect this to themselves so that it is a book worth reading—so that they can make meaning from it for themselves."

Self-Evaluate to Grow

Learners need to evaluate their own reading and writing processes and products. When discussing students' work Linda tells them, "You should be able to write *why* it's important to you." In *Seeking Diversity,* she comments about how her former students taught her the value of self-evaluation:

> The more they were asked to look at their own writing, the better they got at it. . . . I *know* kids can evaluate their own writing; I know that the evalua-

tive process helps them make their writing better; I know that evaluation of writing *in progress* is as important, if not *more* important, than the final product; and I know how to help them learn to do that. (1992, p. 122)

As students reflect on their work in progress it transforms evaluation into a tool for continued growth rather than a process-ending judgment. Self-evaluation means that students find value in themselves and in their work (Hansen 1998).

Socialize to Discover

Education is a social process. Linda says, "I want them to be a community of trusting individuals, where other kids hear what it is they know. [I want them to know] they've got people they can trust—that other people care about them." When students converse, explore, and work together they develop multiple perspectives and a "social imagination" that gives them the ability to read others in the community better (Johnston 1997). Linda believes this leads not only to interdependence among themselves, but also to more independence from the teacher:

They know that the teacher is not the only authority in the classroom. Academically they know that they've got much to contribute to one another, so you've got twenty-seven teachers in the room instead of one. You've got twenty-seven views, so there are all kinds of alternatives and all kinds of ways of looking at the world. . . . There isn't one way of thinking and there isn't one way of learning, so it helps them to see that there is no one answer to everything.

Social learning might transcend the classroom and influence the greater society, at large:

You want kids to care about other people beyond the classroom. I think the greatest pleasure is seeing them informally say, "Listen to this, listen to this. What do you think of this idea?" If you translated that to what happens to them outside in the community, what a great place it would be to live. . . . Then people can respond in positive ways to each other—in ways that value ideas and then build on them.

These roles encourage students to pursue new experiences through their active writing and reading, articulate what they know, and evaluate their own growth. Students begin to share responsibility for discovering the things they need to know.

Teachers' Proactive Roles

Linda sees herself playing several roles. Four of them are *proactive:* they establish an organizational and procedural foundation and promote fruitful conversation, reading, and writing even before she interacts personally with her students.

Offer Choice

"I think you have to offer kids choices about what they do." Linda's students select their own writing topics and reading texts within their general units of study, abandon nonedifying writing and reading, revise writing and re-read books when they need to, decide what and where to publish and with whom to share for response. Choice gives opportunities to students who need a variety of modes of expression, including art and talk.

However, choice is not unconditional. At times, students need direction in order to expose them to opportunities they might not see for themselves. Linda says,

> When I first started teaching I really believed that it had to be total free choice all the time, and then I started writing and reading myself. I realized that there are a lot of times when I want people to ask me to try a certain kind of writing, and I want them to nudge me into some kind of reading. So I would have to say that I think there is a balance of both in the classroom. There are times when I require particular things. There's choice within parameters. There are other times where there is total free choice.

Providing choice teaches students: when the teacher discusses what different choices mean and where they might lead, students learn to make thoughtful, productive choices and avoid those that do not move them forward.

Provide Time and Patience

The student who learns by doing needs *time.* Linda's ideal class time allotment is a five- to ten-minute read-aloud or mini-lesson, followed by a full forty-five minutes for students to read, write, and discuss their work. When students have time, astonishing things happen. Linda recalls a former student who wrote two novels during the school year, each several hundred pages long. "He *wanted* to write those novels!" she exclaims; "I gave him time and permission."

Teachers (including herself, Linda says) often do not give students enough time to think before they give answers. Nor do they give enough time to let students listen to their own work:

> I discovered listening takes so much longer. So I did what I told kids not to do. I picked up their [pieces of writing] and I read them. I took responsibility away from them. I finally said, "I can't do this. . . . " I let *them* read and listen to *themselves*. It doesn't take as long as I think it does and they listen harder to themselves anyway.

Finding enough time is one of the most difficult aspects of a teacher's job. Linda says, "The vicious circle comes in when you've got twenty-eight, thirty kids in a classroom and you're running around the barn and you can never get in! It takes *time*."

"It takes *patience,* too," she continues. Time and patience let students discover their own literacy. Sometimes it takes the entire year and teachers have to fight growing frustration, but, Linda says, patience teaches better than frustration.

> If there's one thing I've learned it's not to get angry with kids who just absolutely refuse to write about anything that seems really meaningful to them. If I get angry it stops them and I'm acting the same way that somebody has already acted to them, which has kept them from writing.

Time is not a luxury for students, but a necessity. Time allows students' thoughts to ripen from the superficial to the profound.

Organize

Careful organization addresses two outcomes. First, it heightens classroom efficiency. Linda organizes time, materials, and expectations. She organizes time through well-planned scheduling and working procedures. She organizes materials using detailed procedures for accessing and using materials, and by designating specific homes for each book, piece of paper, and writing implement. She organizes expectations through explicit statements of how the classroom runs and what she requires of her students. But excessive organization—overly-detailed assignments, for instance—might inhibit students. "I want structure, but I want them paying attention to their *writing,*" Linda says. "I want the structure to be so subtle that it's not even part of the class any more." Organization is truly successful when the room works so efficiently that students do not think about the procedures any more, they internalize them.

Second, organization can encourage specific student activities, most notably talk among students. In explaining her preference for round tables where students sit face-to-face, Linda says,

> The minute you sit kids facing one another you are saying, "I value your talking to each other," and if you don't value them talking to each other then you might as well put them in rows where they're isolated and can't talk. You might as well scream and yell at them when they hand notes under the table to each other. I see kids handing notes to each other all the time! I mean, let them *write!*

But a talking classroom makes organization of procedure and materials all the more important: "If I don't get us organized, I can't deal with the chaos of so many ideas."

Model a Literate Life

Linda's definition of modeling is succinct: "I WRITE. I READ." She also says, "What I value in this class is that these kids leave here knowing they are learners for life. And that's what I have to model for them every day." Her modeling, then, goes beyond simply demonstrating techniques and into "living a life of literacy":

> The literate life . . . includes far more than reading and writing. Literate people have a passion for asking questions, both big and small, a hunger for learning new things and for making connections. In short, they have a particular stance toward the universe: one of constant engagement. (Graves 1990, p. 105)

Linda feels the obligation to share this life with her students. The writing and reading she shares in class are rarely exercises created for the lesson, but come from personal writing and books she reads for her own pleasure and edification. When she does create an exercise, it is essential that she write with her students. She can't spend forty-five minutes writing in class, but she *can* take three minutes to write along with them in her journal. She pushes her own thinking and challenges herself explicitly in class:

> [I want students] to try some things that [they] might not normally try. And *I* have to do that, too. Kids still do say to me, "You do everything you ask us to do." We as teachers have to know that they're watching us like hawks, and if it isn't good enough for me, then it's probably not good enough for them.

Thus, the literate teacher reaps another benefit: she discovers firsthand what isn't good enough for her students. Linda comments on one failed assignment she had given:

> How did I realize the assignment was stupid? I tried to do it. I could *not* do it and I had to reshape it for myself. And I've realized the writing that matters to me now did not come out of [the assignment].

It is the authenticity of the teacher's tasks that makes them valuable activities. "When they see me as real, they tune me in. When I'm a teacher, they tune me out." Participation takes Linda away from the role of a teacher and into the role of a practitioner, doing what she *loves* amidst others.

Teachers' Reactive Roles

Five other roles Linda sees for herself are largely *reactive:* they arise out of direct interaction with students, often on an individual basis, and they help her to address unique situations and needs. They focus more on her students' actions and practices, and thus they require that she carefully attend to her relationships with them.

Listen and Respond

Listening and responding can tie together almost all other aspects of good teaching. As Linda provides choice and time to students and organizes the classroom well, she creates situations where students write, read, and talk in voices that both she and they can clearly hear. By listening carefully, the teacher learns which responses will work best. Linda says, "I'm searching for, 'what do they care about in this piece of writing? What in this piece of writing matters to them?'"

Linda's listening often begins with two questions. She says, "Don Graves taught me how to say, 'Tell me more,' and Don Murray taught me to say, 'How can I help you?'" Students' answers to these questions determine her actions.

Linda defines good listening as recognizing messages that may be subtle or obscured: "A good listener *hears* things that others don't." She looks for "the silence between the words," saying, "Kids say things that if you *know* them well enough you know what they are *really* saying."

Good listening also ensures the appropriate response:

> What makes a good listener? Somebody who acts on what somebody has said to them. Somebody who does nothing but listen as the person is talking to them—who focuses on that person. With teaching, a good listener is

somebody who either changes what they do or continues to do what they do because of what they heard. It's the *acting* on what the child says. . . . You can stand there and write down all kinds of notes and nod your head, but if you don't act on it then you weren't listening well.

Linda acknowledges she is often not a good listener when she is tired, in a hurry, senses kids are not committed to their work, or has read too many journals in a day. But when she sees kids excited about their work and hears "a steady hum" of working voices in the background, she tunes in and responds well. "I hope I model listening," she says.

Appropriate response defines good listening. In fact, the final four roles can all be seen as *response* roles, requiring direct, specific action and interaction with students, which are determined by Linda's perceptions of their needs in each situation.

Nudge Students Forward

Students learn when they need to *pursue* subject matter. It is the responsibility of the teacher to challenge her students' thinking continually to help them forward. Linda says:

Give them real, positive responses to what they're doing, find the things they're doing well, and then begin to push them to try some things that go *beyond* their comfort level. Make them really push their thinking. I'm not sure if kids really know what I mean when I write to them, "You really have to *push* your thinking a bit." I mean push your comfort level. They say, "I can do this, I can do this, and I feel really good and that's all I'm gonna do." I say, "But try some things you might not normally try," and then give them some good, specific possibilities.

Yet one must be careful not to halt the resistant student: "Am I saying things that make kids think, push their thinking, grow as thinkers?" Linda asked, "or do I stop them cold?" She says that a good listener "tries to know the kids well enough to know how much they can handle." This means understanding them on both an intellectual and emotional level: do they have enough background and momentum at this moment in time to move forward into other specific discoveries? Are they emotionally capable of accepting nudges without resisting too much? Monitoring emotional readiness is crucial. Linda offers an anecdote: A few years ago, a boy in class wrote nothing but gory chainsaw massacre stories. Linda tried fruitlessly for months to expand his repertoire, nudging, searching for what mattered to him. Eventually, in desperation, she told him, "Listen, when you decide not to write this garbage, I'll come back and talk with you." She regretted the words as they fell from her mouth. "He did not write for the rest of the year. Sometimes I'll see his mother downtown and cringe, thinking, I hope he didn't tell her what I said to him! Why couldn't I simply have said, 'I can't listen to that anymore'?" Experiences like these affect Linda deeply.

Inform

Teachers must directly offer necessary information that students do not yet possess. Linda says, "You can't hold back information if you know it." She offers most of her information in one-on-one situations or group discussions, often in response to something that has been said by a student. In one instance she provided information about literary devices director Steven Spielberg used in *Schindler's List:* "I want to throw into their ring what I *know* about literary devices like that or decisions that [Spielberg] might have made . . . and I want them to think about that." Specific subject matter is appropriate to give when a situation calls for it in the context of a student's active learning process. It then serves as material to further growth, not merely as an end. In these situations the teacher does not necessarily take responsibility away from the learner. Linda said, "They still *own* the words. I have information that they don't have. I give it to them."

Evaluate

Evaluation is a tool to further learning and growth, not a judgment of competence that often serves to inhibit students. Linda's evaluation of students' work starts with positive commentary and builds on it. "When people tell me negative things, it stops me writing. When people tell me positive things, it keeps me writing," she says. "I'm *always* trying to find something that they did well. And sometimes it's the color of the ink . . . but I *am* trying to find something that they did well." Once students comprehend the positive qualities of their work and can subsequently build upon them, Linda then feels comfortable offering clear evaluations of problems she perceives. She insists on evaluating actual reading and writing work, not test scores. She says, "The kids know that this is real work and they're going to be evaluated on real work, and every skill that anybody's trying to help kids learn in any language arts class is going to surface in what these kids are doing as readers and writers." What stopped her own reading in school "was I knew we were going to have a test on it."

Linda is uncomfortable in her role as grade giver, and at one time contemplated eliminating grading requirements altogether. The concept of grading seems to go against her philosophical stance that learning is a continual process. Grades put an artificial end to the process. However, she hopes that her grading criteria, no matter how imperfect, provide a framework that offers students a direction in which to move. The one imperative she has is that students take their writing seriously. When they do, she says, "they are 'tested' every time they read it or read it out loud to an audience."

Care

"I swear, it wouldn't matter what I taught as long as they know I care about them. I could diagram sentences." For most students, Linda says, "If you don't like them first, there is *nothing* that you're going to get across to those kids." She has a caveat, however. "This is why we should teach good stuff. The kids will follow you [if you don't], but eventually they would be in trouble."

The caring teacher empathizes with the things that are important to the student. Linda tries to remember her own adolescence.

> The big thing, I think, is friends and boy-girl relationships and helping them deal with that. I think that matters a lot more than school. I think *that's* what makes them human beings. And for us to think that the subject we're teaching is the most important thing they're learning is wrong. It's *not* the most important thing we teach our kids.

Because adolescents' perspectives often draw more from the affective than the intellectual, recognizing traumas and emotions is essential. Linda believes she cannot be most effective when she refuses to interact with students on anything other than an academic level. She needs to establish trust between herself and students, forming multifaceted relationships with them. Building trust takes time, but as we shall see, the relationships formed are at the heart of classroom success.

The roles Linda envisions for herself and her students determine the shape of her classroom practice. Her practice leads toward more open communication, creating a safe place where students can take risks and talk about important issues that help define the curriculum. The following chapters will show Linda and her students in practice. They paint a portrait of the classroom in motion, the conversations that arise out of careful preparation, and the complex relationships that are born, and which enrich and challenge the teacher's classroom life.

4
—

A Classroom that Invites Conversation

Good teachers practice what they preach. This is not to say, however, that our practical journeys are smooth or flawless. It is a continual struggle to maintain philosophical constancy in our working classrooms. Just as we do, Linda Rief has to check herself on a daily basis, looking for the spots in her teaching where impatience, exhaustion, or ignorance cause her to flag from the philosophical course she has set for herself. Sometimes she finds great errors in her teaching that make her almost despondent. At other times, she feels the thrill of making just the right move. Her self-evaluation never ends; it is, in fact, necessary if she is to remain true to valuing students' voices. If she does not examine whether or not she has acted according to students' needs, she fails her own mandate.

Let us see how Linda sets her philosophy into action. We will begin by entering her classroom and taking a look around at both the classroom design and a class in action. Both reveal much about what a teacher believes.

The Classroom Layout

Brightly colored posters, made by students, adorn the walls outside of Linda Rief's classroom. The photographs, poetry, quotations, and writing they present depict their lives as readers and writers. The classroom itself is large, square, bright, and airy with comfortable places to work and hide. Students use nooks between bookshelves as sanctuaries from a busy class to read and write in semi-privacy. Mobiles covered with authors' quotes, book passages, poetry, and cartoons hang above every table. The many art supplies throughout the room (including a flower press) assert that literacy includes art. Linda's desk hides in a corner behind a bookcase. She never sits there during class, preferring to walk around the room.

Books

Ten bookcases and several plastic bins, which line the walls, house thousands of books. One case houses information and reference books, videos of literary works, and five binders chock-full of biographical information about authors (Linda has collected articles, interviews, and authors' letters for years). Among the genres and themes within the other cases and bins: fiction, nonfiction, short stories, essays, poetry, young adult literature, writers and writing, human rights, student anthologies from classes past, professionally published children's writing, picture books, cartoon anthologies, riddles, folktales, fairy tales, generations, grandparents, music and musicians, the moon, the environment, Native Americans, journal writing, sketching, art, artists, and crafts. There is a large tape collection of authors and students reading their work and talking about writing. There are issues of *Merlyn's Pen,* a national magazine of student writing.

Obviously, Linda values more than just the standard adolescent fare. She often reads from picture books, pointing out their poetic simplicity and the value of exquisite illustrations to a book's meaning. She emphasizes quality literature of all types, listening for "beautiful language"—powerful words that let us think or feel or see something more deeply.

Walls

Student artwork and writing dominate the walls, and students spend much time perusing their colleagues' work. One wall displays bright cartoon strips made during a joint art-language arts project. (Later, four students will submit their cartoons to a national contest. The head of the contest will call Linda, astounded that all four are finalists even though the judging was blind.) There is a huge mural students made by writing on, decorating, and weaving together long strips of paper (the way a child makes a construction paper place mat). Colorful, student-made masks glare down from the walls. A bulletin board displays notices about writing contests, student publishing outlets, and articles about authors who have visited the class. These are literate walls.

Furniture

A futon where students read rests on the floor under a window. Six rectangular tables, and a large round table sit at strange angles to one another. Students sit four to a table. A smaller round table serves as Linda's working table. The tables appear to be in random arrangement, but Linda always meticulously returns each one to its particular spot. The arrangement ensures that no table has quite the same view—that there is no obvious focal point as there would be if desks faced the same way or in a circle. At the tables, students sit across from one another, which invites talk.

The careful design Linda puts into the room upholds her philosophy. It is a place that promotes talk and brings her into conversations rather than isolating her in front of the class or behind a desk. It is a place that values book variety and authentic, creative student work over a more limited and manageable repertoire of classic books and skills work. Linda's choices give rise to new problems as well as new opportunities, but her arrangement clearly indicates the direction she wants to take as she practices her craft and interacts with her students.

The Class in Action

I portray this scene as a single class, but it is actually a composite of my observations of several classes on a single day. In each class I looked at different elements of the same lesson. In reality there is no such thing as a typical class, but this composite portrays the look and feel of Linda and her students in action.

Easing In

At 7:45 Linda's group of fourteen advisees meet in her room for home base. Home base eases kids into the school day. Linda often uses this time to find out what is happening in their lives outside of class. Today, the art teacher, Beth, brings her own advisees to Linda's room. The kids have brought in coffeecake, donuts, bagels, and juice. As they eat, some kids write or do homework; others read. Four kids sit on the futon and pore over a book together. Talk undulates, low and pleasant. Linda kneels on the floor and talks softly with Beth, who sits in a chair. As first-period class time draws near, Linda reminds the students, "Folks, I would greatly appreciate it if a couple of you could clean up the breakfast area." Dodge, as usual, hems and haws and then volunteers another student. Linda laughs and volunteers Dodge. Some students wander out to other classes while the rest stay for Linda's.

Linda Reads Her Writing

At 8:05 class begins. Twenty-eight students cheerfully buzz as they settle into their seats, teasing one another and telling friends what they did the night before. Linda moves toward the small round table and quietly scans their faces; most of them settle quickly. "Would you take out your journals please." Yesterday she handed out a list of five spelling rules to help students as they write. Today she reminds them to paste the rules into their journals for easy reference.

She begins her lesson. Where do writers get ideas for their writing? Today she shows a poem she is writing, which was inspired by Cynthia Rylant's book *When I Was Young in the Mountains*. The book took Linda back to her own childhood. She places a transparency of her typed draft up on the overhead projector and reads it for the class:

WHEN I WAS YOUNG AT THE OCEAN

(With thanks to Cynthia Rylant for *When I Was Young in the Mountains*)

When I was young at the ocean, I sat at the edge of the wooden pier and dangled my toes in the water. Like tiny rowboats my toes skimmed the rolling waves, ever alert for sharks. Sometimes I sat cross-legged in shorts and Tee-shirt, a bamboo fishing pole stretched to catch mackerel. No one ever told me to bait the hook.

When I was young at the ocean, I cracked open mussels and periwinkles and clams, and ran my fingers across the gushy insides. I squished seaweed nodules between my forefinger and thumb, anxious for the pop and spray from the moist insides.

When I was young at the ocean, I burned my shoulders and smelled of Noxzema through the entire month of July. I drank in the aroma of hip roses, salt water, and seaweed. At low tide I played croquet with the Queen of Hearts, flew the moon in a hammock, and fed my dolls deviled ham sandwiches in the shade of the screened house.

As the tide came in, water lapped at the rocky shore. The skin of my feet toughened as I paced those rounded stones, my eyes searching for skippers. When I was young, I never wished to climb the mountains, or live in the city, or camp in the forest. The ocean was enough. It still is.

Those who look carefully at her paper can see that Linda has already begun to revise her poem. There are check marks next to the words and lines Linda particularly likes: "gushy insides," "Noxzema," "hip roses, salt water, and seaweed." These are the types of descriptive words and phrases Linda endlessly exhorts her students to find in their own writing. At the bottom of the page are her handwritten notes of other memories she might include next: "Clam digging with Grampa . . . hoist me on his shoulders . . . dominoes—penny candy—root beer barrels . . . walkway—peonies—lily of the valley—clothesline—white sheets . . . moon across the ocean . . . combine-connect summer-ocean." An arrow juts from her words "rounded stones" in the last stanza and points to a possible replacement, "ragged stones."

A Quick-Write

Linda tells the class, "Every piece of writing, professional books, kids books, observations . . . give me ideas." It is not improper to borrow lines or phrases from others to get you started, she says. "I want you to borrow the line, 'When I was young at. . . .' I want you to write for two minutes as quickly as you can about a place that's just for you. I want you to write about the sights, the sounds, the smells. . . ." Every eye is on Linda as she speaks, attentive and ready to write. Almost. At the farthest table a boy whispers to his friends from behind his hand, "When I was young in my bedroom . . . spanking my monkey!" They burst into uncontrollable giggles, trying to stifle themselves with their hands and tucking their heads into their shoulders, but it is no use. Linda hears them and looks up, but she does not address them. Instead, she waits until the giggles subside. Then she begins to write for herself.

The class is silent as they, too, write in their journals. Linda stands, cradling her own journal in the crook of her arm. She moves over to a table of students, sits in an empty chair, and continues.

Three minutes pass. Linda looks up. "Okay, even if you're not done, stop. A trick my teacher Don Murray taught me is, if you're in the middle of a sentence, don't finish it. It helps you pick up where you ended when you come back to it." Linda asks if there is anyone who would like to read what they wrote. A student volunteers. He clears his throat and speaks:

> "When I Was Young in the Woods." When I was young in the woods, I could hear the leaves beneath my feet crackling and the trees creaking left and right, swaying to the rhythms of the wind. I can hear the busy beaver gnawing at the wood, I can hear the howl of the coyote deep in the woods. I do not wish to be anywhere else, just right here, deep in the woods.

"Wonderful!" Linda exclaims, "I love the creaking of the trees." Over the next few weeks, the student will take this passage and carry it through three revisions to create a richly descriptive poem, which will grace his portfolio as one of his best pieces. Many will never follow through with this quick-write, which is perfectly acceptable. It is meant only to create possibilities.

Two other students read their quick-writes, and Linda comments, "Those are the startings of poetry—the sights and sounds." She then reads what she just wrote. The scribbles on her original poem have given rise to another memory:

When I was little I couldn't wait to visit Gram and Grampa Mac. I would swing open the door at the top of Beltram St., leap from the car, and race down the root-filled pathway towards their house. Dodging rocks, exposed roots, through the white swinging gate, past the lilies of the valley, past the holly hocks, under the clothes line, my hands pushing aside damp white cotton sheets flapping in the summer breeze to fall breathless into my grandmother . . .

"I didn't know I would write this," Linda tells her class. Ideas most often come *during* the act of writing, not before. She asks, "What was the purpose of doing this?"

"Getting our imaginations going," replies Annie.

"That's right. And we'll continue to do something like this two to three times a week, in different ways, to keep your writing going."

A closer inspection of the paper from which she just read reveals other scribbles. Linda has been writing notes to herself on it since early this morning:

What struck you from *Radical Reflections*? What did you learn from *Voices*? How might you go about teaching *The Giver*? Holocaust—p. 60–61, p. 68–71. We have choices? p. 74–79. *The Giver*—w/ *The Velveteen Rabbit* (comfort objects). W/ military—very regimented.

These notes indicate that Linda is already thinking about the months ahead, when she will introduce her students to the Holocaust and the class will read *The Giver* (Lowry 1993), a book in which the characters sacrifice freedom for comfort, which leads to oppression and death. Linda writes notes like this to herself continually. There is also one other line on the paper. It says: "Kelly: My teacher said, my moon was wrong." Often, when a student like Kelly says something that appeals to Linda, she will write it down for future reference.

"So we're spending this period writing," Linda continues; "I don't mind if there is quiet talk. I mind if I can hear individual voices." She reminds students of some writing possibilities: they might choose a new topic, write in their journals about something they are reading, continue with their "When I Was Young" leads, or continue with a preexisting draft.

Linda Confers

The students have no trouble getting to work. They know their options, and many have planned ahead. Linda begins to move from table to table, listening for students who need help. She shows Mandy and Lynn how to cut and paste their spelling rules into their journals. Damon has drawn a beautiful illustration, inspired by a fantasy book he is reading. He is now creating characters for his *own* fantasy story. Amy reads a letter and Linda admires how Amy moved from general to very specific comments. They both agree that Amy is ready to edit it for spelling, grammar, and punctuation.

Another table. Linda sits with George, who yesterday filled out a questionnaire, which asked, "What can I expect from you this quarter? What do you really want to do as a reader and writer? What do you really need to work on? How do you plan to do that? What do you expect from me? How can I best help you?" George shows her his answers. He has written that Linda's requirement of three to five journal pages a week has simply been too much and that she can expect one to three pages from him. Linda weighs his offer, debating in her mind how much to challenge him. Knowing George's history, suspecting that his offer is sincere, and realizing that one to three pages will be an improvement, Linda says, "One to three pages is good." Hal works on a story. He says he has an idea where it is going, so Linda leaves immediately.

A third table. Raef is frustrated. "I can never come up with any ideas to write about," he moans. He thinks he wants to write about science fiction, but his tone of voice seems to belie his interest. Linda casually asks him what his interests are. "I don't know," he says, but his face gradually softens. He loves to snowmobile. Linda does not suggest he write about snowmobiling. Instead, she remembers that Aaron's mother recently wrote an article for an outdoor magazine and she thinks that it had an article about snowmobiles in it. She will get it for him. She asks, "What's your favorite book?" Raef replies, "*Jurassic Park*." Linda smiles and gets up to leave. Raef begins to write, perhaps about snowmobiles, perhaps about dinosaurs, perhaps about something entirely new.

Linda moves to Dodge, who has lost his muse. Linda suggests he expand his quick-write into a story or poem. "If you take every line and write as much as possible about each one, you'd have a lot of pieces." Her nudging fails. Dodge ponders a few ideas, but Linda never hears excitement in his voice. She gives up for the present and moves on.

Linda confers with Leo, whom she had as a seventh grader. He tells her he wants to start reading more this year, but he is discouraged because he is not that good at it. But Linda has been carefully tracking his work and counters, "You *are* reading more this year." Knowing his reading tastes, she writes in his journal the names of two books she thinks he will like, then asks him what books he has liked recently. Leo says he really enjoyed *Roots*. "Okay," says Linda. She writes down another title: "*Black Boy*, Wright."

Elena reads Linda her new poem and suddenly it is the end of class. Linda tries to make it a point every day to bring the class full circle by using the last five minutes as a whole-class share where a student reads something he or she has written, someone reads a professional piece, or the class discusses their day's discoveries. But sometimes class ends with her and her students absorbed in their own work. Linda asks herself, are the students hearing enough of one another's writing?

The students file out quickly. Linda calls several back to slide their chairs underneath their tables and pick up crumpled papers off the floor. As the last student wanders out slowly, she reviews the class. She was particularly impressed with Damon's journal illustration. "For a kid who's not awake," she exclaims, "he was really there. If you say the right thing to him he wakes up." She wonders how she can counteract this resistance of some of the reluctant writers in class. Then she sits down to rest for one minute before the next class begins.

Other classes throughout the year consist of workshops by local authors, lively whole-class discussions about literacy and social issues, and trips to the theatre and museums, but this class depicts many of the types of activities that occurred on many days. Linda's sharing of her work and others' work, her immersion into students' activities, and her one-on-one conversations with them help define the tone and tenor of the class. As we will learn, it takes much time and patience to create this smooth, complex, atmosphere in which students work and converse confidently and independently.

5

Classroom Expectations

Many of the expectations Linda has for her students can be found in her books *Seeking Diversity: Language Arts with Adolescents* and *Vision and Voice: Extending the Literacy Spectrum.* Weekly, students read for half an hour each night, write three to five pages of reflections and responses, maintain a list of books read, maintain a list of difficult spelling words, define three to five difficult vocabulary words from their reading, take class notes, and create three to five pages of rough draft writing. She expects them to complete two final drafts every four weeks, set goals, and self-evaluate.

Literacy Journals

Literacy journals are the primary repositories of student writing. Here, students accumulate a vast number of observations, thoughts, and ideas for potential writing. Literacy journals include drawings and other artwork, which express ideas differently than words. Journal entries become students' primary sources for the ideas they eventually take to draft. "I would like you to collect fragments of language," Linda tells students. "This becomes the seedbed of all writing you might do." Responses do not have to be about reading books, but about anything students want to preserve or remember: aspects of good writing, experiences and memories, reactions to books, conversations, questions, self-evaluations, and artifacts that show who they are as writers, readers, thinkers, listeners, observers, and participants. These are the observations that influence or inform future writing.

Portfolios

Portfolios are the places where students present and evaluate what they deem to be their most effective writing, reading, and artwork at the end of each quarter. They also include artifacts that represent other aspects of their lives, giving a more comprehensive portrait of their talents and proclivities.

Process Papers

Process papers are documents included in quarterly portfolios. Students use them to describe how their chosen portfolio pieces originated, from conception to final draft. For each piece they evaluate and grade: (1) their writing processes, (2) the content of their pieces, and (3) mechanics. Linda then assigns her own grade to each of these areas and determines a final grade by averaging her grade with the student's. If there is a large discrepancy between her grade and the student's, they meet to discuss it. (For an example of a similar process paper, see Appendix Q of *Seeking Diversity*.)

Evaluations of Writing and Reading

Evaluation of writing and reading questionnaires included in quarterly portfolios detail students' views about what makes someone a good writer and reader, what they have learned and how they have grown, what goals they have met, what new goals they have set, how Linda has helped them, and how she might better help them in the future. As students answer the same questions each quarter, they and Linda can track their growth.

Curriculum Themes

This year the curriculum is divided thematically into four quarters of the school year.

Quarter One: An introduction and immersion into reading and writing. Linda familiarizes students with classroom structures and procedures; discusses their histories as readers and writers; and introduces processes of finding a topic, writing, and revising. Students create projects that link literacy and art. They have almost complete freedom of topic choice.

Quarter Two: An author study. Each student chooses an author to read extensively. Though they still have choice in their reading and writing, a portion of students' work has to show what they have learned about literacy from their authors.

Quarter Three: A unit about human rights, which focuses on the Holocaust. Students choose books from the extensive selection of human rights literature. They have much autonomy in what they read and write, but they must read at least a few self-selected books about the Holocaust. Along with their free-choice work they also create pieces of writing and artwork devoted to the Holocaust. They devote over a week to reading *The Giver,* by Lois Lowry, out loud as a class. They use *The Giver* and movies about the Holocaust as prompts for whole-class discussions.

Quarter Four: Reader's/writer's research projects. Students have complete freedom to use their literacy skills as they deem fit. As a class they also read and discuss *Romeo and Juliet,* view two movie versions and a stage version, then write reactions and responses through a variety of genres. Finally, they work together to link the language arts and music classes. This year, all four classes collaborate to write and perform a full-length musical for the school. Students' final portfolio presentations may show some connection to music.

Creative Expectations

The above expectations and themes create structure for students. They provide maps that guide the creation and organization of work products. They allude to a work ethic that will create a large body of work upon which they can carefully reflect. But Linda has another, perhaps more important set of expectations, creative ones, which reveal habits she feels all good writers practice. She discusses three particular habits more often than any others.

Write About What Matters to You

Before the class reads the short story "Eleven" (Cisneros 1992) together, Linda lists "the elements of fiction" on the board: "beginning, characters, conflicts, setting, dialogue, journey, ending, theme." Now, students discuss the emotions they felt while reading about the girl humiliated by a teacher who forces her to wear a filthy red sweater. They recount their own stories of being shamed. Linda lists their words on the board: "bad feelings," "helplessness," "injustice," "unfairness." She pauses. She looks at the separate lists. She points to the "elements of fiction" and says, "In my experience, this is *not* what you pay attention to *first.*" She then points to the list of emotions. "You pay attention to *this* first." Start with what matters, then use conventions to enhance your message.

Linda says clearly to students: write about what you know and what is important to you. Read what interests you and stirs your imagination. If a student is not gaining pleasure or edification from a book, he or she should find another one. Linda's responsibility is to help students identify their cares and passions—what is meaningful. She often uses quick-writes like the "When I Was Young . . ." exercise to elicit what is important to the writers. Students interview one another and make lists of loves, hates, and wonderings. Linda also shares students' journal entries that show their investment in their topics. "Here's an entry," she says one day, then reads and comments:

> "I think this is one of the most emotional books I read [*One Child,* Hayden 1995]. Every joy Torey and Sheila has is fragile, like a weak berry branch in a heavy storm. It showed me how precious love is. You can't live with it, you can't live without it. I really believe that. I finished this book standing in the bathroom and cried. My mom, who'd been passing by, asked if I was okay and spoiled the moment."
>
> I would hope that every book you pick to read is so wonderful to you that somebody interrupting you spoils the moment . . . that you *love* it that much. And if you can't find some books that you love that much this year, then I have failed—we both have failed to really help each other out as readers. That's how important books should be to you. It doesn't mean you're summarizing it. I want to know what you're thinking about that book.

Linda wants no summaries, no traditional book reports. "Do you love book reports?" she asks one day.

"No!" shouts the class.

"I *hate* book reports. I want you to discuss what interests *you*. I want you to find what you think is absolutely beautiful language." When students do decide to write reviews of books, Linda encourages them to write what is memorable to *them*: the unique sentences, striking images, and moods that matter to them.

Give Specifics

Linda repeats a pet phrase over and over again: "Give us the sights, the sounds, the smells. . . ." Whether they are journal writing, draft writing, responding to others' work, giving answers or explanations, goal-setting, or self-evaluating, students should supply their audiences with unique and relevant details. Linda constantly asks the question she had learned from Don Graves: "Tell me more." As Mark writes down in a piece that he loves "food," he already knows what Mrs. Rief will say when she hears it: "Be more specific," he predicts as he rolls his eyes.

The more specific and descriptive the writing, response, or evaluation, the more valuable the work. Even on pieces that Linda or the student consider "failures," a detailed case history of what happened, how it happened, why it happened, and what was learned becomes the primary evaluative focus. It greatly influences Linda's portion of the grading process. Specifics give every form of expression the individual student's unique stamp.

Write a Lot

Linda does give specific whole-class assignments: autobiographical posters; graphs that chart students' loves, hates, and wonderings; and the daily responses in journals, to name a few. The assignments serve the singular purpose of having students create a large cache of preliminary writing out of which nuggets of good writing will appear. These bits can then be crafted into quality pieces. Linda often paraphrases Don Murray's line, "Write badly to write well" (1993, 145), suggesting to students that the more they write, whether they deem it good or not, the more chance they will find quality lines within it to develop further. As Don Murray analogizes,

> A few times I've worked on stories with well-known photographers, and I was struck with the fact that where I would shoot a roll of film they would shoot dozens and where I would choose a picture to print they would choose that picture to crop and shade and redevelop. What they were doing was finding from abundance something that worked and then making it work better. (1985, p. 138)

Linda often tells her students, "You have to do a volume of writing to get good writing. These assignments generate a volume of writing out of which the writer might find a topic or a line or a *thread* to follow."

Troubles with Expectations

Linda believes that the classroom foundation she creates will help students work responsibly, independently, and creatively. But the path to important, passionate reading and writing is complicated. Many concepts arising out of the classroom setup and Linda's expectations prove to be extraordinarily difficult for some students to navigate initially.

What Do I Do with Choice and Time?

Nineteen of one-hundred-and-ten students know Linda's classroom, having had her as seventh graders. Many others enter on the first day with an entirely different conception of language arts class. They are used to being assigned books and writing topics. Some, like Peggy, who have never been taught writing as a process, panic. Linda says, "She's been taught that you write, hand in a piece, get it back." Revision is foreign to many. They expect to hand in first drafts as final work.

Many students shun their freedom of topic choice and don't know how to exploit their extended work time. During the first few weeks some seem obsessed with getting Linda's explicit approval before they take initiative to write or read. Their questions begin with, "Can I . . . ": "Can I put more than one poem in my journal?" "Can I cut out pictures from bike magazines?" They will not begin unless Linda first approves their choices.

A few exploit writing time to socialize and ignore work, but most of the students who aren't writing look chagrined. Time to create without explicit direction from the teacher freezes them. They appear not to know how to begin. In previous classes, their teachers guided their procedures by assigning books and pages to read, handing out materials when they needed them, or passing out work sheets. In this class students find their own books and working materials. Those who have never had these responsibilities become confused. Questions abound about how to check out books, where to find drawing paper, and where to store folders and portfolios. In the early days it is a logistical nightmare for those unused to the workshop atmosphere.

What Matters to Me?

Many students have little trouble identifying their passions but many others do. Adolescents beginning to question their identities, relationships, and societal roles (Barbieri 1995; Erikson 1950; Gilligan 1982; Marcia 1980) often have greater difficulty identifying the aspects of their lives that are most important to them, are reluctant to reveal those aspects for fear of ridicule or ostracism, or simply do not believe that the things they value might also have value to others.

Their lack of experience in creating their own topics (which prompts the familiar complaint, "I don't know what to write about") certainly contributes, as well. But, remarkably, some students who have difficulty in class finding writing topics demonstrate a deep value of writing outside of school. One student, Kurt, shocks Linda with his diametrically opposed attitudes toward in-school and out-of-school writing. Linda says about Kurt:

> Literally, my rank book is a blank for him. Well, come to find out, he's writing for a computer magazine! He has published at least seven articles this year, but he didn't think it mattered! And he didn't think to *mention* it! I said, "You're going to win a Pulitzer Prize and you're going to stand up

there and you're going to say, 'I did this despite my language arts teacher!'"
He has a zero in the class! But he goes home and he works on the Internet.
He's got an editor he works back and forth with; he's fourteen years old and
writes for computer magazines and mountain biking magazines. . . . I said,
"Could you bring in, Monday, the letters that have gone back and forth with
your editors, the e-mail that you've done, the pieces that you've published?"
He goes, "Yeah."

Kurt has been writing for two on-line magazines for about a year, after
stumbling across a want ad for a columnist on the Internet. His job requires
him to read and research extensively and write columns that present technical aspects of mountain bikes. He never thought to put this work in his portfolio. He says, "It never just came to me that you could include it for writing."
He suggests that Mrs. Rief tell students what kind of writing she accepts. In-
credulously, I show him numerous examples from my notes where Linda had
specifically exhorted students to bring in out-of-school writing. "Yeah," Kurt
shakes his head and smiles sheepishly. "I really don't know why I didn't include it."

Kurt knows what is important to write about, but does not know it is
important in the context of school. He says that past experiences taught him
teachers wanted "pieces of writing that had to be on a certain topic." That
Linda has explicitly welcomed the exact type of writing he is doing demonstrates the highly ingrained nature of students' difficulty understanding what
"important" means in her classroom. It also demonstrates the magnitude of
her challenge in overcoming that difficulty.

What If I Just Don't Care?

While a student like Kurt secretly appreciates writing, some students—many
of whom are fantastic oral storytellers—hate to write or seem indifferent to
it. Linda says,

> There are kids who don't really care about reading and writing. That could
> be because there are things going on in their lives that I have absolutely no
> control over, and reading and writing don't matter to them at the moment.
> But it doesn't mean I'm not going to *try* to offer them experiences that I
> think are good for them. I'll be as patient as I can, I'll always be there, but
> I can't continually spend my forty-five minutes working with those one
> or two kids who still, at this point in the year, are not doing work.

Linda is torn between devoting her time to these students or to the already interested students who clamor for her precious attention. She hopes
that the work of their classmates will somehow model literacy's importance

better than she can. For these students she often shifts away from academics, toward simply trying to help them work through problems beyond her direct influence.

Why Do I Need Specifics?

For students less invested in writing, the notion of supplying rich detail seems to be either bewildering or a waste of time. Even fine writers sometimes give general descriptions and resist Linda's attempts to lead them toward detail. Writing in generalities is one of the most prevalent difficulties among all students.

Lloyd, for instance, writes a poem in which he enthuses, "Hockey is my life, hockey is everything," but has not supplied any descriptive details. In a conference Linda encourages him to list the sights, sounds, and smells of hockey, but his next draft is largely unchanged. Linda gives him an exercise. She asks him to revise the poem under one condition: he cannot use the words "hockey" or "winter." Lloyd looks grim.

How Many Pieces Are Due?

At the beginning of the year, some students worry about how much writing Linda expects from them. Linda initially exacerbates this worry by requiring a certain number of journal entries each quarter. In October questions such as "*How* many pieces are due?" and "If you do two pages in your journal does it still count as only one entry?" prevail. Linda is frustrated. Students are not concentrating on the quality of their writing.

The danger Linda runs in stressing quantity to *find* quality is that students misinterpret the quantity as the focus of the assignment, which turns their writing superficial. Ultimately, she says, the number of pages has little effect on her final evaluation. She expects fine products upon which students can thoughtfully comment, regardless of numbers. She simply knows, as a writer, that fine products come about with more writing. Though she explains this several times, quantity still sticks in some students' minds as *the* major consideration when writing.

6

Organization

As teachers, we want to establish an atmosphere that promotes talk and writing that is relevant to our students. Linda's role as an organizer helps reduce the difficulties students have. Her careful organization offers direction and context to students overwhelmed by their newly found freedoms of choice and time. Without this foundation they are unable to attend as well to her subsequent instruction and Linda has a harder time listening. Organization gives stability, which enhances receptivity.

But it is crucial to understand that Linda's efforts pay off only in the long term. Proactive organization cannot be practiced sporadically or judged on a daily basis. Consistency in action and patience are essential to success. Linda does not obtain immediate results. In fact, this year she spends close to two months at the beginning of the year teaching students how the classroom runs. It is not until they are sufficiently familiar with its layout and procedures that they immerse themselves fully into writing and reading.

Organize to Meet Expectations

In Linda's classroom every paper, every pen, every table and chair, every book has its place. As she familiarizes herself with students' ways she modifies organization and procedures to increase efficiency, but at any point in time she knows where each artifact resides and how every procedure functions. "Perhaps I'm a fanatic perfectionist!" she says. "I can't work in a messy environment, and the more I have to do, the more organized I have to be!" Here are some of the elements of her organization.

Procedures and Logistics

Linda's mini-lessons at the beginning of the year often are not "mini"—she sometimes devotes entire classes to familiarizing students with the room's setup, procedural expectations, and book borrowing. Students learn how to check out books by placing check-out cards in the plastic card files (one for each class) on top of one bookcase. They learn where to put supplies, how to sign up for conferences, how to catalogue and cover new books, how to write down assignments, how to clean the classroom, and how to sign out to go to the bathroom. While some of these procedures are familiar to anyone who has attended school, what is significant is the weight Linda places on them and the extensive amount of class time she spends reviewing and reinforcing them.

The Books and the Room

Linda's book organization begins before the start of the school year. She organizes picture books on shelves by theme or genre. Chapter books are shelved alphabetically by author. She catalogues, in her computer, each new book she has bought or received. All hardbacks receive plastic library covers and stickers with Linda's name on them. She writes her name on the inside front cover of each paperback and covers them with contact paper. (As the year progresses, students take over the responsibility of covering all new books.) If there are multiple copies of a book, each gets an identifying number. She places her homemade library cards in the middle of each book.

Cardboard shelving systems in one bookcase organize reading lists, conference sheets, permission slips, and paper. On a wall hangs a system of file cards and paper pockets used to designate weekly student jobs—attendance taking, handing out papers, etc. There is not a physical artifact that cannot be put away where someone else can find it.

Students are free to roam the room, but Linda assigns each to a table. She wants those who can help each other to work together. She tries to ensure that each person sits with at least one fairly close friend, but friends can also inhibit work, so she keeps alert to dynamics. At tables students face each other and, as we shall see, Linda encourages social talk, but she continually struggles for balance. Table organization must create social talk that influences the students' literacy work, but does not break down production. She fiddles with arrangements and rearranges tables a couple of times a quarter in order to introduce fresh viewpoints.

Journals

Every student organizes his or her journal in the exact same way. Using white tabs, they divide their journals into four sections: *Response,* where they put book responses, thoughts, or artifacts that informed their reading, writing, and thinking; *Notes,* where they write mini-lesson information; *Vocabulary,* where they write unfamiliar words; *Spelling,* where they write personally misspelled words. Inside the front cover, each student staples two pages of directions about how to use the journal and a *Reading List* to document information about every book they read.

Journal setup is nonnegotiable, and Linda explains why: she reviews over a hundred journals, and she intends to be thorough. If everyone arranges his or her journal differently, she has to rummage to find what she wants. If she spends just two minutes searching for reading lists and other work in each journal, she loses more than three hours of precious time.

Portfolios

At the end of each quarter, students include the following items in their portfolios: (1) their best four or five pieces of the quarter, with the most effective placed on top and the least effective on the bottom (each piece includes every draft, with the final draft on top, and earlier drafts underneath), (2) Case Histories and self-grades of their two or three best pieces, (3) their quarterly Evaluation of Writing and Reading (see a similar survey in Appendix I in *Seeking Diversity*), (4) a Readers'/ Writers' Survey that outlines their literacy beliefs, talents, tastes, and needs, and (5) any other work or material that is important to them.

Draft Folders

Each class has a color-coded file folder bin. Each student has a folder in which to put working drafts. Anyone who wants Linda to read a draft places it vertically in his or her folder in the bin. Linda then knows to read and comment on it.

Conference Sheets

Each student has a Conference Sheet. During a conference, the student hands the sheet to Linda. The sheet has boxes where both student and Linda write commentaries and questions while talking. Students use Conference Sheets extensively for the first two months, but as they internalize procedures they generally abandon them. They begin to write questions and comments on the drafts themselves. (For an example of a similar conference sheet, see Appendix N in *Seeking Diversity*.)

Take *Time* to Organize

It is essential to understand that the road to an organized, smoothly running classroom is a long one. Students do not become competent after hearing directions only once, no matter how clear our explanations. At the beginning of the year, Linda goes over organization and procedures time and again, alternately bemused and frustrated when students continue to ask sincere questions about what to write in their journals. Students read and write every day, but reviewing procedures eats real time.

During this year it is October, and some students still use journals as places to write their formal drafts. In class, Linda tells them, "I'm really worried. I took too many leaps with this journal." She again explains the differences between journal responses and draft writing. She spends the rest of the class moving from table to table, helping students reorganize their journals and folders and explaining what she expects in terms of entries and rough drafts.

A few days later, Linda reviews the journals. She is sorely disappointed. Students still have not organized according to her written directions and mini-lessons. Some have not been recording responses to their readings. On Monday Linda abandons her intended mini-lesson and refocuses on journal requirements. "We're going to start over at the very beginning," she says as she puts up a transparency of a journal's Reading List on the overhead projector. Though they have reviewed the material many times, many students still struggle. "This is confusing!" whispers Annie, softly, as Linda speaks.

It is a low point in the year for Linda. She is uncomfortable with her classes, even now, because she does not yet know her students through their writing. School is over a month old and they still struggle with classroom operations! One night she talks on the phone with Nancie Atwell, who empathizes with her. "I hate all the organizing!" Nancie tells Linda. "It takes a full month!" Will these students ever learn? Linda wonders. Weeks later, after the class has begun functioning smoothly, she laughingly admits that she feels the same panic at the beginning of every year. She always remembers what last year's students did in *June* and forgets the same struggles she encountered with them in the first quarter.

Linda's persistence—her unwillingness to drop organizational issues even when they seemingly take away from literacy learning—quite suddenly shows results in the first week of November. Almost miraculously—within the span of a few short days—students begin to organize and use their journals according to her expectations. They quit tugging at her sleeve. "Can I . . . " questions drop precipitously, as do questions about the location of supplies and books. It is November. Linda *now* begins to confer more often with students about their work.

Organize to Put Students in Charge

Linda's organizational design helps guide the freedom and time students need to enhance their creative processes. She standardizes the organization of classroom resources and the presentation of students' products, but does *not* want to control the content or process of students' work. This is sometimes a difficult feat. In October, some students interpret one requirement as an appropriation of their writing. Linda announces that she expects each student to complete at least five pieces of writing by the end of the month, because she wants them all to have enough quantity and variety from which to find true quality work. One of these pieces will be a "major piece" of five pages or more. The other four can be "minor pieces"—short prose or poetry. Over the next few days, confusion ensues as students try to figure out which of their pieces are "majors" and which are "minors." There are exchanges like this:

Student: Is this long enough to be a minor piece?

Linda: It's a major-minor.

The assignment's definitions are not clear in anyone's mind. Things come to a head. Laura has written a short poem she loves and announces that it is her major piece. No, Linda disagrees, a major has to be five pages. "No!" Laura cries out; "I can't do it!" She feels her short piece deserves the honor of being a "major." Why, she asks, does Linda insist on evaluating pieces according to their length rather than their quality? Later in the day, frustrated with herself and the students' apparent inability to understand her motives, Linda changes the rules:

> I'm not going to count major or minor anything any more. [Just write] what is important to you. That's all that counts. I don't care if you do one piece or twenty as long as it's something you care about.

Students like Laura resist Linda's assignment as they sense their autonomy as writers being wrested from them. Her organization has cut too close to the creative product for those who *welcome* creative freedom. Linda vows in the future to tell students they simply need enough writing to be able to unearth material worthy of carrying forward into final pieces.

Keep Up Organization

Subsequent days prove that effective organization also requires vigilant upkeep and maintenance. Procedures that students internalized weeks before sometimes break down as familiarity breeds disregard. On one weekend Linda comes in to shape up the room. She finds books that are misshelved, backwards, and upside-down. Some books have no check-out cards. She takes immediate action. On Monday, once again, in detail, she reviews proper book organization and check-out procedures, then refers students to another detail she has just added: reference signs that describe where books sit. Periodic upkeep like this continues throughout the year.

Linda's devotion to organization, even though it initially takes away from vital reading and writing time, offers students procedural boundaries within which to conduct their work. It gives direction to their freedom of time and choice. Further, the efficiency it eventually engenders *creates* time: time for students to talk, ponder, read, and write in the long run, over the course of the entire year. It also gives Linda time to listen to and observe students, which informs her responses to them. She knows she will read and respond to extraordinary amounts of student writing, listen and respond to extraordinary amounts of student talk. It is impossible to respond thoroughly or well if the classroom does not function smoothly. Students must flow through the day without interrupting Linda with problems they can learn to answer for themselves. Her ability to listen to a student's process of creation, rather than just the final product, depends completely on more time.

7

Read, Write, and Share

Only when students internalize organization and procedures can they fully attend to Linda's literacy instruction. Linda teaches literacy by sharing authentic writing with students. She teaches almost exclusively through three sources of writing: students' writing, professional authors' writing, and her own writing. Through them, she examines method, style, and conventions. She eschews workbooks, basals, and other materials created directly for school instruction. Importantly, Linda also reads and writes with students during class.

Sharing, Modeling, Finding Solutions

In this atmosphere where the teacher teaches by doing and sharing real writing and reading, students are better able to grapple with their difficulties finding a topic, generalizing, and focusing on quantity, even with their indifference to reading and writing. Seeing other authors' real struggles, students begin to see possible solutions to their own difficulties. Solutions lead to greater interest and more enthusiastic talk and writing.

Sharing Student Writing

Linda copies and shares hundreds of pieces of student writing she thinks are exceptional. The writing spans all genres, including journal writing and quick-writes. It teaches a multitude of lessons. It demonstrates procedures (how to set up journal entries, reading lists, evaluations, and portfolios), progressive drafting and other aspects of the writing process, and topics other students consider important to write about. For example, one day Linda reads Tim and Kelly's letter to a local newspaper protesting their class's treatment by a visiting presidential candidate. The letter is so exceptional that *Harper's* magazine picked it up and ran it. Linda asks the class, "Has anyone made you feel so strongly that you had to write something? Has there been a time when you have been either humiliated or embarrassed? Have *you* ever done anything that humiliated or embarrassed someone? Jot them down. They may turn into writing."

She demonstrates student writing with rich, specific description, like this journal entry of a former student who wrote an entry on a train. Linda says, "She's just noting what she sees and hears—the smells . . . ":

> Black train, seats pink like Pepto-Bismol, rubbing knees with Hannah, curled on the seat beside my own. Moon in the waning stage, illuminating snow piles out the window, which we rush by, rattling. Orange lights pierce darkness, a white church steeple . . .

Sharing Professional Writing

The professional writing Linda shares comes from primary sources. It encompasses every genre imaginable: fiction and nonfiction, young adult and juvenile, poetry, picture books, art, nature, how-to, humor, travelogues, cartoons, short stories, histories, pamphlets, speeches, newspaper and magazine articles, advice columns, sketchbooks, and journals. She wants students to relate writing to their own lives. "Write down anything this reminds you of, makes you feel, makes you think," she says.

She shares to examine particular elements of writing or the writing process. To show students how they might incorporate artwork into their journals, she shows illustrated journal entries from authors Jean Craighead George and Karen Ernst. Just as often, she simply reads out loud to show the raw power of words, challenging students to look for "powerful" or "beautiful" language.

Linda has met some of the authors whose works she shares. She has inside information about the creation of their books, which personalizes them. Discussing revision, she holds up the book *Wombat Divine* by Mem Fox (1996). Before she reads it, she tells the students that Fox had given her a copy of the first draft. She reads, juxtaposing first draft text with final. "Can you hear the big difference?" she exclaims. "*Huge* differences."

Sharing Personal Writing

Linda also exemplifies a wide array of literacy styles, genres, and conventions through her own writing. She rarely shows, however, her final drafts. She chooses instead to focus on journal entries and works-in-progress. Her writing reveals the writer's inspiration because she traces pieces back to their original sources. To show how journal entries inspired further writing she shares an entry about meeting Miep Gies in Germany. She then shows a letter she is drafting to Gies which expresses her admiration for the woman who hid Anne Frank.

Linda also teaches conventions through her own writing. In one instance she shows a poem draft, detailing the proper formatting for her title, with quotation marks and important words capitalized.

Writing and Reading with Students

"Mrs. Rief doesn't *listen!*" Jade jokes one day, "All she does is *write!*" In most instances, Linda completes in-class assignments with her students, directly modeling the behaviors she wants them to acquire. This year she drafts an autobiographical sketch, interviews students, and creates a comic strip. She writes and shares quick-writes and comes to class with a book. Sitting at a table with students or alone in a corner, she reads, underlines passages, and writes rapidly in her journal. When visiting authors conduct workshops, Linda participates as every student does.

As students become more familiar with reading and writing on a daily basis, Linda often limits herself to quick-writes; the rest of the time she devotes to conferring. Nevertheless, when there are bits of time to be had, Linda wades back into the middle of the crowd to read and write with her students again.

Her reading and writing powerfully influence students' work. Because she takes her own literacy seriously, students respect her requests for an atmosphere conducive to work. They adopt her learning stance. Linda notices, "The kids watch me *really* carefully. The kids who want to do well really watch me to see what I'm using. It confirms for me that they are really conscious of what you do as a teacher." Gretchen says, "I look at examples of her writing and it gives us ideas. She read [a piece] to us a couple of days ago and *I* got an idea from it." When surveyed, students overwhelmingly state that Linda's practice and sharing of her own literacy is invaluable. It offers them new writing ideas and perspectives, challenges their thinking, and helps them find new books. It makes reading and writing more personal, tangible, and accessible.

Finding Inspiration for Stories that Matter

As Linda presents personally relevant work, both she and her students have frequent and sudden flashes of empathic recognition: one person's story elicits others' personal stories (Kaufman 1995), which Linda encourages them to share. Linda's own stories can be remarkably intimate. She shares a poignant quick-write about her father's alcoholism and how she tried to hide his bottles as a child. Several times she strongly insists that writing about something important does *not* have to mean something intimate or intensely private; nevertheless, her shares expand the boundaries of what is acceptable classroom conversation. Students feel more comfortable discussing more of their lives. They talk about families, boyfriends, and girlfriends; swap jokes; complain about school; discuss their weekends; disagree and argue. Social and personal concerns begin to inform academic ones, introducing the subject matter Linda feels is most important to their writing.

One example occurs as Tina, Melanie, and Lynn talk socially about Tina's trampoline. Jumping on the trampoline reminds Tina of an autobiographical essay she is writing. Her story provokes her friends to talk about their own families, which, in turn, inspires them to develop their own autobiographies. Notable is the continual pulsing and shifting between academic and social talk. Stories feed into one another, giving rise to progressively more stories. The informal stories influence their texts.

This social talk is productive because the students continue to work on their writing while talking, or shift back to work during lulls in conversation. The social talk eventually leads students to ask questions about assignments, read their writing to friends, and ask for help. Now focusing on their work, they confer. Finally, they attend directly to drafting and revising, utilizing their peers' feedback. The conversation then shifts to new work concerns and new social topics. The cycle repeats.

But the social talk cannot overwhelm the task at hand. If students do not attend to work on a continual or regularly patterned basis, social talk becomes "goofing off." In one instance Dustin, Kip, Robert, Ashley, and Greg talk about sports and dating, but none of their social talk translates back to the page. Some of them, in fact, do not have pens. Their ideas, so similar to those Tina, Melanie, and Lynn discuss, vanish once spoken.

Finding the Balance

It is a delicate balance the teacher has to listen for. Students' personal lives drive their writing, and talk is the primary method by which they explore life experiences before committing them to the page. The teacher has to evaluate each talk situation to see if it enhances writing or takes time away from it. How can Linda tell? "The noise!" she says. "They seem to be having *too* much fun that has gone beyond the bounds of personal talk contributing to actual asks." Volume is a fairly reliable indicator of its value to writing. If the noise level rises above an acceptable "working hum" to where the teacher can distinguish individual voices, it indicates that students have become temporarily oblivious to a requisite of productive work: a quiet enough atmosphere in which to think. When they attend to their work, they heed the rule of relative quiet, in need of it themselves.

On the other hand, if students are unwilling or unable to discuss personally relevant issues, their talk holds less academic value. For example, at the beginning of the year two students, Walter and Tim, interview each other in order to write short biographies.

Walter: What's your most favorite thing you like to do?

Tim: I like to play hockey and draw.

Walter: Why?

Tim: Hockey's the best sport on earth.

Walter: And drawing?

Tim: Because I'm good at it. . . . How long have you been in school?

Walter: That's stupid. You know that. . . . What's your favorite spot to be when you're angry?

Tim: My bedroom, because that's where I get sent. . . . What are your favorite hobbies? Is that a good question?

Walter: I like to read, play the computer, and draw. . . . What do you want to be when you grow up?

Tim: A hockey player or animator.

Walter: Why?

Tim: Will you stop with the why questions! That's what I like.

The talk here is perfunctory and a little stilted. Tim doesn't elaborate for what may be any number of reasons. He may be shy in front of someone unfamiliar. He may feel that the things he likes aren't important enough to share. He may be reluctant to participate in talk that leads to writing. He may have come from classrooms where personal lives do not inform the formal curriculum. Whatever the reasons, no easy conversation gives rise to potential new writing. Instead, talk follows the unadorned line of the assignment: to ask and answer questions. In this sense the questions are as dryly academic as possible, purely following the teacher's directions, unembellished by personal curiosity or enthusiasm for what is being said.

However, Walter subsequently asks Tim who his favorite character to draw is. Tim responds, "Moe. Want me to draw it?" He draws a picture of a little man with a large nose and a mustache. This is the only point in the interview in which Tim volunteers unsolicited information, drawing enthusiastically and easily. Drawing, I learn later, is the form of expression with which he feels most comfortable. Tim isn't one for small talk, and he loathes writing.

The question that arises, then, is what happens to the student who either is not a natural talker or is unable to associate personal conversation with the academic agenda? For Tim, Linda tailors her approach. She encourages his drawing and he creates a wonderful cartoon and poem about his hatred of writing! It is excellent writing and receives a finalist award in a national contest.

Most others, though, learn through Linda's consistent, persistent message that talk and writing do in fact inform each other. Students begin to use talk as one of their primary modes of predrafting.

8

Social Talk at Work

To illustrate how social talk informs and enhances students' academic work, let us look at a conversation where it occurs. Here, at a table of students, talk is generated by participants wholly comfortable with one another. Their words have in some ways been inspired by the academic agenda presented them, but social talk sustains the conversation and influences subsequent writing (Barnes 1992, 1995; Britton 1993; Wells 1986).

Science Talk

As class begins, Linda suggests that students work to complete any unfinished pieces they want to include in their portfolios. Kelly, Gretchen, and Anna, three close friends, rummage through their writing. Gretchen decides to work on a science assignment. She has to observe a natural phenomenon daily over several weeks and record any changes. (Linda has recognized that these observations might lead to writing ideas, so she has arranged it with the science teacher to have students record their observations in their language arts journals.) That the first conversation at this table is about science underscores the expansion of acceptable topics in Linda's classroom.

Gretchen: I have to observe. It's not gonna be hard to observe stuff about nature, but every day it looks the same, so I don't know what to write.
Kelly: I know! You'd be, like . . .
Doug: No, it doesn't. As a matter of fact, who was it? I can't remember whom I was talking to yesterday, but they said, "I have to have an observation," and

they looked out yesterday, and I said, "What did you see?" And they said, "Nothing." And I go . . .

Gretchen: I don't see . . . I see the same thing I saw yesterday.

Kelly: No, it was raining yesterday!

Gretchen: No it wasn't.

Kelly: Yes it was.

Anna: It was raining in the morning and . . .

Gretchen: Well, I didn't write about that. I wrote at night yesterday.

In conversation, a person's speaking turn provokes recognition within another person, who then uses personal knowledge to respond. Kelly empathizes with Gretchen's complaint, and shouts, "I know!" I, who had heard another student's similar complaint, challenge Gretchen's opinion. Gretchen's statement has evoked unique personal experiences from both Kelly and me. My statement then reminds Kelly of another experience. She extends my commentary, reminding Gretchen of yesterday's rain.

Gretchen's statements now inspire Kelly to write her own science observations:

Kelly: I'm writing now. It's like blue sky, and, see what kind of clouds there are. There's cumulus clouds out . . .

Gretchen: When it was dark. Around five thirty. It wasn't really night, but it was dark. It's been getting so dark early.

Anna: [Adding to Kelly's comment] . . . and they're moving really, really fast.

Gretchen: What do you write about cumulus clouds? They're *boring!*

Anna: They're moving really fast.

Kelly: Well, *yeah!* But that's an observation, isn't it?

Doug: What does it mean that there are cumulus clouds?

Gretchen: They're puffy.

Doug: Yeah, but what does cumulus clouds mean?

Anna: They're cotton balls.

Gretchen: Oh! Does that mean it's nice weather and it's sunny?

Anna: Yes.

Gretchen: Cumulus, I forget. I know the sign. It looks like that. [Draws a symbol on her page]

Kelly: Yeah, me, too. That's the sign for it.

Gretchen: I know. I just said that.

Again, exchanges prompt reactions that supply information and provoke thought. The tone here is informal; it is talk among friends. But it is also academically informative—a collaborative science lesson. Significantly, the nature of this talk precludes rules that might diminish one's willingness to contribute. Whereas a teacherly question might compel the student to conjure up a "right" answer, here none of the students feel that explicit responsibility.

Individual Interests

This table talk has another layer of complexity. The students here discuss one topic as their personal experiences offer them entry into the discussion, but each student also has an *individual* agenda riding in the undercurrent. For instance, at this point in the conversation, Anna works on her own project. A few days before, she had read Linda a poem she wrote about lost childhood innocence. Linda, had cried, "That's beautiful! It's fabulous! It makes me cry! I don't think you have to change a word," but had added, "I can see somebody putting this to music. Can you hear the rhythm?" Today, while she talks clouds, Anna also revises her poem and pulls a new line of conversation to the surface:

Anna: I had to rewrite the poem because I made another verse. And now I'm upset because I hate writing this thing.

The students continue to discuss science observations. Anna contributes to the conversation but also hums a tune she has written to accompany her poem. The tune catches Kelly's ear and redirects the conversation.

Kelly: Is that your little song?
Anna: Yeah. Those are the words. Well, not all of them.
Gretchen: I made up my own tune after listening to yours.
Anna: Yep. [Sings]
Gretchen: They're sort of similar.

Anna's writing had already influenced Gretchen's writing: a day or two earlier, Anna had sung Gretchen her song-in-progress, which inspired Gretchen to compose her own music—a project she otherwise would not have attempted. It was a familiar phenomenon: one student's statement or activity inspires another to begin a new project or revise current work. We see here, also, how new topics arise and veer in surprising directions at a rapid pace, changing according to the unique experiences of each participant. During these conversations, many topics arise in a short time, contrasting with more academic discourse, which focuses on a limited number of topics at a time in a very ordered fashion. The trade-off is that while a lesson, for instance, can clarify a specific topic or concept, social talk provides a vast array of potential writing topics.

Informal Tones

Talk dominates the room, and students mill from table to table. They initiate conferences with an informal: "Do you like this line?" or "Read this." The ensuing talk holds the same informal tone, but contains valuable academic feedback as the respondents address the writers' concerns. Today, for instance, Charlie comes to the table, hands Kelly a play he is writing, and asks, "Do you think this is neat enough?" The ensuing conference involves the whole table. Gretchen and Kelly praise the piece's humor, laughing and pointing out parts that work. Anna offers specific help to Charlie's questions about neatness and spelling, and a pointed criticism: "This is stupid! Nobody would go that far on a dare! It's a good story, but nobody would go that far on a dare." The tone is different than conferences where the teacher formally assigns students to confer. Instead of formulating responses guided covertly by a teacher's academic agenda, they respond as friends answering one another with what immediately comes to mind.

Charlie leaves. Gretchen writes her observations. Anna works on her song, turning her attention to its meter:

Anna: I have to write this on, you know the paper with the lines? I have to write it as music notes, and it's *really* hard because I don't know what time it's in. I don't know if it's more four-quarter or three-quarter.

Kelly: Do you want us to figure that out for you?

Gretchen: Sing it.

Anna: [Sings] "Have you forgotten what it's like to float among the clouds, to ride the. . . ." Definitely not all quarters.

Gretchen: That's two-two.

Kelly: That's four-four. That's four-four time.

Anna: That's what I thought.

Kelly: And then you can just put it in quarter notes.

Anna: Okay.

Over the next few speaking turns the topic shifts several times, providing students a number of potential writing ideas—the oral equivalent of the entries stored in their journals. Gretchen laments that she can't sing like Anna, and Anna insists Gretchen has a beautiful voice. Gretchen replies she can break windows. This prompts a discussion about how certain sound pitches can shatter glass. Kelly announces she just wrote "cumulous clids," which prompts Anna to review the spelling in her lyrics. "How do you spell *among?*" she inquires. The girls write silently for a while, until Gretchen begins to hum again, whereupon Anna and Gretchen compare their tunes.

At this point, Diane comes to the table. She wants feedback to some watercolors she is painting to illustrate a poem. The table has now conferred about multiple literacy genres: science writing, a play, song lyrics, music, and painting. They have also discussed spelling conventions. By the end of class, this list will increase.

Diane receives response from three people. Kelly points out the picture she finds most appealing, Gretchen notes how the picture's shading works well, and Anna suggests further shading ideas. The sheer amount of information exchanged is one defining feature of this type of conversation.

Talk with the Teacher

Linda comes over to the table. All three students immediately vie for her attention. Anna reads her new verse out loud. Kelly picks up a book she wants Linda to read. Gretchen asks to confer about a piece that has, in fact, come from her science observations:

> The fog is thick, giving a heavy feeling to the air. Lugging a large doubt in the mind of a wanderer. He hugs his oversized coat in close as he shivers from the early morning chill. A breeze blows by him and his imagination takes over. He sees himself getting carried away by the wind, just like the sand that's stinging his face. He is a bird, a bird of mysteries. A mysterious wanderer, roaming around with no particular place to go.
>
> The figure keeps walking down the path. The long, winding path that he is no stranger to. In his mind he can see every root, every rock, every slight imperfection disturbing the smoothness of the path.
>
> I follow him steadily, curious where he is going. He takes his time, one faded footstep after another. Ahead I can see a lake. The mist gives an eerie, smokey feeling to it. There he approaches it cautiously, as if he's looking it over and deciding it's suitable. He starts walking faster. Picking up speed as if he were going to splash right through it. Feeling the cool water riding over his body.
>
> He stops at the edge and prepares for whatever he plans to do next. My mind is racing, clueless as to what's happening. I show a blank expression on my face. I wonder if he knows I'm watching.
>
> As my curiousness expands he begins forward, drifting across the hazy darkness of the water. Almost magically, the fog engulfs him and he is gone.

Gretchen: Do you like that?

Linda: I *like* this.

Gretchen: But . . .

Linda: Um, there are a *couple* of things I'm wondering about.

Gretchen: Uh-huh?

Linda: It's almost like it's not a he. It's really the *fall* that you're seeing.

Gretchen: I know! It is.

Linda: Okay. It's *almost* like, I mean, you've got this saved on the computer?

Gretchen: Yeah.

Linda: I mean it's fine as it is, but the one thing . . . it's almost like I need to have *one* phrase or something at the end, like, "He is gone . . . or is he?"

Gretchen: Right. Okay.

Linda: It's almost like there's *something* that I'm just waiting for that . . .

Gretchen: Right.

Linda: *Right.* That one little thing. The other thing I want to mention, and it's fine that you did this: you've got a whole bunch of fragments all the way through here.

Gretchen: Uh-huh.

Linda: Now, if you've done them with intent, that's okay. It's almost like it works that the fragments of your thinking are going in and out of the fall, so they're not complete sentences. If you're doing it with that intent, then it works. If you just made a mistake . . .

Gretchen: No. I like . . .

Linda: Okay.

Gretchen: That's what my mom said. She was helping me, and she said, "This is an incomplete sentence." I said, "I know, there's *not* complete sentences all *over* it. That's the point." It's not really a story. It's just . . .

Linda: It's images.

Gretchen: Yeah.

Linda: Then, that's *perfect.*

Gretchen: I like it that way.

Linda: Then that's the way you should keep it.

Gretchen easily initiates the conference, clearly wanting Linda's feedback. She asks, "Do you like that?" in the same tone and manner she addresses similar questions to her friends—directly, with a hint of excited anticipation in her voice. She is comfortable with the procedure and with Linda.

Linda's tone is slightly different than that of Gretchen's peers. Her words, voice, and mannerisms indicate a more conscious awareness of the impact her responses might have on Gretchen. Whereas these students directly told one another their opinions (Gere and Stevens 1985), Linda uses more introductions ("Um, there are a couple of things I'm wondering about . . .") and qualifiers ("The other thing I want to mention, and it's fine that you did this . . .") to soften the blow of any statement that Gretchen might interpret as criticism. Linda knows that her words carry a different weight, derived from her power as class leader and official evaluator. Her verbal approach illustrates a key difference between casual peer conversation and more traditional academic talk. In the latter, responses are more consciously measured, informed by a more specific agenda. In this instance, Linda's agenda is to help Gretchen with her writing, move her forward, but not alienate her. She has to weigh her words to find that balance. Friends' talk, guided by the different rules of confident social relationships, allows for blunter commentary and more informality.

Linda likes the piece, but suggests an addition to Gretchen's ending of ". . . and he is gone." Gretchen's response is noncommittal: "Right. Okay"; "Right"; "Uh-huh." Her tone of voice indicates she isn't at all sure she wants to do that. Linda then questions Gretchen's use of sentence fragments. But note that she does not order her to fix them. Instead, she explores the possibility that Gretchen wrote them intentionally, for effect. Linda applauds breaking conventions if the writer knows what she is doing. She tells her class on one day, "Does a sentence always have to have a noun and a verb? No it does not. Some of the best authors play with language." In this case, Gretchen indicates that it was indeed a conscious strategy to establish mood. She had already talked with her mother and made her decision. Linda responds, "Then, that's *perfect*."

In the conference, Linda again addresses Gretchen's ending:

Linda: And the *only* thing would be . . . something at the end that makes me stop to think. It's almost like I'm still thinking it's a *person,* and then I'm thinking, "No, it's not. It's *fog*. . . . or *is* he, or *is* it," or *something* in there. Just something that leaves us thinking at the very end.

Gretchen: Okay. [Reads the piece to herself] Okay.

Linda: And it could even be, "Will he be back tomorrow?" I mean, I don't want you to give *too* much away, because you've got, I don't know. It might just be, "Or is he?"

Gretchen: Okay.

Linda: Just think about what that last sentence could be. But that works *really* well. . . .

Kelly: Can I read this, Gretchen?

Gretchen: Yeah.

Linda: And I *really* like the fact you know that's what you meant.

Kelly's seemingly innocuous statement, "Can I read this Gretchen?" is very important. When Gretchen's conference begins, all other talking at the table stops. Kelly and Anna listen intently. In effect, Linda gives a conference to all three people. They all hear Linda's complements, questions, suggestions, as well as Gretchen's explanations and justifications. This one-on-one conference has a more wide-reaching effect.

Thinking and Challenging

Linda leaves the table. Anna reaches over and takes Gretchen's piece.

Anna: [Looking at Gretchen's piece] See, I *like* that. I would say that would be the ending. [Reads] "As my curiousness expands, he begins forward, drifting across the hazy darkness of the water, almost magically, fog engulfs him and he is gone." [She adds] "Or is he?" I don't like that. I just like, "and he is gone."

Gretchen: That's what *I* like. I don't like the other way.

In effect, Gretchen's conference is not over. Anna heard the conference and disagrees with Linda's suggestion to change the ending, and Gretchen concurs (which one might have predicted from the tone of her responses to Linda). That she had not challenged Linda's suggestion in conference may indicate her sense of respect for a traditional teacher-student relationship, a fear of contradicting Linda, or a need to mull over the suggestion. In any case, she now has a collegial ally and another opinion to weigh when she revises.

The talk at the table again begins to shift and flow and intertwine. Anna shows a cartoon she has drawn, Kelly works on a social studies report. Diane returns to confer about a poem and another illustration. Gretchen debates Linda's suggestion some more.

Gretchen: I think it's weird.

Anna: I like it how it is. "He is gone."

Gretchen: I didn't know what to write in the bottom, 'cause I had this part up to, "I wonder if he knows I'm watching?" When I was *typing* it, I was like, "That *can't* end. It's just *stupid*." [Laughs] And it was due the next day, so I just kinda *wrote* something. Well, actually, I spent a little time with the thesaurus, but . . .

Work that Belongs to Students

A week later, when Gretchen hands in her portfolio, her completed piece will end with, ". . . and he is gone." In her Case History she will admit, "Ending it was/is a problem for me. I could picture what I wanted to happen, but I couldn't describe it." But Gretchen feels enough comfort and control over her own writing to weigh and then *dismiss* Linda's suggestion, which defines the classroom behavior Linda tries to engender.

This class ends with Kelly reading to her friends her autobiographical fiction about an eighth-grade girl struggling with overbearing coaches, rude teachers, and snobby classmates. Each character is based on a real person. It is a fitting story with which to end because it highlights vividly the connection between students' personal issues and the academic product. These students exploit the extraordinary variety of opportunities with which their conversations present them. They create literacy products important to their own lives. Their own talk plays a critical role in their learning and discovery; their subject matter and enthusiasm indicate their commitment. The class that begins with a solid organizational foundation enables students to receive more clearly the presentation of real reading and writing, which in turn enhances their own classroom conversations.

But there is another facet of our instruction needed to promote educative conversation, specifically in regard to our own personal interactions with students. The dynamics of the teacher-student relationship are often more difficult to navigate than those of friends. Teachers must adopt a more sophisticated approach that addresses a wider spectrum within students' personalities. In the next section we see Linda's one-on-one interactions with students, particularly her writing conferences with them. They demonstrate the conditions a teacher might establish to achieve more effective interpersonal communication, enhancing listening and response.

9

Conference Procedures

A writing conference is any conversation between a teacher (or student) and an author (or coauthors) about a text or writing ideas. Conferences sometimes suck in other curious students sitting nearby, the way Linda's conference with Gretchen drew in Kelly and Anna. These others listen intently to the conversation and sometimes join in, providing their own commentary. They ask questions, give the teacher background about the author's piece, and offer advice. In short, conferences sometimes become social events that revolve around the author's work but which also inform, and are informed by, other listeners. This phenomenon teaches students more than if the teacher is the sole respondent.

Most of Linda's conferences with students have a basic framework—a general pattern of interactive elements. However, it is tremendously dangerous to call them a formula. In fact, the following chapters will show how a teacher must vary her approach to meet the diverse needs of individual writers. Instead, we might call this pattern the *proactive* element of Linda's approach—a foundation upon which to begin, which is born out of years of experience. It is based on what she knows *usually* works and what she wants students to accomplish. Her approach has six basic steps:

1. Initiating the conference
2. Learning the student's needs
3. Listening to the text
4. Praising the text
5. Questioning, suggesting, explaining
6. Closing the conference

Initiating the Conference

Both Linda and students initiate conferences. Linda often roams the room searching for writers who appear to need help. She requires students to confer with her about any piece they intend to include in their portfolios.

Students initiate conferences by putting their names on a list on the board. However, time often runs out before Linda reaches the bottom of the list. Those particularly eager for help lobby for a few minutes of her time before she goes on to the next name on the list. At other times the list disappears and students simply approach Linda.

Learning the Student's Needs

Linda begins almost every conference by asking, "How can I help you?" It forces the student to identify and focus his or her needs. The student's reply orients Linda's listening focus and shapes her subsequent approach. "How can I help you?" starts the conference in the writer's hands: the writer controls the topic and Linda addresses the stated needs before she can impose her own agenda.

After Linda asks her orienting question the student either clearly articulates a specific need or *cannot* identify or articulate a need. In the second case, Linda cannot orient herself and assume a clear listening stance, so she might ask the student to clarify a too-vague answer or analyze the problem further, ask a series of questions to orient both of them, or ask the student to read the piece so she can comment according to what *she* perceives to be the student's needs.

Listening to the Text

Once Linda understands the student's need and other necessary background, she asks, "Why don't you read it to me?" When students read their own writing the teacher can ignore mechanical problems of early drafts and better hear the author's true intentions. It also forces the author to hear and analyze his or her own work.

Praising the Text

Upon hearing a piece, Linda's first response is to praise the student's text, writing process, or talk. A praise implicitly reveals what ideas she feels should be nurtured during subsequent work. Linda praises *specific* aspects of a text or process. A praise at the beginning of a conference provides the writer with a solid footing upon which to build. The teacher's praise must be legitimate, revealing something she truly finds important or appealing so that the student builds from an authentic foundation. Random or vague praise in pursuit of a generic notion of building self-esteem does not instruct.

The following excerpt shows how Linda uses praise to instruct. She confers with Judy, who is drafting a letter to author Carolyn Coman. Judy is an ice skater and loved a description of ice in the book *What Jamie Saw*. Linda sits down and Judy tells her about the letter.

Linda: That's a wonderful piece of writing. I like the way you went from a general comment to something really specific. Writers love to see that. . . . What do you think you need to do to the piece now?

Judy: Edit it.

Linda: The only thing I see is that you talk about three different things. You should have three paragraphs.

Linda begins with legitimate praise for a specific aspect of the work. Judy now has a good sense of Linda's perception of the merits of the piece and may now build off of them. Linda *then* segues to aspects of the piece that might need work (Slattery 1993), and Judy formulates her *own* perception of what the piece needs: editing. Linda concurs and offers advice.

Questioning, Suggesting, Explaining

Linda has now gathered enough information to fashion personalized responses, and she blends questions, suggestions, and explanations together in a multifaceted approach. She gives students new literacy knowledge, offers them options, and nudges them to think about what they have done and what they want to do. She pushes students to find a *direction* for their subsequent work.

Questions

Linda's questions attend to matters beyond the printed text. They help students to build the story behind their writing: their intentions, expectations, difficulties, and confusions. Her questions create a dialogic partnership with the author that begins and sustains forward motion.

The questions fall into two general categories. First, there are questions that teach Linda. They give her a basic background that guides her subsequent approach. These questions provide background about students' knowledge or experience. They clarify unclear practical information, the status of students' work, and information about schedules, organization, and procedures.

Second, there are questions that make students analyze. They provide background information, as well, but also push students toward critical reflection, challenging them to take control of their own work. Here, her expectations for students reveal themselves. She asks them to analyze what they are doing and how they are doing it, what they know and how they are growing, and what they have created and how well they have done. These questions tap into what is personally important to students. They also encourage students to analyze and evaluate oral or written description, ideas, concepts, purposes, and finished products.

Two conference exchanges highlight how Linda's questions emphasize her expectations that students write about personally important topics and supply descriptive detail.

Questions: Finding a Focus

In the first conference, Anna tries to write about her father's heart attack. She has a very rough draft and can't find a focus for it. "It's just this and then this," she says, worried that the draft is a series of disjointed facts. Linda asks Anna simply to tell her the story of the incident. Anna finds it much easier to *speak* the story; she immediately describes being upstairs when she heard her father scream, "Call 911!" She says she was so frightened that she almost asked, "What's the number?" Linda replies, "That would be a great lead: 'Anna, Call 911!' 'What's the number?'" But Anna still believes she has a larger problem with focus, so Linda tries a different tack:

Linda: What are you trying to get across in this piece?

Anna: I don't know.

Linda: What do you love about your dad? What do you *like* about your dad?

Anna: I don't know.

Linda: Well, maybe that's why you need to start writing, so you can to find out. What do you like . . .

Anna: His car.

Linda: Why were you scared?

Anna: 911 could be anything. He could have been dead down there.

Linda: What would you miss about him?

Anna: That's hard. What do you miss about your dad?

Linda: That he was there, though he didn't do a great job all the time. He was an alcoholic, but when he was sober he was the nicest, most wonderful man. He kept a roof over our head. I loved going to the dump with him. He was smart, a CPA . . .

Anna: You're too good at this, Mrs. Rief! [Anna thinks and talks a bit, trying to come to terms with this question.] I would *not* go to the dump with my father. He's annoying.

Linda: Why?

Anna: He focuses on the bad instead of the good. If I clean the entire kitchen and don't empty the dishwasher, he'll come in and say, "You didn't empty the dishwasher!"

Linda begins by questioning Anna's purpose. When Anna can't answer, Linda asks a series of questions designed to help Anna discover what she really cares about, which will define her purpose. Question after question she chips away at Anna's lack of focus.

When Anna then turns the tables on Linda and asks a question back, Linda gives a remarkably personal answer that exemplifies one type of answer Anna might provide. Finally, something that is important to Anna—her annoyance at her father's demeanor—*does* begin to come out. This is a potential focus for her writing. With work she might incorporate it into her original topic about fear over her father's heart attack or she might abandon the first topic. In either case Linda's line of questioning nudges Anna forward.

What Linda has learned from her questioning subsequently inspires her to create a novel approach on the spot. "I'm going to give you a strange assignment," she says. She asks Anna to think about her father and formulate sentences that follow the construction, "If I _____, he'll _____." She gives Anna a prompt: "If I clean up the kitchen without being asked, he'll . . ." and then says, "Put down at least thirteen things he'll do." Finally, Linda tells Anna to answer two questions about her father in her journal: "If something really bad happened to him, what are three things that would really change for you?" and "What are three things that you would really miss about him?"

This assignment caters to Anna's unique problem. It gives Anna more questions to contemplate. Her answers to them might elicit the essentials of her relationship with her father, reveal a focus to her piece, and provide her with written material.

Questions: Finding Specifics

A second exchange highlights Linda's emphasis on descriptive detail. Kim has written a poem draft called "Wonder":

> I sit and wonder,
> about everything.

How the world will be,
tomorrow,
next century—will there be any wilderness left?
I sit and wonder,
about what will become of me.
Will I be rich?
Poor?
Will I have a job?
What will it be?
I sit and stare,
at the outdoors.
Next time I look, will the fall leaves be on the trees?
Or will they be a carpet on the green grass. I love the swing—
how it dances in the breeze.
Will it remain?
Will I feel safe anymore?
I sit and wonder,
about my friends.
Will I be wanted?
Who will they be?
What will they look like?
I sit in silence.

Linda sees potential in the piece but worries Kim has not supported the grand issues she ponders with enough details, which will personalize the theme and make it relevant to her readers:

Linda: Where are you sitting and wondering?

Kim: My front porch.

Linda: What do you see?

Kim: Just the trees and the grass, the swings and the flowers that are dead now.

Linda: What do you think is going to happen to those?

Kim: They're going to be gone, or something.

Linda: What would you miss?

Kim: It being natural.

Linda: What do you see that you take great pleasure in?

Kim: Trees and grass.

Linda: Is it colors, shapes . . . ?

Kim: They seem just so quiet and peaceful. I don't know. It just seems more comforting.

Linda: When you think of the word *comforting,* what words come to mind?

Kim: I don't know. Just feeling *wanted,* I guess. I don't know. Feeling safe.

Linda: Good. Okay. Where in the whole poem could you add some things that could give us the strong feelings you have? You have some very generic lines here . . . this is not Katmandu. What are specifics? The leaves are carpeting the grass. What does it look like? . . . You want to give the sights, the sounds, and the smells that you treasure. . . . Your words are going to take us in and out. . . . But it's *lyrical.* It sounds like a song. What are the two or three lines you might repeat as a chorus?"

Linda's questions focus on specifics. They force Kim to think about how she might change her pieces for greater effect. Kim uses general terms like "natural," "trees," "quiet," "peaceful," and "comforting" without enhancing them with specific imagery. Linda wants qualities that make universal concepts unique and personal. She asks Kim for details that will set her words apart from others' words on the same subject.

In this instance, as Kim subsequently analyzes Linda's questions about specifics, she realizes that deleting certain generic lines like "about everything" will help reduce generalities.

Kim: I could cross it out.

Linda: Yeah. Does it change the poem if you take it out?

Kim: No.

Linda: Look for lines like that, that you can take out without changing the integrity.

Here, Linda recognizes a legitimate strategy, drops her own agenda for a moment, and builds off the *student's* idea, thus putting Kim in a position of greater control.

These excerpts exemplify the nature of Linda's conference questions. They are not questions that require yes or no answers, but are overwhelmingly thinking queries. They discourage a traditional Initiate-Reply-Evaluate approach because they do not require a "right" answer, but a *thoughtful* one.

Suggestions

Suggestions propose actions for students to consider. Linda presents suggestions to provide options for writing—writers *always* have the right to reject suggestions. By increasing choices, suggestions promote critical thinking. Most of Linda's suggestions consist of ideas to improve specific aspects of a given piece of writing. (Directives, on the other hand, are commands to revise work. They offer students no options to weigh, and thus provoke less analysis. Linda's directives focus on writing conventions—spelling, punctuation, and grammar—rather than ideas. Linda used vastly fewer directives than suggestions.)

Linda's questions often try to draw out what a student cares about, and her suggestions carry the message further. They advise the student how to *use* the subject matter important to him or her. She gives suggestions only after she has picked up cues from the author. In this example, David knows what he wants for his science fiction piece. He says, "I want to make it a little longer, but I'm not sure what to stretch," so Linda moves directly to listening to his piece. David reads his futuristic tale about an apprentice scientist and his best friend who work together in a lab specializing in gene splicing. Despite the high-tech nature of the scientists' jobs, David's portrait of the future is somewhat bleak. When not in the lab, the protagonist lives in a tin shelter with his pet "iguanoid" (a gene-splicing experiment gone wrong) and keeps all his food rations and other "treasures" in a garbage can. David finishes reading and Linda responds:

> Everything you've done, David, I really like. I mean it's just a fun piece to read, and I honestly almost believe you. This iguanoid, the rations, the PET lab, the scales instead of feathers, the whole splicing, the dialogue, the admitting that he prefers to be the best. And the grandfathers . . . that's really wonderful, and it all works. A place that you might add *on* to this is, what does this tin shelter look like? Maybe it's not like home, but by the time you get to the very end of it you don't *mind* it being home. I'd really like to hear more about how you would describe this tin shelter. . . . The other thing I'd like to know is what does this lab look like?

Linda starts with specific praise, then segues to her suggestions, which respond directly to David's desire to find legitimate places to lengthen his story. Her response to elaborate on the shelter comes from what she, as the audience, wants to know more about.

But Linda also presents perceptions of a piece that are independent of the writer's stated need if she feels the writer can contemplate them without blindly accepting or rejecting them. As this particular conference continues, she suggests that David might use the friends' relationship to create conflict, which she feels is missing from the story. David responds that he already has an idea to bring in another character to create tension. Linda thus ascertains that he is in control of his writing and she might therefore offer even more pointed suggestions.

Linda hopes David will use at least some of her suggestions because they represent an informed, professional opinion. But in the long run, what matters to her is that he thinks about them carefully. If he can justify his ultimate choices in his Case History, Linda will count that most in her own evaluations.

Explanations

Explanations, one might argue, are at the core of traditional classroom instruction. A teacher's lecture provides an almost unending stream of explanations about a topic. Explanations offer students potentially new information and resources that help them better navigate the world. Explanations are the teacher's presentation of her knowledge, ideas, opinions, speculations, interpretations, clarifications, analyses, and evaluations.

Some of Linda's explanations simply provide context and background information to students, which help them understand subsequent comments. Others provide potentially essential new subject matter that helps guide students' thinking about their work. In this example, Gretchen has written a piece addressed "to those who really don't believe the Holocaust happened." After Linda praises Gretchen's topic selection and use of repetition for emphasis, she makes a suggestion and then offers an explanation to help Gretchen comprehend the suggestion:

Linda: What I would suggest that you do here is put an epigraph.

Gretchen: A what?

Linda: An epigraph is just like a sentence or two, almost a statement *from those people.* We read this epigraph saying, "We no longer believe the Holocaust happened. It's a bunch of malarkey." And then the reader knows that everything you're going to write here is an *answer* to that epigraph.

Closing the Conference

When the conversants recognize that the writer has new insight with which to continue writing they close the conference. Usually Linda gives the final word, ending the conference with a word of praise, "This looks great. I'm really glad you did that."; a question to verify that the student is on track, "Okay, so you know what you want to do with it?"; a final suggestion, "But *tell* us something about this creek."; or a final evaluation, "It's ready."

Response Reflects Values

What are some of the salient features of Linda's conference talk with students? To find out I analyzed twenty-one transcribed conferences: six first-quarter and five third-quarter conferences with males, and five first-quarter and five third-quarter conferences with females (Kaufman 1998).

Value Ideas

I placed each of Linda's conference utterances (a complete sentence or independent clause) into one of three categories adapted from Sarah McCarthey: (1) *ideas,* which include comments about content (plot, character, setting, etc.), the writer's process of crafting ideas, and students lives and interests that might lead to text creation, (2) *mechanics,* which refer to spelling, grammar, punctuation, and other conventions, and (3) *logistics or procedures,* which relate "to getting materials, reading or sharing a piece of writing, or classroom management and organizational concerns" (1992, 56). While McCarthey showed that some teachers who are learning how to confer focus a great deal on mechanics, Linda focuses overwhelmingly on *ideas* (in 82 percent of her utterances). This percentage is consistent between the first and third quarters (Kaufman 1998).

Value Learning from Students

Linda also asks a large proportion of questions, especially at the beginning of the year. In the first quarter, almost half of her speaking turns (48 percent) contain a question, meaning that students are offering her a great deal of information to which she can listen, learn, and adapt her approach.

However, in the third quarter the percentage of speaking turns containing questions drops to 31 percent. My observations suggest a possible explanation. As Linda gets to know each student, she has to ask fewer questions at the beginning of each conference in order to learn the writer's tendencies, tastes, styles, and thinking processes. In fact, as the year continues, Linda's beginning-of-the-conference questions to those students we both consider to be enthusiastic and receptive drop off precipitously. With these students she sometimes launches almost immediately into suggestions or explanations. In conferences where Linda is still not as familiar with the student or the student's work, a larger percentage of speaking turns are still questions. Linda also asks a slightly greater percentage of questions to males than she does to females in both the first quarter (52 percent to 45 percent of her speaking turns) and the third quarter (35 percent to 28 percent) (Kaufman 1998). In the next chapter I will discuss the effect of gender on Linda's general conference approach, and its possible influence on her questions.

Linda's conference procedures offer her a foundational context for conducting conferences. Her approach comes from her experiences of what works, in general, for students. But they guide her much *less* than might be imagined. There is something much more important to creating effective conferences. When we welcome students' personal lives and passions into the text, they bring with them unique perspectives and ways of negotiating that generalized responses cannot address alone. We must primarily focus on building *relationships* with our students in order to create more open and harmonious conversations, which better inform their texts.

10

Conference Relationships

Good conversations depend upon good relationships. For the teacher seeking diversity through students' individual lives, a formula is not enough. First, a variety of factors contribute to many students' inability or unwillingness to *express* their diversity. The teacher has to build relationships with them that overcome powerful resistances. Second, when students do begin to share, the teacher then has to recognize and address the unique dynamics of their individual personalities. In both situations, not only do we have to attend to the *cognitive* domain, attempting to enhance students' thinking and evaluative processes, but also to the *affective* domain: the emotions, moods, feelings, attitudes, motivations, and self-perceptions that influence literacy activities.

In essence, we try to develop a relationship with each student that in many ways matches the productive socio-academic relationship students have with one another. For most students, a prerequisite to successful communication with the teacher is rapport: a sense of social and emotional (as well as academic) comfort and trust between them. Rapport allows students to discuss the personally relevant topics that drive the curriculum, giving the teacher material worthy of listening to. At the same time, rapport makes the teacher more willingly receptive to each student's unique passions and problems, further enhancing her listening and response. This chapter examines the influence of teacher-student rapport on the student's social construction of literacy.

Tapping the Writer's Interest: The *Spark*

There is a standard prerequisite for a productive conference (a conference in which the student leaves with a clearer direction in which to take her piece and a new willingness to move forward through revision): the student has to have an interest in what she is writing. If she knows what that interest is at the beginning of the conference, she has to be able and willing to articulate it to the teacher. If she cannot identify her interest, but nevertheless wants to improve the piece, she must articulate her willingness and also be willing to explore possibilities that arise out of what intrigues the *teacher*.

When a student shows no interest in a piece at the beginning of a conference, Linda helps the student unearth or create an interest by examining the important aspects of the student's life. Sometimes Linda describes her own interests to inspire hidden or immature interest in the students. If neither Linda nor the student can tap an interest or shape one into writing, then the conference can move no further on its own. At these times Linda often says to students, "If there is nothing there, then go on to something else." But lack of forward progress with one piece does not necessarily mean lack of success. It means the student can abandon the place where there is no interest and move forward into a place where there is.

Helping One Student Find His Interest

At the beginning of the year many students have some difficulty finding writing topics. When Linda sits down to confer with Andrew, he does not know how she might help him, only that he doesn't know what to write about. Linda had not taught Andrew as a seventh grader and she knows little about him. The first thing she does is ask him to read the goals he has written for himself on his Reading-Writing Survey. "I need to work on liking to read," says one. Linda takes this as a starting point:

Linda: Have you ever read a book you absolutely loved?
Andrew: Yeah, I found some. . . .

Andrew's voice trails off and Linda seems to conclude from his lack of enthusiasm that she might learn more about him by shifting focus to his trouble writing:

Linda: What has been difficult for you as a writer?
Andrew: Just writing a lot. I like to write; I just can't write that much.
Linda: So, don't worry that much about quantity.

Linda: Do you have anything you want to write? A letter . . .
Andrew: I could write a story. . . . About sports.

Linda: Why don't you write a page that starts, "I think I'm going to write a story about sports." Don't worry about the writing right away.

Andrew's response reveals much to Linda. That he says he likes writing focuses *her* response. Linda immediately tries to erase the obstacle that apparently stands in his way: his stated inability to write a lot. In her effort to keep Andrew moving forward, she tells him not to worry about writing a lot.

Then it is back to her primary focus. What does Andrew care about? His speculation that he might write about sports is the first time he has been able to articulate a possible topic. But there is no conviction in his voice. Linda senses that he is unsure about this topic. She suggests he write down what he is *going* to write about, which may spur an idea.

Linda doesn't leave the conference yet. She chats informally with Andrew about his other work. He tells her that he's copied some poetry into his journal and wants to know if it counts toward his weekly requirements. One of the poems is by Shel Silverstein and begins, "I've never roped a Brahma Bull . . . " (1981, 36). It is a poem about desires. Linda reads it and seizes upon the concept. She suggests stealing the beginning, "I never" and writing a piece that includes that phrase. She continues to try to learn what is important to Andrew.

Linda: What is it you absolutely want to do?
Andrew: Skydiving!

For the first time Andrew shows enthusiasm during the conference, and it is only at *this* point that Linda stands up and ends the conference. As soon as she leaves, Andrew begins to write.

This conference exemplifies the focus of Linda's listening. What stands out is Linda's patience and gentle persistence. When Andrew hopefully suggests that he write about sports, she doesn't leave the conference as might be expected. She keeps looking at his journal, asking him questions, and making suggestions. She reacts to Silverstein's "Brahma Bull" poem immediately, exploiting it to find Andrew's true passion. When Andrew almost shouts, "Skydiving!" she knows that this idea holds infinitely more promise for him than a sports story. Only *then* does she get up and leave Andrew who, free from his writer's block, can now create.

This is a pattern in Linda's conferences: she waits until she sees excitement in the writer's eyes and hears it in his voice. "Yes!" says Linda. "Something that catches in the writer's throat—a spark!"

A *spark*. Linda listens for a spark. Until she catches that spark, crackling out of the student's already burning interests or ignited into existence with her help, her further instruction holds much less promise.

Developing Rapport: The Flint for the Spark

Very often when we teach, we listen for answers we already know, but the listening teacher listens to *learn* through the student's enthusiasm and commitment. But herein lies the rub. The optimum conditions under which students will discuss their passions and emit sparks exist within a certain relationship between them and the teacher. The students who gain the most from teacher-student conferences are those who develop rapport with the teacher. While rapport doesn't guarantee a successful conference, all successful conferences reveal some element of rapport.

The nature of this relationship is complex. It has to let students take risks and reveal important thoughts without fear of humiliation. It does not necessarily require an extraordinary amount of friendship or social camaraderie, although most relationships have them. Instead, the mutual trust and respect upon which it is based (Oye 1993) creates an understanding on the student's part that the teacher is a resource and ally, as well as an evaluator, and an understanding on the teacher's part that the student is sacrificing time-honored, self-protective behaviors in order to move forward. In order for a student to be willing to discuss personally important matters, his or her relationship with the teacher has to be free of intimidation—it has to feel safe and comfortable.

The result is a conference that often looks and sounds unacademic. The image that comes to mind is that of a book club where people chat amiably, sometimes passionately, about writing from an informal, personal perspective. In a good teacher-student relationship, the *social* dialogue often fuels the academic agenda.

Linda says that her most successful conferences often shunt academics to the side. In casual conversation where Linda begins by learning who the student is as a person, students often find writing topics because they are talking about themselves. "Tell me about yourself," Linda urges, then she simply listens carefully. Linda says:

> I've had people say to me when they're watching a conference, "It's almost like you're acting like a *psychologist.*" I'm not really sure what they're talking about because I've never had a psychology course, but I think I *am* trying to gain some relationship with that person so I can understand what they're writing about, because writing, even if it's an essay, should be personal. It's what you think, believe—not necessarily what you feel, which I think is what some people mistake all writing for: your deep inner feelings. It certainly is your ideas and your beliefs, and that *is* personal. So I think I am trying to make a link with them.

Linda sees learning as socially constructed. Her comparison of herself to a psychologist highlights similarities in her conference style with Carl Rogers' person-centered psychotherapy approach (Rogers 1951, 1961, 1969), which several writing teachers have examined as a potential influence on effective conferences (Carnicelli 1980; Taylor 1993; Thomas and Thomas 1989). In Rogers' approach, the therapist is a facilitator rather than director, someone more responsible for creating and organizing a proper environment in which people can reflect and express themselves free of fear or embarrassment. Instead of taking a role as a scientist or evaluator, which may objectify a client, the therapist establishes a personal, subjective relationship with him or her. Instead of directing the client toward the proper course of action, the therapist removes obstacles and creates situations that allow the client to self-evaluate and move toward independence and self-direction. These are Linda's goals. She provides the same acknowledgement and reiterative feedback to what students say, letting them make self-realizations, which help them move their writing forward. The challenge becomes to create easy conversation that also serves a purpose:

> The other day [a colleague] was talking to me about quilting. I said one of the things that I think is missing today—and maybe it's why everybody goes to therapists so often—is that there are no quilting circles where women get together and chat as they're producing something. I guess that's what I think of conferences. It's a good healthy chat as you're *producing* something. And you have a hard time committing yourself to that production of something if you don't feel comfortable in the place where you're producing it.
>
> Beautiful things happen even in a casual way. Quilts turn out to be the most beautiful pieces of artwork, but people weren't concentrating so much on the product as they were forming that relationship with each other and listening to each other. And they're still stitching away. That's kind of what a conference is like.
>
> And yet the *purpose* of that good healthy chat is getting that writing to be the best that it can be, the same way with a quilting group. They enjoy each other's company so they get together, but they want to also be producing something at the same time, and that seems to be the focus. The subtext *is* that conversation that's going on—that relationship. I really don't think people have thought a lot about the relationship between the teacher and students when you're talking about conferencing. If they don't know you're *really* interested, which comes from that chat, then you're probably not going to get them to really move. The more I focus on academics *first*, the less I get them to move, I think.

Linda's social conference talk tends to be nondirective, letting students discover personally relevant issues through "a good healthy chat," while her academic talk tends to be more directive: questioning, suggesting, and explaining concepts as well as introducing them to matters of technique, expression, and concerns for audience that they might not discover for themselves. Her quilting metaphor introduces her vision for a proper balance between the two approaches. Talking one day with a group of visiting teachers, she again ponders this dual relationship:

> I almost can't have an academic relationship until I've got a social relationship with the kids. But that social relationship can't be pushed so far that it's a playful relationship. You're always walking a tightrope of social, academic, social, academic. [Kids] trust me not as a friend so much as a *learner,* but it's a balance of both. They trust me as a friend, but they trust me as a teacher and then trust me as a learner. Somehow, they've come to the understanding that I can be all of those things to them.
>
> . . . [Conferencing] is *much* more confusing than I ever thought. All the things that you have to keep in mind about each of those kids, going from one conference to the next! You have to know the students, you have to know their work, you have to know what stops them writing, what keeps them writing. And you know that if it's true for this one, it might be the absolutely wrong thing to say to the next student. When conferences last a long time, it's because I'm not really listening to those kids and remembering all of those things—that *history* that they bring that I'm already aware of.

Linda focuses on being a good conversationalist. As soon as she orients her approach in this way, students accept and enter more readily into the conversational performance. Working in a relationship of camaraderie, she is better able to elicit and recognize the things that interest them. Then she can say to the writer, "Look at what you just said. Get it down on paper!"

Creating Comfort to Create Discomfort

When the teacher creates a sense of emotional and intellectual comfort and security, she can then push a little harder. By gaining students' trust she can begin to create a sense of *discomfort* within them, challenging them to expand their intellectual boundaries by trying new approaches and taking risks. This discomfort provides the impetus for students to try new experiences. "I'm trying to respond to [you] so I can push your thinking a little bit," Linda tells her class. For example, When Marty writes a draft about mountain biking,

Linda sits next to him and says, "Ah, this is excellent!" Then she points to one section, "What are you trying to say here?"

Marty describes his great love of mountain biking and Linda asks him to be specific for her. Marty says he has never been competitive in sports, but he now wants to compete in mountain biking.

Linda: Why do you want to compete?

Marty: It seems like the thing to do. I've never been competitive. I really like this sport. I have a lot of natural ability in acting. I don't have to work as hard, but with *this* I've really had to work hard to get as good as I am.

Marty speaks with passion and intensity. Importantly, he is comfortable enough with Linda to converse with her. Linda now knows she can begin to prod—create the discomfort and tension that will force him to extend his thinking and evolve his work.

Linda: Everything you've just said goes in here. . . . This is pushing your limits. Tell us *why* you like doing this, put us *on* the bike. What does it feel like sitting there? I think you're taking us too much through a day that doesn't matter.

But Linda has to monitor her pressure to ensure that it does not become miseducative, actually halting the student's thinking or initiative. At the beginning of the year, for instance, Linda cannot nudge as hard as she can later, when students have grasped the concept of writing as thinking and have successfully exercised their own thinking skills. Linda says, "At the beginning of the year my eye, ear, and heart *see* things kids could do to make their writing better, but I realize they may not be ready yet." She believes that at any given point in time the teacher can challenge students only so far from their current foundation of experience, ability, and desire—that pushing any further will fail until they gain more experience. This is the practical application of students' zones of proximal development (Vygotsky 1978), on both an intellectual and an emotional level. Her response decisions are sometimes quite difficult when working with both confident and reluctant writers. She discusses one confident writer, Sonja:

> Sometimes she's willing to revise and other times she's not. She likes some of the stuff the way it goes down and so sometimes I have to accept *what* it is, depending on the body language she gives me. It's kind of her eyes and face and the way she responds to something I might ask her. I know I have to let it go and just let her keep it the way it is. But because this is the second year I've got her, I want to *push* her thinking a little bit. In seventh grade I let them enjoy what they've written and be comfortable with it. But I don't

want her too comfortable. I'd like to make her a little uncomfortable and push her thinking.

But, at the same time, Linda says, "I want her to know that she *does* do some *very* fine writing, some very fine thinking, and I have to be careful that I don't push her *too* hard." The proper balance between the two, she believes, will lead Sonja, and others, to surprises. She says, "I guess that's what I'm looking for in kids. The ones I know, the ones I *don't* know, I want them to surprise themselves."

Her great care also goes into her relationships with reluctant writers. In one instance, Hugh, an unconfident writer, completes one of his first pieces, a poem and an accompanying illustration about a girl who had broken his heart. He has handwritten his final draft and drawn a dark black border around the poem and picture. His writing is difficult to read and his marker lines look sloppy, but he has carefully traced straight lines in pencil so that his border will be square. Linda likes the poem and the illustrations very much, but because of the messy parts she can't decide if it is ready to present. In a conference she suggests to Hugh that he type the poem, but he refuses. She goes so far as to type his piece at home and bring him copies. He tells her he wants it in his own handwriting. Linda acknowledges to herself that despite the draft's relative messiness, it is the first time she has been able to read Hugh's writing. Clearly, he has done a lot of work and is very proud of it.

Linda struggles for the right response. Should she say, "Good work" and put the piece up on a wall because it is the hardest and best work Hugh has done to date, or should she again encourage him to clean up his piece so that it meets her own standards of show quality? What will move him forward and improve his subsequent work? If she rejects what might be a breakthrough effort from him, will she stop his growth? These are the key questions all of us must ask in these situations. In this case Hugh's handwritten draft hangs on the wall three days later. Discomfort must push forward, not halt.

"Stealing" Ideas

Recent research, much of it arising out of the works of Vygotsky (1978, 1986), Bakhtin (1981), and Bruner (1986), maintains that composing processes are socio-cultural events (Bruffee 1984; Dyson 1993; Floriani 1994; Flower 1994; McCarthey 1994; Myers 1992; Sperling 1990): One's ability to create arises out of social interactions, and learning moves from interaction between individuals to an internalization of knowledge within an individual (Vygotsky 1978). In the case of writing, this interactive knowledge-building influences what appears on the page. As a teacher and a student engage in a writing conference, the teacher's continual nudging and the extended talk that occurs produces empathic epiphanies and compromises that guarantee co-creation—a *social* construction of the student's text. The teacher cannot completely separate herself from a student's writing; by simply responding to it she inevitably collaborates, influencing it for better or worse.

While Linda listens to learn what students know and care about, she also inevitably influences their writing through her own interests—the elements in the student's text that she finds most intriguing. She often responds viscerally rather than searching for academically correct writing. For example, when John reads her his futuristic story of a United States wracked by depression and impending war, Linda nudges him to discover his own solutions, but also shares what has most affected her: "The interesting part to *me*, John, is the bomb shelter, because it always struck me why people would go into one of these and then come out to *nothing*." She reminisces about her relatives in Switzerland, forced by the government to build bomb shelters in their houses.

The thoughts and emotions that John's story arouse come from Linda's stance as a captivated appreciator of a text, not just as an academic evaluator looking for flaws. She allows the story to affect her aesthetically. In the same way that each individual brings his or her own life to a book, constructing a unique interpretation of the text influenced by personal experiences (Rosenblatt 1978), Linda constructs her own personal vision from John's text. Since this is a writing conference where the text is still in *process,* her vision can affect the final product. Linda's statements now challenge John's own ideas as well as offer him new perspectives. He may use some of her ideas to alter his text.

So the question becomes, where is the line between authentic collaboration—social construction—and teacher appropriation of the text? How do we determine whether the student has moved forward intellectually or has blindly obeyed the teacher's orders? The answer appears to lie in the student's final perception of the teacher's information. At the end of each quarter I interviewed students about where they had gotten ideas for their pieces. I asked about aspects of the texts that I knew had been influenced by Linda's conference suggestions. In most instances where we all had considered the conference productive, the students stated they had arrived at the ideas on their *own*. In most instances where we had considered the conferences unproductive, the students said, "Mrs. Rief told me to put it in."

In essence, writers' retain control of their socially constructed text by *co-opting* Linda's ideas and internalizing them as their own. This may occur when students know their own intentions well enough that they recognize when the teacher's idea matches those intentions *or* when it somehow provokes other personally relevant ideas. They internalize the teacher's idea more readily because it already fits into their own preconceived vision of the text or ways of looking at the world. An effective response then, is one that the student can connect to a personal conception, internalize, and then use to move his or her work forward. The students in these cases have intellectual and emotional control of Linda's ideas. Linda says, "The skill for the kids is when they are ready to take our suggestions and know what to *do* with them, and have the ability to accept them or reject them for the right reasons." These students have that ability.

11

Relationship-Building

It is not always easy for students to have intellectual independence and thoughtfully weigh the teacher's ideas. Most students need a strong relationship with the teacher before such synchronized communication and subsequent epiphany occur. Relationship-building is often a complex, tricky affair. Some students take an instant liking to Linda, and their burgeoning social relationships nurture their academic ones. Others develop trust in her gradually through the months, after they learn her tendencies. Still others never develop rapport with her. Some who respect her as a teacher, or even say they like her, never feel comfortable enough with their writing or with her to open themselves up to a true dialogue with Linda. There are a number of factors that appear to discourage good social relationship-building.

Troubles in Relationship-Building

Gender

Linda admits, "The kids I've had the toughest time with have all been boys." She says, "There's still an incredible resistance on boys' parts, [who say], 'I am *not* gonna *write* about that!' Our society says to them, 'You shut up anything that has to do with your life.'" Linda often has to tell boys it is not necessarily the "personal" she wants them to write about.

Linda: It's what *matters.* I mean, that's where I have a problem with some of the kids, and especially some of the boys. They think that what I'm after is something personal. When you use the word 'personal,' they misinterpret that.

Doug: As touchy-feely emotions.

Linda: Yes! Right! And it doesn't have to be that. It's what are you angry about or what do you care about? What *matters* to you? Is football the biggest thing in your life and you'd do anything to get to a professional football game, or do you love being at Fenway Park? But trying to get some of those kids to do that is so difficult.

Another gender difference that seems to influence rapport-building is the student's initial desire to form a personal relationship with Linda. Linda's students of both sexes are very well behaved and friendly toward her, but girls engage more socially with her. They come in to eat lunch with her, tell her stories about their personal lives, and ask her questions about her life.

Finally, boys' writing genre preferences sometimes influence Linda's conference effectiveness. This year, boys are much more prone to write science fiction or fantasy stories—genres that do not appeal to Linda. Her own more emotionally-based genres do not appeal to as many boys. Because Linda focuses on helping students discover their *own* solutions to problems, genre choice is not usually problematic. However, when a boy can't find his own way out of a writing dilemma, Linda has more trouble helping him.

For instance, Linda's conference with Tom is perhaps the longest of the year—twenty minutes—because Tom has difficulty articulating his problem and Linda can't conceptualize it for herself. Tom has written a science fiction adventure. He likes it, but the detailed plot has him confused. Linda asks Tom question after question, to which he replies, "That's what I don't know yet." Linda finally says, "Oh dear! I don't know what to do to help you, Tom, because I don't know that much about science fiction stories." Neither she nor Tom can tackle the plot.

Tom finally says, "I have a *slight* idea." A cue like this usually prompts her to have the student talk the idea out, letting it flower in oral expression before he commits it to the page. But today Linda does not ask Tom to elaborate on his idea. Her lack of confidence may have influenced her attention.

Conferences like this, I suggest, account for the difference in the percentages of questions asked between males and females in the conferences I analyzed. Situations like Tom's compel Linda to ask many more questions as she searches for the elusive educative response.

These difficulties, of course, are not drawn in absolute lines between males and females. Many girls hesitate to write about personal things while many boys easily express their personal passions. A great many boys form close relationships with Linda, while some girls do not socialize with her. Some girls choose genres or topics that Linda has trouble handling, whereas she feels wholly comfortable with many boys' genres and topics. Just as many boys succeed in Linda's classes as do girls. What I observed are *tendencies* that show a general demarcation between the sexes. Some of these tendencies, whether attributed to male or female, make rapport more complex to attain.

Adolescence

To teach eighth graders is to witness in wonder the beginnings of astounding transitions into adulthood as students discover aspects of themselves and the world they previously could not have imagined (Siegel and Shaughnessy 1995). It is also to experience frustration as their moods pitch and yaw, as they search for their own authority by questioning others, as their attention ricochets in a variety of directions.

Adolescence is the time where the physical and biochemical changes of puberty, the emergence of a new sense of sexuality, great strides in cognitive development, redefinitions of social roles, and, often, an abrupt transition to a completely new style of schooling (Eccles et. al. 1993) intersect to create tremendous social, emotional, and intellectual volatility. Adolescents are intensely preoccupied with peer socialization. They test the definitions of the child-adult relationship, which leads to an apparent withdrawal from this once most powerful bond (Ianni 1989). All who have lived or worked with adolescents can attest to the silent figures who refuse to engage with teacher or parent, but who suddenly transform into bright, lucid, articulate participants when friends come around. As they test their independence from their protectors, adolescents also feel a tremendous need to conform with their peers. What results is a child sometimes unwilling to disavow the implicit rule that authority figures are not to be trusted. Their reticence to jeopardize newfound autonomy and risk social stigma is not insurmountable, but it generally increases the students' hesitation to share the most important experiences of their lives.

The effects of adolescence are often apparent in conferences:

Linda: Why don't you read this to me?

Jade: No!

Linda: Why not?

Jade: Because it's stupid! It makes me sound like I don't have a life.

On various days students burst into tears, withdraw sullenly, and sometimes respond rudely. Linda speculates on the personality traits that sometimes complicate adolescents' willingness to carry conversation into writing, or their *ability* to write about some issues:

I think it is one of two different things. They'll talk about things and then they'll say, "You already *know* that. Why would I write it down?" They don't see it as important. Or, it's *too* important. There are a *lot* of things going on in kids' lives that are so important to them and so close to them that they can't even write them down yet. They're not far enough away from it. Also—and I think that's where this is really complicated—there's that *trust* factor again.

She also sees some students' reticence to write as arising from a new-found sense of independence and ownership:

They *own* this information; if they write it down they give it away. We do give stuff away the minute we write it down, and it's ours so long as we are keeping it to ourselves. And in adolescents, particularly, it's pulling in and pushing out all the time: "What do I keep for myself? What do I give away?"

The vital characteristics of the age, though, can powerfully influence her and her students for better as well as for worse. Her approach needs to value their social worlds in order to develop trusting relationships with them, where they willingly share those worlds with her through their writing:

Everything matters to adolescents. It matters what you're wearing, it matters how your hair is, it matters who you're sitting with at the table, it matters who's standing at your locker, it matters what you're eating for lunch, it matters if you're going or not going to the dance. *Every* single thing they talk about is important in their lives, and it's important to let some of that talk go on! Because then they know that you value them as people and that what they're thinking really *is* valuable. . . . If you don't let some of that talk go on then you're not going to hear some big things like, "Where do I fit in this world?" . . . If we don't know how they think about themselves as adolescents, as young women or young men—the things they're concerned with—then the big things that we want to talk to them about—the way we deal with each other as human beings, the way we treat each other—they're not going to listen to; they know you're not listening to what some adults may think are the little things in their lives. Just somebody calling on the phone and a parent saying, "You can't talk to them; you're not allowed to," that's *traumatic* to that child. They don't want to disappoint people, but they're so into friends and the little things that we think are minuscule, and we *laugh* at them. But they weren't minuscule to us when we were adolescents. I think we're never going to hear about the things that *we* think they should be concerned with, and teach them some of those big things in life, if we don't pay attention to and value the little things that are important to them.

Personal History with Literacy

Many of the students identified by teachers and specialists at the beginning of this year as having had difficulty with reading and writing in the past are the students who try to avoid conferences, resist engaging in detailed conversations, and thus develop less rapport with Linda as the year progresses. Some students never initiate conferences. Their previous histories with literacy seem to contribute to their unwillingness to ponder teacher feedback. They either accept or reject it out of hand. Some students speak of negative experiences with former teachers, which affected their attitudes.

Joe: I didn't have any positive responses [to my writing] except seventh grade.
Linda: What did that make you think?
Joe: That I wasn't good.

Dean tells the class, "My third-grade teacher turned me off writing. All she did was correct my spelling." Julia says:

> I think it was sixth grade. [Our teacher] told us, "Okay, now I want you to write a mischievous story that happened to yourself, and you have to write it sort of like Mark Twain." And, you know, it's just like, "What?" . . . She was trying to help kids try different styles of writing so they could find their own, but the thing is, you learn to write by your style, by reading everything and mixing it together. That was disastrous. Especially when you're asked to write about something that happened. Because sometimes you just don't feel like you've had anything that's *really* funny happen to you; *that's* one of the biggest [problems] I had. I was just like, "Oh my God. What funny thing happened to me?"

Many reluctant students speak of textbook work, assigned topics, and spelling tests that "got old." But perhaps the best indication of how some resistant students view the typical language arts class comes when I ask Damien, "What makes a teacher a good listener?" He replies, "But teachers don't listen to us. We listen to teachers."

Some prior experiences aren't necessarily defined as negative by students, but they engender expectations that conflict with Linda's own expectations and teaching style. Cate is astonished when Linda will not accept her final draft that is simply a neater, better-spelled copy of her first draft. Linda's class can be frustrating for students who have been taught to measure success by quick creation, quantity, and neatness, rather than by the thinking process that goes into writing.

Linda understands many of the students' frustrations, for she experienced them herself. She often discusses with her students the teacher comments that inhibited her own writing when she was young. She says,

> I don't think I have a really significant history as a reader/writer. In high school it was more spitting back—taking notes, and writing the paper that spit back everything. None of it was mine. Ever. I think when I finally got into teaching I said that's what I *don't* want to happen for kids.

Personality Differences

Sometimes relationship-building is difficult for no other reason than that the teacher and the student have different personalities and interests. Linda says she has had students who simply do not like her: "I've had kids who told me to fuck off, who have stomped out of the room, who have slam-dunked their portfolios into the wastebasket." Sometimes personality clashes stem from home lives Linda cannot control, sometimes from a simple dislike of language arts. Linda says,

> There will always be kids who don't value reading and writing, and I am the example of everything they hate. There are kids who I had a fine rapport with, who hated math, and Michelle stood for math. They hated her and said things to her that were brutal, and they would be kind as anything when they walked through this door. And I had kids who would do just the opposite. They hated it so much in here. They did beautifully in math class. They loved it.

On the other hand, the teacher's attitude toward the student has just as much, if not more, to do with successful relationship-building. Linda admits that every year she has one or two students whom she has difficulty liking or whom she likes personally but whose overt disdain for language arts makes it difficult for her to feel close to them on more than a superficial level. She knows it affects her instruction.

> I occasionally raise my voice because I lose my patience. I say things that I know, the minute they're out of my mouth, I should not have said—that they were hurtful to those kids. I forget that they're adolescents. I forget they're children. I want them to like me as much as they want me to like them, and I forget that sometimes.

Success in Relationship-Building

The predictable sequence of Linda's conference approach, her question, "How can I help you?", her praise, and her displays of genuine interest all contribute to relationship-building. But other elements also help establish a good communicative relationship. Some of them are conscious acts, some arise naturally out of her personality. Always, maintaining rapport is a delicate balance of subtle strategic moves, instinct, and an awareness of the students' multiple and rapidly changing needs.

Living the Life of a Learner

Linda's participation in the activities she assigns to her students—sitting among them and reading when they read, writing when they write, sharing her work, participating in interviews and taking part in authors' workshops—not only demonstrates skills and processes, but also promotes student trust and motivation that carries over into conferences. Many students comment on its impact. Kim writes about the ideas she gets from Linda's work and also says, "It also reminds us that teachers do work too." Ivan comments, "It tells us who the teacher is, and you feel as if the teacher is involved with the process also. You feel more or less an equal." Fiona writes,

> I think one of the best things a teacher can do is put themselves in the student's chair. You take us seriously because you want us to take you seriously. You show you're not only a teacher, but also a reader and writer. I really enjoy it when you share with us.

Kelly says,

> It shows us what we need to do and helps us feel more comfortable because we know she's not giving us an assignment and she doesn't do it. It's a better atmosphere for everybody to work in, and if she shares her writing then we feel more comfortable to share our writing.

At other times, Linda's in-class work has the effect of making her invisible to the students. She blends into the rest of the classroom, kneeling at a table or tucked into a corner with a student while the class continues, busily humming. Aaron looks up one day and asks, "Where's Mrs. Rief? Oh, she's sitting over there. She looks like everyone else." Her modeling seems to indicate to students that she trusts them enough to not watch over them at all times. The effect is reciprocal. Once Linda enters a conference she is already more trustworthy than she otherwise might be.

Listening Deeply

It is a general rule that one cannot interrupt Linda while she confers with another student. One day early in the year, pairs of students interview each other. Linda teams up with Julia, whom she doesn't know very well, and the two go into the hallway. Linda sits with her back to the classroom and immediately blocks everything behind her out. She and Julia laugh and write together. The noise behind her rises and falls as people work but she seems oblivious to anything except her conversation. She is absorbed! Linda later responds,

> I should have had Julia's back to the class *but* I wanted to start off right with her and let her know I really cared about her and all she had to say—individual attention. With my back to the class I could ignore them, still knowing you were there and wouldn't let anyone do anything *really* dangerous!

Linda's deep listening serves commensurate roles, with the first role enhancing the effectiveness of the second. Her engrossment promotes rapport, which encourages the sparks—the personally relevant issues students discuss enthusiastically. Sparks are the important subject matter in which she becomes engrossed and about which she gives pertinent, individualized responses.

Kneeling, Watching, Notetaking

Linda's consistent body language during conferences also indicates her deep attention. She never stands, but either kneels on the floor or sits on a chair. This brings her eye-level with students. She does not sit opposite students. Rather, she sits next to them or at the adjoining side of the table so that she can scrutinize a text without taking it from them. These are all strategies that show to students the teacher in the role of "advocate" rather than the role of "adversary" (Graves 1983, 98).

Donald Graves also discusses the power of eye contact, saying, "Now in the conference if I look away, not wanting to see the child's hurt, the child may think I don't care for him" (98). But Linda's body language reveals a more complex dynamic: as Linda interviews Julia, she looks directly into Julia's eyes as she asks questions. But as soon as Julia begins to speak Linda puts her head down to take notes. She keeps it down, but occasionally looks up and smiles when Julia says something amusing. Julia's voice becomes more animated and Linda eventually stops writing and looks up for an extended period. As soon as this happens, Julia's language pattern changes. She replaces words with facial and hand gestures. Her sentences become less coherent and more interspersed with the intensifier/interjection "like." ("It was, like, weird.") Linda's initial avoidance of Julia's face forced Julia to be more articulate. Later, Linda says, "The person who is doing the talking is clearly doing the thinking. Some teachers who watched me criticized me for not looking at kids during conferences. But I think it really makes them talk differently. They have to use *words*."

However, Linda consistently reestablishes eye contact with students when: (1) *she* talks and questions or (2) the student says something that surprises her, makes her laugh, or moves toward personal topics. In other words, she looks at students during the *social* moments of their conferences because eye contact engenders a sense of kinship and social connection. But her intense, head-down notetaking indicates her deep value of their work: an academic respect for their words.

Speaking Indirectly

Linda's directives often look like suggestions. "You might want to go out in the hall to finish that," she will say. She softens other directives by using a passive sentence construction, as in "There shouldn't be any talking." In conferences she softens her statements similarly:

Linda: Okay, you've got this quote and that's from you. And who's Trent Reznor?
Joe: He's the lead singer in Nine Inch Nails.
Linda: Okay, so you might need to put the group that he's part of, okay?

In this instance, since Linda wants Joe to clarify a fact rather than revise ideas, her statement is more a directive than a suggestion. However, her sentence construction softens the charge. Her indirectness may imply that the student has shared control of the situation. Linguist Deborah Tannen explains the benefits of indirectness.

> If you get your way as a result of having demanded it, the payoff is satisfying in terms of status: You're one-up because others are doing as you told them. But if you get your way because others happened to want the same thing, or because they offered freely, the payoff is in rapport. You're neither one-up nor one-down, but happily connected to others whose wants are the same as yours. Furthermore, if indirectness is understood by both parties, then there is nothing covert about it: That a request is being made is clear. (1990, p. 225–226)

However, Linda's style is problematic in one area. Lisa Delpit (1995) quotes research that finds white and middle-class teachers are more likely to use indirect speaking styles than black or working-class teachers when giving commands, and that both white and black working-class students are disadvantaged in classrooms where teachers are indirect because the students misinterpret directives as suggestions. However, in Linda's primarily white, primarily middle-class classroom, an opposite misinterpretation sometimes occurs: students who have had little power in previous classrooms often take her frequent suggestions as *directives*. A good relationship takes longer to establish if a student does not learn the difference between a suggestion and a directive.

Linda is ambivalent about her sometimes indirect approach. "I wonder if I'm too tentative by doing that. Is it effective?" She recognizes that for students with different backgrounds (and this may apply to some males in her class) her approach might have the opposite of its intended effect. She says, "Maybe my choices send all kids without some structure in their lives the same message: 'You don't care about me either!'"

Caring

Linda repeatedly says that caring makes any style of teaching more effective. Nel Noddings (1992) defines caring as an engrossment that results in a desire to "respond in a way that furthers the other's purpose or project" (16). This caring enhances the receptivity and responsiveness of the one being cared for. Linda's own concept of caring also emphasizes demonstrating friendliness to students as well as attention to their nonacademic concerns. In terms of developing relationships it means that, with students who hate language arts or are intimidated by teachers, she sometimes has to prove her care, friendship, or respect before she can address academics. We will see later how these dynamics play out.

12

Successful Conferences

Rapport usually results in a productive conference in which the student leaves with new perspectives, a clarified direction for further work, and a renewed enthusiasm. Several conditions are present in the conferences that Linda, the students, and I define as productive. A conference does not have to contain all of these conditions to be productive. Instead, the conditions strongly indicate that the conference *will* be productive.

Students Initiate

Teachers can initiate many successful conferences, but a student-initiated conference indicates that the student can articulate a specific concern or at least values the piece enough to seek response. Furthermore, it indicates comfort in interacting with the teacher. The student trusts her enough to initiate a dialogue and seek her feedback.

For example, Janine is a reluctant student who often cuts her classes. For the first couple of months she interacts little with Linda academically, though the two get along well socially. In conferences, Linda works hard to pull words out of Janine's mouth. But one day after class, Janine hands a poem to Linda, telling her that once she writes things down she can't figure out what she is trying to say. Linda reads the poem, tells Janine she did a wonderful job, and says they will go through it together in class to correct spelling and punctuation errors. This conference is a long-term success. Although Janine still participates infrequently during class, she writes poetry for the rest of the year outside of class, often sneaking back into the classroom to share it. Her willingness to enter Linda's class after hours is the first sign that Janine trusts Linda.

Sharing Control

Students have an investment in productive conferences that gives them co-control. They negotiate a conversational course with the teacher that takes into account their agendas as well as hers. Thus, they are better able to get their specific needs addressed.

First, students not only initiate the conference but also initiate and own many of its *topics,* which is necessary for a collaborative teacher-student relationship to develop (Sperling 1990). If the student doesn't have a say in the topics, the conference turns into a teacher-dominated forum similar to an Initiation-Reply-Evaluation approach (Dunn, Florio-Ruane, and Clark 1985). The student contributes fewer ideas, opinions, and emotions to the relationship, thus discouraging rapport. When the teacher controls all the topics, students are less invested.

Second, students discuss and challenge the teacher's statements more often, clearly articulating their own visions for their work. They feel comfortable saying no to the teacher and presenting alternatives. In conferences where Linda and the student have not developed rapport, the student either simply agrees with Linda's suggestions without discussion or resists adopting suggestions without articulating reasons or alternatives.

Third, students usually talk more. Researchers suggest that students who are more engaged in the conversation, who share control through their amount of talk, have more successful conferences (Fletcher 1993; Harris 1986; Jacobs and Karliner 1977; Sperling 1990; Taylor 1993). This willingness and ability to sustain talk also indicates rapport—a comfort level that allows the student to dominate, at times.

Here is part of a conference that exemplifies shared ownership. Linda, the student, and I all consider it productive; the student leaves the conference motivated and with a clear direction for revision. The conference results in extensive revisions, which incorporate both Linda's and the student's ideas: Sonja has read a draft of her new poem, "Sunset." Linda praises her descriptive words: "wait for the night," "muffled," "fade," "Queen of the night," "cloak," then begins to challenge some of the vagaries. She suggests that Sonja list "the array of wondrous colors" she writes about.

Sonja: Well, I don't really like *listing* the colors. Maybe if I have one color and then I wouldn't want to say, "Reds, oranges, and yellows." I'd want to say, "as red as the cardinal's wing," or something like that.

Linda: Yeah! Yeah.

Sonja: List the colors like that.

Sonja is not afraid to challenge Linda's suggestions and offer her own legitimate alternative visions. As the conference continues, Sonja is a controlling partner:

Linda: You talked about how they become "muffled," and they get covers thrown over them. So, how are they blending together?

Sonja: Yeah. I have actually the same sort of thing in a different piece that I was doing. I was just sitting by the window and describing what I was . . . writing what I was seeing. [She reads an extended passage from her journal about looking outside at a "gloomy, foggy, silent morning," contemplating her future, and noticing the amazing array of vivid colors]

Linda: If you're going to do something with that, you've got to get us back to decision. Because the whole point of this staring into space is about decisions. So, somehow you have to get us back to that.

Sonja: And then [Taking out another poem] this was the *next* day. This is part of the next day, where it was like almost the exact same kind of day. [She reads another extended journal passage about the cold fall wind: ". . . I love this kind of day—cool, misty, drizzly, and refreshing to spirit and soul."]

Linda: I like that. You know what, Sonja? I think all the pieces that you've read, you've got some really strong lines in each of them, and it's almost like you need to work to get *all* three of these . . .

Sonja: Yeah. I figured this one and the one before could all go together.

Linda: Yeah. I mean, it's not like you need every line, but *particularly, definitely,* these two go together.

Sonja: Yeah.

Linda: So you might . . .

Sonja: And I thought that "Heaven is Harmony" and "Sunset"—they both came from very similar pictures I had. "Heaven is Harmony" came from that one [Points to painting in her journal], and then [Shows another painting] "Sunset" came from that one. They're very similar.

Linda: Yeah, they are. Well, you know what? Those might even be . . .

Sonja: They might be part of a major.

Linda: Yeah. Definitely. And you might even take these pictures to a finished draft, too.

Sonja: But I think this one could go a little longer, too, the one that I read aloud in the group. I added some more verses to it, too.

Linda: Yep. I'd just play with those. Then you might have these that go with your drawings or illustrations, and these might be combined to be one piece. That would work pretty well. Okay.

Sonja: So I could do a minor with this one, and I could do a minor with the misty ones . . .

Linda: Yeah.

Sonja: And then, I could . . .

Linda: Well, you could . . .

Sonja: . . . end up with another one to make this into a . . .

Linda: Yeah. And you could end up, if you combine that with a more finished draft of a couple of those illustrations . . .

Sonja: That would make a major.

Linda: And that could make a major.

Sonja: Okay.

In this conference, Sonja initiates, owns, or co-owns the discussed topics much of the time—when she insists on reading pieces other than the original conference piece and when she suggests how she can combine smaller pieces into bigger "majors." Sonja also wrests topic control from Linda by either cutting her off or anticipating what she is about to say and then finishing or redirecting her sentences. Whether or not Linda is going to suggest combining pieces into a "major" piece, for instance, the idea becomes Sonja's, and she begins to speculate on how she can arrange her pieces for final draft.

According to a word count of the entire conference, Sonja and Linda speak almost exactly the same amount, not including Sonja's reading of her journal entries. And by reading her own work Sonja controls the tone and agenda even more. In this case Linda does not even ask Sonja to read her entries; Sonja thrusts them into the conference to satisfy her own agenda.

The notable exceptions to the trend of co-ownership of talk within productive conferences are some conferences later in the year, where Linda clearly dominates. If a student already has a strong working relationship with Linda, he or she might request Linda to indicate, for example, "stuff that you don't like." In these cases, Linda sometimes launches into specific suggestions or explanations immediately. Rapport gives the student a more open ear and allows Linda to dominate when requested to do so.

The point is important because it suggests that how much a student talks is not *necessarily* a key determinant of a successful writing conference, as long as the teacher is still focused on the student's agenda (Walker and Elias 1987). When middle school students develop rapport with their teacher, they better understand that the teacher has valuable knowledge. They develop a willingness to engage in a more teacher-dominated format *if* they determine it meets their needs. In most successful conferences teacher and student share control but, importantly, rapport allows the successful conference to take a wider variety of forms, each of which can address students' unique needs in different, context-specific ways.

Taking Suggestions as Suggestions

While some students misconstrue Linda's suggestions as directives, many others do not. There is a clear pattern: students whom Linda and I identify as having a good rapport with her are those who interpret correctly her myriad suggestions *as* suggestions—statements of well-informed opinion meant for serious consideration, not blind adherence (Fletcher 1993). Students who have not developed a rapport more often comply with, or refuse, her suggestions without any reflection.

Sonja's working relationship with Linda illustrates this point. Here, she has written a poem draft, titled "Second Heaven" (I've added numbers for reference).

> When one thinks of heaven,
> One may think of the storybook version.
> But I have come up with my
> Own picture of heaven.
> 5 I don't see angels and pure
> White puffy clouds
>
> My image of heaven has no
> Shape or form.
> Heaven is a feeling.
> 10 A feeling of complete bliss
> And happiness
> Of contentment where
> There are no more "wants,"
> And all needs are fulfilled
>
> 15 Heaven is the payment for a
> Job well done.
> Heaven is a piece of mind
> A state of beauty and peace
> Of quiet and tranquility.
> 20 Heaven is harmony,
> Within one's self

Sonja gives it to Linda, who responds to it in writing the next day, writing five comments that Sonja considers as she revises.

Later, Sonja tells which comments she used to change her text and which comments she didn't. Here are Linda's five written comments (in italics), followed by Sonja's revision responses:

1. Line 2: *"What else?" [and an arrow suggesting she move lines 5 and 6 to below line 2]*. Sonja says, "I did this. I put the lines together."

2. Line 10: *"What gives you complete bliss?"* Sonja says, "I couldn't really describe what complete bliss was. It just didn't make sense in the poem." She did not use this comment to revise or add.

3. Line 13: *"What do we spend too much time 'wanting'?"* Sonja clarifies her text by adding the line, "For unneeded possessions."

4. Line 16: *"How would you describe 'job well done'?"* Sonja says, "It would be too long and wouldn't work in the verse." She does not use this comment to revise.

5. The last five lines: *[Linda writes a star that corresponds to them.]* Sonja says that Linda starred this section "because she thought it was really, really good. She stars stuff she likes." She keeps this section as it is.

Sonja uses two of the comments to change her draft, ignores two others, and acknowledges the last comment as praise, which identifies what she should keep. She also makes other unsolicited revisions, changing "payment" to "gift" (line 15) and moving part of "a state of beauty and peace" from line 18 to line 17 after getting rid of "piece of mind."

Sonja says that she doesn't look at Linda's comments as commands but as *suggestions*. "She doesn't get upset if you don't use [her suggestions]. They make you *think*." Linda's suggestions serve their purpose. Sonja estimates that she uses "about half" of Linda's suggestions. When I interview other students I identify as having rapport with Linda and ask how often they use her suggestions, the most common answer is "about half the time." They feel comfortable to self-evaluate and make decisions without fearing some covert teacher agenda.

Discussing Ideas

As we saw, Linda talks about ideas with her students more than eighty percent of the time in conferences. However, in many less successful conferences when Linda cannot encourage the student to discuss ideas, she begins to focus on mechanics in a last-ditch attempt for some kind of progress. This is her unconscious fallback strategy. It indicates frustration, perhaps even failure because, philosophically, she wants to address mechanics only after ideas have been organized, clarified, and enhanced. Reflecting on her tendency she says, "I think *I* focus on the mechanics and the academics more because I can't get a handle on anything else." She speculates that the solution is to work harder to form relationships with those kids.

Talking, Laughing, Enjoying

In productive conferences, the participants' voices and bodies *move*. Their eyes focus more intently on each other and the work. In less productive conferences, voices are often more monotone with less verbal emphasis. Eyes more often scan the room.

In productive conferences humor abounds; participants joke more often with each other. Though this joking isn't an infallible sign of a successful conference (students sometimes joke to avoid focusing on their task), productive conferences contain more laughter. One sees those ritualistically social activities that often make conferences appear like chats rather than academically focused events. In many conferences, exuberance, informality, and camaraderie not only indicate rapport but also nurture and sustain it.

13

A Poem Is Born

Good relationships inspire good conversations. Good conversations influence good writing. Let us see how the elements of a good working relationship look in practice as a student creates a text over the course of several months. It is important to note that each of the following conferences takes only a few minutes. While Linda and the writer talk, the rest of the students work and confer on their own. By now they have internalized classroom expectations and procedures and know how to work independently. They know that if they need Linda she will be available shortly.

The student, Laura, had Linda last year and knows her well. She and Linda constantly joke and tease each other, but Laura knows the line between informality and disrespect.

Helping the Writer Listen to Herself

Early in the year Laura tries to piece together her autobiography. She has written a bit:

> Laura was born February 10, 1983 at Exeter, New Hampshire. She has grown up at Durham, NH. All of her life she has lived in the same house.
>
> When she was two and a half her sister started playing the violin. Everything that she did always looked so good to her that she wanted to play also.

But she is now stuck. Linda sits down to confer with her:

Laura: This is really boring. I don't know what else to write. I thought maybe about my violin, but I didn't know.

Linda: [Reads what Laura has written] Yeah, you're right, that is really boring.

Laura: Thanks, Miss Rief [Laughs].

Linda: You're welcome [Laughs]. Well, you want the truth, don't you? [Laughs]

Laura: Yes.

Linda: [Inquiring] You've done nothing in your entire life that was really interesting.

Laura: [Whispers] I stuck a carrot up my nose! [Laughs]

Linda: You stuck a carrot up your nose.

Laura: Yeah. How many times are you gonna have to repeat that!

Linda: That was the most interesting thing you've ever done in your entire life.

Laura: No, I started playing the violin when I was two and a half.

Linda: That's really interesting! What got you into the violin when you were two and a half? Did your mother make you do it? Did they lock you in a closet and say, "You are to play the violin," or did you say, "Oh, wow! This looks *so* interesting!"

Laura: I don't really remember! [Laughs]

These two share a great camaraderie. Because they know and feel an affinity toward each other, they are already aware of each other's needs and boundaries. Instead of leading off with praise, Linda has no qualms about immediately *teasing* Laura—"Yeah, you're right, that is really boring"—and Laura has no problem understanding the tease and laughing with her. Lack of praise at this juncture of the conference is very rare, indeed; Laura and Linda are unusually comfortable with each other.

Linda, however, is there to help Laura expand her topic. She segues into a gentle provocation: "You've done nothing in your entire life that was really interesting." Laura jokes again, but when Linda persists Laura reveals more— not only did her sister start playing the violin when Laura was two and a half, Laura did *too!* Linda is fascinated. She cannot help but assume that violin playing is a passion of Laura's. She wants to learn more.

Linda: Do you still play the violin?

Laura: Yeah.

Linda: What do you like about playing it?

Laura: You can get your feelings out.

Linda: Okay. What are some of the favorite melodies or compositions that you do, or your favorite composers?

Laura: I like to play "Meditation" from *Thais* and Pachelbel's *Kanon.*

Linda: All right. And, how much do you practice every day?

Laura: Forty-five minutes.

Linda: Where? Think about, when you get your violin, where do you go to play?

Laura: Well, my sister has a stand in her room, but usually I wander around.

Linda: And just play.

Laura: Just playing? Well, it's different between practicing and playing.

Linda: What's different?

Laura: Playing, you just play, and practicing, if you get like a note wrong you have to go back and fix it.

Linda: And, when you're playing, if you get it wrong you just go right by it?

Laura: Yeah.

Linda: Okay. Why don't you start with the sentence, "I've been playing the violin since I was two and a half."

Linda's several questions draw out specific details about Laura's playing. Laura answers easily and enthusiastically. She simply chats about the thing she loves.

Information accumulates with each of Laura's answers. When Linda feels there is enough to push through Laura's block, she makes a suggestion: "Okay, why don't you start with the sentence, 'I've been playing the violin since I was two and a half.'" In this exchange Linda has adopted a deeply receptive stance, asking many questions to which she really wants to know the answers. The information she learns produces a response that directly addresses Laura's stated need, "I don't know what else to write." Linda's suggestion is specific but framed in a slightly indirect, softened fashion. Note that her suggestion comes directly out of Laura's own oral story. It is easier for Laura, as it is for most students, to tell her story rather than write it. Essentially, Linda tells her to copy down what she just said. Conference teaching is most successful "when the teacher helps the student realize what the student has just learned" (Murray 1982, 164).

The conference continues. Laura responds to Linda's suggestion, saying, "Okay. But I started on a cardboard box, like this big." She accepts Linda's suggestion, but is still excited to continue her story.

Linda: Well, that's great! You started what? What do you do with a cardboard box?

Laura: I had a ruler attached to it and I thought I was playing beautifully! [Laughs]

Linda: [Laughs] And did anyone mention to you that you were playing beautifully?

Laura: My mom, probably. My dad's so tone-deaf he probably thought I *was* playing beautifully! [Laughs]

Linda: And is that when you were two and a half? [Laura nods, yes] You know what? Listen to everything that you just said: "I started playing the violin when I was two and a half. I started on a cardboard box with a ruler. My dad was so tone-deaf he never complained about it, and my mom was *always* encouraging, telling me what a beautiful job I was doing." And then talk about what you do now with the violin. Show us the kinds of compositions that you're doing.

Laura: Like, what part *shows*, like . . .

Linda: Well, just name some of those that you really like to do.

Laura: Okay.

Linda: But start with the violin and take us right through the violin. Because that's a real important part of your life.

Laura: I also play soccer and I play the piano [Laughs], and I do a lot of other things.

Linda: Right! And you could add that at the very end. But you want to focus on the violin. That's a very special, unique thing that you do. And what else do you do?

Laura: I row. Like crew.

Linda: For crew? How do you fit all that in?

Laura: I don't [Laughs]. I don't do my homework! [Laughs] Just kidding!

Linda: Really! [Laughs] All right, start with that and then just tell us everything you can about you playing the violin.

Again we see the confluence of social and academic as Laura and Linda joke with each other. Linda asks in mock incredulity if anyone found Laura's cardboard box-playing beautiful and Laura teases her father. Linda continues her effective listening, repeating Laura's oral story and suggesting she write it down. Laura again accepts and again shares more of her story. Though Linda attempts to focus her on one topic, Laura's enthusiasm is fertile. She continues to create potential subject matter for her writing.

Laura immediately begins writing as Linda leaves. In a few minutes she has a new paragraph:

> She started on a small, about an inch thick 9 inch by 9 inch box with a ruler coming out of one of the sides. It slightly resembled a violin. Of course, no noise came out but her mother and father would tell her how wonderful it sounded.
>
> Laura started the Suzuki method. She studied for 6–7 years with Heather Staley but she moved to Concord. Her family made the commute for a year but finally realized that it was too hard. So she found a teacher in Exeter, Caroline Biggs. She only studied with her for one and a half years because

she moved to Chicago Illinois. Caroline by far was her favorite teacher. She taught her all sorts of new violin techniques and had her play much prettier music than Suzuki. Right now Laura is studying music with Sandi Shoemaker. Laura's favorite three pieces are La Foria, Meditation, and Pachelbel's Kanon.

In addition to violin, Laura and her sister are very close. Laura is very committed to soccer, rowing crew, swimming, and her schoolwork. She hopes to get into the Exeter Orchestra and get a scholarship for either violin, swimming, or crew and go to a really good college and become a physical therapist.

The conference unblocks Laura. Linda has helped her hear herself. She moves her writing forward, creating a richer portrayal of the major events in her life. Linda's listening and response has been effective.

Shaping Ideas

Linda does not expect students' autobiographies, written at the beginning of the year, to become pieces of writing they put in their final portfolios. Instead, they are an exercise to create more potential topic material. Laura's autobiography serves this very purpose. Almost two months after she writes it, she approaches Linda, journal in hand. She has written three similar drafts she thinks might lead somewhere. The third draft reads:

Violin

My music is a part of my life
My music is a part where I couldn't not pay attention to or
   brush away
My music is everything, it is my mood my talent and my
   hobby.
My music is my family and my home
I can play and nothing else is important.
It is special and it lets my mind wander into beautiful trances
   of happiness and peace. It is where no one can touch me or
   my feelings.
My music is a part of my life.
My music is a part of me.

Laura shows Linda a beautiful close-up photograph of Laura's hand on the neck of her violin with sheet music as a background. She wants to incorporate the photo into the piece. Laura reads her third draft and Linda responds.

Linda: "It is my mood, my talent, and my hobby"—I love this line. [Reads] Oh, I love it! "It is my family and my home." It's kind of like a metaphor. I like the peacefulness and the whole mood of it. . . . That's a beautiful picture Emily took. See how Emily moved in incredibly close to the hand and the music? You need to move in close with your *writing*. When you say "mood," how do you describe it?

Laura: Aggressive . . .

Linda: What kind of music do you like to play?

Laura: Vivaldi and Bach.

Linda: What does that mean? I know nothing about music. . . . How would you describe the mood of Vivaldi?

Laura: [Has trouble explaining]

Linda: Do you have special words for how you hold the neck or the wand? What's that thing called?

Laura: The bow [They both laugh because the answer is obvious].

Linda: Do you have to hold it in a particular way?

Laura: You have to hold it in a special position.

Laura picks up a pen and draws a picture of the handle of a bow to show Linda how it's shaped, and then demonstrates with her hand how to hold it. "When I pick up a bow my hand just drops into that position because I've done it forty-five minutes every day," she says. Laura can play any note immediately if she hears it, but she's still trying to get better at playing when someone calls out a note. Linda and Laura then discuss music jargon—words like "pianissimo," "forte," and Linda asks, "Besides Vivaldi and Bach, what others are your favorites?" Laura says every time she hears "Meditation" from *Thais*, it sends shivers up her spine. She goes to sleep to violin music every night.

Laura's rush to Linda with her draft indicates her commitment to the piece and her comfort with Linda. There is no need for Linda to help find a topic of interest. Laura already has a spark in her throat as she talks.

Laura also shares control of the conference. She launches into extensive talk about how to hold a bow (she even draws pictures!), her ability to play notes, music terminology, losing herself while playing, and what it feels like to play. She is animated through the entire discussion. She and Linda focus exclusively on ideas. Linda then begins to offer suggestions.

Linda: All the places where you say, "It's my mood," you have to get into those moods.

Laura: [Tells Linda that when her parents get into a fight with her she sometimes goes and plays a fast piece on the violin] . . . Sometimes I'll play a piece and I haven't even thought about it. I'll be thinking about what's out the window. . . .

Linda: [Tells Laura what she should do before she writes another draft] Start with every line. Say everything you can about *that* line. [Reads] "Music is a part of my life." What do you *mean* by that? Go down through every line. We want to hear about your "mood," your "talent." . . . You want to explain this in as much detail as possible. . . . "It is special and lets my mind wander." We need to know, wanders to *where?* . . . What's going on in your head when you're playing? We want to get as close to the music as Emily got to you.

Laura: [Referring to her last lines] Is that a good way to end it?

Linda: I don't know until I see what else you write. . . . You need to add sounds: "pianissimo," "forte." There are no sounds in here now.

Laura: [Discusses what it's like to play—she says that when she plays it's like her fingers are walking]

Linda: Your fingers—"It's like walking"—*Now* you're getting into the sounds of poetry.

Linda again formulates her responses out of what she has heard in Laura's talk. Laura, as do most students in the beginning of the year, expresses herself with generalities (referring simply to "my mood"). Linda requires specifics. She suggests Laura take each one of her lines and fill it in with more details. As Laura describes what it feels like to play, Linda recognizes the wonderful poetic imagery of fingers walking, which gives her a strong suggestion—again simply repeating back Laura's own words—with which to end the conference.

The next day, Laura has written another draft. It has some significant changes:

Violin (Draft 4)

My music is a part of my life
My music is a part where I can turn to it. The music is everywhere
   I look and everywhere I am
      My music is in every thought I have. Everywhere I turn music is
        within me.
      I can rest my hand on my violin and reality disappears.
      My life is now circled around my feelings and my thoughts.
      My mood is brought out by every note on the page. The notes
        flow into a ocean of rhythms and each note lapping and
        swarming upon each other like a wild ocean. Calm and
        relaxing one minute and intense and alarming the other.
      I sway with the motions of my fingers.

Laura has not adopted all of Linda's suggestions. She does not incorporate new music jargon or musical sounds, for instance. But she does use Linda's suggestion to attend to the mood of the piece, crafting an ocean metaphor and noting music's ever-changing personality. Finally, she uses Linda's last comment in the conference, ending the piece with the motions of her fingers.

Linda clearly influences this draft but has not overwhelmed it. Laura makes the decisions. She also continues to move forward independently: she ponders Draft 4 and recognizes some new lines with real potential. On her own, Laura sees a new lead buried in the middle of the draft. She redrafts and substantially changes the feel of the piece, expanding the metaphor of music as a journey through nature and weather. The piece moves forward, translating a richer sense of Laura's violin-playing experiences.

> **(Draft 5)**
>
> I rest my hand on my violin and reality disappears.
> I am free with my emotions and feelings.
> I blow through the wind, circling through the branches and down
> waterfalls and brushing against every grain of sand in the desert.
> I roll through the mountains and valleys and swim through puffs of
> clouds and glide across the smooth ice plains into beautiful fall
> leaves of New England.
> Every note on the page brings out another emotion. The notes flow
> into a ocean of rhythms and moods, each note lapping and
> swarming upon each other like a wild ocean.
> Calm and relaxing one minute and intense and alarming the other.
> I sway with the motions of my fingers growing more and more in
> depth as the music goes on.
> I have captivated myself deep and deeper into the pages and pages
> of the song.

Finding the Right Words

The draft is much different now. Laura says it really is like another piece to her. She needs to get Linda's perspective again and rushes over for a conference. The two look for more ways to tie music images into ocean images. Laura marks changes on her paper and Linda writes down notes and suggestions on a conference sheet. Linda asks Laura to think of words that describe grains of sand against your body. Laura comes up with "burn" and, then, "sinking." Linda replies, "Great word! Because you sink into the music the way you sink into the sand." Linda writes Laura's words in the margins of the draft. She then begins to nudge: *You've* got the emotion [in this piece], now you just need to find the words. She questions some more:

Linda: Okay. What are the sounds and smells?

Laura: Crunchy? I can hear it . . .

Linda: You are so good at sounds.

Laura: Crackling?

Linda wants to learn more. "I don't know anything about notes," she says. Laura tells her about different kinds of notes: half notes, quarter notes, eighth notes. She claps out the rhythms to help Linda understand. By teaching Linda—drawing on her own knowledge and life experiences—Laura learns about herself. Again, Linda has an opportunity to say, "You've taught me what is important. Now write it down."

The conference continues:

Linda: What are the emotions? What are the words you would use? Is it ever anger, or is it only wonderful emotions?

Laura: It's anger. It's *every* emotion. Calm, happy . . . not happy . . .

Linda: Contentment?

Laura: Contentment.

Linda: Do you ever feel envy?

Laura: When I listen to my sister. My teacher doesn't think I give myself enough credit.

Laura tells Linda that she listens to her sister play in an orchestra, but she doesn't want to play in it. However, she can't stop listening to the orchestra—she can't take her eyes off of it. The music sends chills down her spine. "I have a passion," she says; "I feel really sorry for people who don't have it." She says her sister and her father understand, but her mother will listen to music and, when the rest of the family becomes moved, she will say, "What? What is it that made that better than something else?" She badly wants to hear and understand what the rest of them are hearing and understanding, but she can't.

Linda: [Writes on Laura's draft as Laura talks] I've written down every word you've just said: anger, calm, content, envy, chills, moved, sigh. Take us through all of these sounds, but one of these stanzas has to have the words of music: highs, lows. . . . At the end [of the piece] you might be watching someone else playing.

Laura: What if I say I was at a concert?

Linda: It doesn't matter. Remember yesterday when you said you were playing and you said you just went out the window? It doesn't matter where you are.

I love when you said, "I feel bad for people who don't have this passion for sound." You've *got* this piece! I don't know why you don't think you have it.

There is a slight shift in the tone of this conference. Where previously Linda helped Laura search for more general concepts and ideas—an attempt to get hold of "moods"—here the two begin to refine, searching for specific *words* to highlight the moods. The piece has a better shape and they sculpt the details. Laura is able to generate a whole list of mood-enhancing verbs, adjectives, and nouns—specific "sights, sounds, and smells."

Laura's extraordinary "I have a passion . . ." monologue tells much. Her rapport with Linda allows her to speak with ease, and her ease allows her to say extraordinary things that might otherwise go unsaid, and thus undiscovered.

This speech, in fact, inspires a new ending to her piece. Leaving the conference, she buries herself between two bookcases and writes, while Linda confers with other students. By the end of class Laura has a sixth draft:

(Draft 6)

I rest my hand on my violin and reality disappears.
> I take a deep breath drawing in down my lungs and through my
> > body. I bring my bow to the violin and begin.
> I am free with my emotions and feelings.
> I race with the wind circling the tree trunks up to the
> > outstretched arms of their branches.
> I slope down, riding, tumbling through waterfalls. I brush and
> > sink into every grain of sand in the desert.
> I swim through puffs of clouds and glide across the smooth
> > glaciers. Rolling up and down mountains and valleys, falling
> > through the raked leaves of New England, crunching and
> > stomping in the pale to brilliant leaves of yellow, orange,
> > and red.
> Every note on the page of music turns into a thunderous
> > stormy ocean, crashing, lapping, and breaking upon
> > each other, each growing to a climax and falling rapidly
> > into a slower allegro and building itself faster into a forte
> > of my feelings.
> I sway with the motions of my fingers, growing intensity as
> > they pound down on the strings, bringing out my
> > aggressiveness with every placing on the wood.
> I draw my bow to a close, never shutting the door
> > completely of my emotions. They are trapped inside of
> > me until I turn the page to another piece.

I am moved and have chills from the music that was played.
And in the window seat I am glued. I feel bad for those who
  don't have the attraction, passion, and love for sound as I do.

The piece now races along with sharp verbs, a large palette of colors. It splashes the reader with specific mood. Laura also, finally, incorporates Linda's repeated suggestion to use music terminology, a suggestion that I feel weakens the line somewhat. It seems forced and it is perhaps why Laura did not take Linda's suggestion in the previous conferences. However, Laura still clearly controls the piece. The rest of the words have come out of her mouth; Linda simply repeated them back and highlighted her views about them.

Crafting Conventions

But Laura is not done. She types another draft at home, making more revisions to her ending, including a line where she sits in a seat and listens to someone else playing. Again she comes to class and approaches Linda. This time the conference has a much different tone than the previous ones. Linda reads the piece out loud, feeling the rhythm and testing the sounds:

Linda: [Reads] ". . . I bring my bow to the violin and *draw* it across the strings." Okay. "I am free with my feelings and emotions. I *race* with the wind . . ." That's lovely. ". . . circling . . ." How about if you just say, "Circling *tree trunks*"?

Laura: Okay.

Linda: And, if you're having to go *up*, what are you doing, especially when you . . . what's the word?

Laura: I'm riding the wind?

Linda: All right . . . what do you do to a tree, though?

Laura: Hm, um . . . cuddle it [Laughs]. Hugging . . . climb in it.

Linda: Oh, climbing! [Composing out loud] "Circling tree trunks, climbing or hugging your outstretched arms of branches," *or,* "*Climbing* to their outstretched arms."

Laura: Ooh, I almost did that! [Laughs]

Linda: Okay, [Reads] "I *slope* down, riding, tumbling through waterfalls. I brush and sink in every grain of sand in the desert." That's really nice, too. "I swim through . . ." How about just "*puffs* of clouds," not "*the* puffs"? [Reads] ". . . puffs of clouds and I glide across smooth glaciers, rolling *up* and down mountains and valleys." What are the words from music that mean up and down? Is there a word that's smooth?

Laura: A crescendo is kind of like, um . . .

Linda: And what's a falling? Is a crescendo up and down? Okay, even if you just drop the word "crescendo" in there and see how it sounds . . . [Reads] "rolling *up* and down mountains and valleys." I don't know. Maybe that won't work. "Falling through fresh raked leaves of New England, *crunch* . . ." Probably a comma there. ". . . *crunching* and stomping . . ." Is it "stomping" or "kicking"? In the music, what is it more like?

Laura: Nah, I was thinking stomping was kind of like the staccato, like doon-doon-doon-doon [She taps out the beat on the table with her pen].

Linda: Okay, good. Good. ". . . on the pale to brilliant shades of yellow, orange, and red. *Every* note on the page of music turns into a *thunderous* stormy ocean, crashing, blackening, breaking upon each other." This is where you might use the words, of all the ones that were here. "Staccato," "crescendo." I mean, you drop some words in here that you have not used here. Just words that show this gliding is *up,* it's down, this rolling, and this *stomping.*

Laura: Mm-hm.

Linda: "Crescendo," "allegro. . . ." See, I don't even know what they all mean. I just know they're words. And, put them right there in between. "My music grows to a climax and falls rapidly into allegro and rising to a forte of my feelings." So, if you drop the words there—all words, but not *those* two.

Laura: [Writing] ". . . a climax . . . and rapidly . . ."

Linda: Okay, "I sway with the motions of my fingers growing *intensely* . . ." Is that what you mean? Or, "growing with intensity"? Because that could be "*with* intensity." [Reads] ". . . as they *pound* down on the strings, bringing out my anger and aggressiveness with *every* placing of my fingers on the wood." Is it just anger and aggressiveness? This whole piece sounds really positive, and anger and aggressiveness throw me off.

Laura: Okay.

Linda: What else could it be? I think you had it right. You had words on the other draft.

Laura: [Reading from notes on a previous draft] "Anger, calm, content."

Linda: I don't know. You might even want to have, like, "Bringing out my contentedness, my anger, my aggressiveness with every placing . . ." You need one calm word there.

Laura: Mm. [Composing] "My calmness. . . ." I don't know what to use.

Linda: Yeah. I know. But all you need to know is you need a positive word in there. [Reads] "I draw my bow to a close." What does that mean? What do you do with the bow?

Laura: Lifting it off the strings.

Linda: Okay. [Composing] "I lift my . . ." Then, why don't you say that? [Composing] "I lift my bow off the strings . . ." comma, "never shutting the door on my feelings . . ." See, this kind of slows this down: "that-still-will-be-with-me."

Laura: Yeah.

Linda: How about if you just say, "That *stay* with me?"

Laura: Oh, that's what I was looking for! [Softly, slowly, as she writes] "That stay with me." How about, "until I turn the page"?

Linda: Yeah. Good. All right, now you're going to put a double space here . . .

Laura: So, like a double paragraph. Like a double . . .

Linda: Yeah, just white space that's doubled. I would just put, "I *adore* music." Period. [Reads] "Chills trickle down my spine. I am *truly* moved."

Laura: Maybe I should take out the concert.

Linda: I think you might take that out. Because, this is all about you. Because that's how it happens for *you.* [Reads] "I am truly moved. I feel bad for those who don't have the attraction," comma, "the passion, and the love for sound, as I do." It's ready.

This conference focuses on very *specific* ideas, concepts, and on mechanics. Here, Linda takes much more control, asking fewer questions, and making more suggestions. The suggestions focus on smaller details: refining word choices, cutting unnecessary articles. Linda feels less uncertain about offering more directive statements and taking over the conference because they are dealing less with Laura's larger ideas and more with details, but also because of the inherent security in their rapport relationship.

We also see that Linda, for the third conference in a row, encourages Laura to add more music terminology. She makes another suggestion: soften the word "aggressiveness," which stands out like a sore thumb in comparison with the rest of the piece, by supplying other mood words.

Laura, however, is not passive. As they talk she discovers that her new line about sitting and watching a concert doesn't work. She is still thinking independently.

A Poem that Belongs to the Writer

Laura leaves and soon writes two more drafts, one incorporating the changes inspired by this last conference, and one to edit some minor grammatical errors. Here is her final draft:

I cradle my violin under my chin. I rest my hand on the neck and
    reality disappears.

I take a deep breath drawing it down my lungs and through my
    body. I bring my bow to the violin and draw it across the strings.
I am free from my feelings and emotions.
I race with the wind, circling tree trunks, climbing up to the
    outstretched arms of their branches.
I slope down riding, tumbling through waterfalls. I brush and sink
    into every grain of sand in the desert.
I swim through puffs of clouds, and glide across smooth glaciers.
    Rolling up and down mountains and valleys. Falling through
    fresh raked leaves of New England, crunching and stomping on
    the pale to brilliant shades of yellow orange and red.
Every note on the page of music turns into a thunderous stormy
    ocean, crashing lapping and breaking upon each other. The
    music grows to a climax and falls rapidly into an allegro and
    rising into a forte of my feelings.
I sway with the motions of my fingers growing with intensity as they
    pound down on the strings, bringing out my contentment,
    happiness, anger and aggressiveness with every placing of my
    finger on the wood.
I lift my bow off the string, never shutting the door of my feelings
    that will stay with me until I turn the page of music.
I adore music. Chills trickle down my spine. I am truly moved.
I feel bad for those who don't have the attraction passion and love
    for sound.
    As I do.

Again we see Laura's control of her piece. She does *not* incorporate more
music terminology. She does, however, use Linda's suggestion to expand
upon the emotions music brings out of her, not just anger and aggressiveness
but also contentment and happiness. She excises the line where she sits and
watches, stating instead, "I adore music."

"Violin" becomes one of Laura's portfolio pieces. In her Case History she
writes:

When I first started this piece of writing it was a totally different form and
all it started out with being [was] "My music is a part of my life." It was
nothing like my final and there were no emotions in it. I decided to take the
different parts out that I did because it really added to the story. I made
every sentence a closer so I couldn't add on to it.

This piece makes me think of standing in my living room on the blue
carpet and after walking away leaving my two tiny to big to bigger foot
prints on the rug after standing there for awhile.

My first draft is in my log with what I started from. I have my interview [Conference Sheet] in with this piece because it helped me make it the piece that it is.

Sometimes when I think about this piece I want to send it to a publisher and make it a picture book. I wish I could draw.

Another thing about this piece is I know that I liked it and enjoyed writing it because after every draft I wanted to share it with you (Mrs. Rief). I could tell I was happy with it because of that and how proud I was to be able to write what the piece ended to be.

Laura gives herself an *A* for process ("I went draft through draft to make this piece of writing."), an *A* for content ("I think this was an effective piece of writing because of the way I worked so hard on it. I made it the BEST that I could and even now enjoy reading it to my family."), and an *A* − for mechanics (". . . I have done endless amounts of rough drafts, fixing sentences that according to me didn't fit well."). Nowhere in her analysis does Laura mention Linda's influence on the ultimate content. She has internalized it and adopted it as her own. Laura had recognized a passion; that passion became the driving force in an intensive process of analysis and creation.

I identify Laura as someone doing exactly what Linda wants students to do in class: find their passions and use writing to explore them. Laura does, as evidenced by her nine drafts, her deep thought, and her drive to craft her piece. Fueled by both personal motivation and careful relationship-building, she gains a powerful rapport with Linda that allows her to share control in her conferences. Linda's agenda does not overpower her. Instead, the two work together to construct the piece. Laura is the driver, secure enough to listen to her guide, Linda, but also controlling the direction her piece ultimately takes. The social relationship she built with Linda allows her to discuss freely, to engage in a good healthy chat where interesting ideas flow.

These conferences also serve as a testament to the profound influence oral language has on written language. Nothing is so powerful an antidote to writer's block than the ability to talk about one's interests with an interested other. All the listener then has to do is reiterate and clarify that which has already been spoken.

14

Relationships and Emotions

Rapport between a teacher and her students promotes conversations in which students speak with sparks in their throats, enthusiastically discussing personally relevant topics that become the subject matter of their writing. This is the material to which the teacher listens and responds, relaying it back so that students can better hear themselves. In this concept of rapport, participants pay deeper attention to interpersonal relationships that move beyond cognitive, intellectual connections into affective, emotional connections, as well.

In terms of reading and writing instruction, there is some literature about teacher-student relationships—the thoughts, feelings, attitudes, beliefs, and expectations we have about one another, which powerfully influence our classroom triumphs and failures (McLeod 1995; Tobin 1993)—but it is sparse. There is a little more research addressing how affective states, including emotion and motivation, influence the literacy learner (Brand 1987, 1991; Fleckenstein 1991; McLeod 1987, 1991, 1995), but again there is a relative paucity.

Recognizing Emotion

This is surprising, because emotion is an integral component of almost every psychological and developmental theory that literacy teachers and researchers cite as influences. Erikson, Piaget, Vygotsky, Bartlett, Kohlberg, and others have all noted the necessary role affect plays in social, cognitive, and moral development (Brand 1987; Fleckenstein 1991; McLeod 1991). Speaking of the relationship between intellect and affect, Lev Vygotsky warns,

114

Their separation as subjects of study is a major weakness of traditional psychology, since it makes the thought processes appear as an autonomous flow of "thoughts thinking themselves," segregated from the fullness of life, from the personal needs and interests, the inclinations and impulses, of the thinker. (1986, p. 10)

Kristie Fleckenstein (1991) suggests that affect and cognition are integrative in that they lie along the same continuum. On one end of the continuum lie the experiences of emotions, feelings, moods, and preferences, which are most affective in nature. Next are attitudes, beliefs, motivations, and evaluations, each generating a progressively more powerful cognitive stance (see also Brand 1994a, 1994b). Fleckenstein likens this conceptualization to Louise Rosenblatt's (1978) description of the difference between *aesthetic* reading, in which the reader focuses on the more visceral associations, feelings, attitudes, and ideas that the text arouses within, and *efferent* reading, in which the reader focuses on reading for information, solutions to the problem, and directions. Just as no reading experience is ever purely aesthetic or efferent, no human experience is ever purely affective or cognitive. Instead, each is a combination of both in varying proportions.

Fleckenstein's model can help us examine what types of responses we may use to move a learner forward. For instance, we can see that Linda Rief's philosophy, teaching style, and expectations integratively span the entire continuum from most affective to most cognitive. Her expectation that students write about personally relevant topics means that they must tap into their emotions, feelings, moods, and preferences; that their attitudes, beliefs, and motivations help determine how and what they write; and that they will engage in continual cognitive evaluation of themselves and their work. In another classroom where the teacher focuses on subject matter, the affective end of the continuum may not receive as much attention. The listening teacher, devoted to valuing students' voices, naturally expects them to recognize and exploit their affective dimension more than the teacher who controls the subject matter of the class.

Because of this we again have to acknowledge our momentous responsibility: by inviting in the personally relevant, we invite in many sets of emotions, feelings, moods, and preferences. We must attend to them all, lest they wither from neglect.

Yet, once we invite the personal and/or emotional in, we often ignore them. We say, "Now that you have brought me your precious life, I will teach you the *process* of how to craft it." We focus only on the intellectual aspects of literary creation. Though we insist on students' emotional investment, we often treat the teacher-student relationship as purely academic. Sometimes it can be, but more often we need to deal with students emotionally as well as academically before their lives can be crafted into text. When the teacher pretends that students' spoken or written words are somehow disembodied from the personal investment that carries them—treating them as emotion-neutral bits of intellectual information waiting for sculpting—she discovers that the students become unwilling to reveal what is important to them. They recognize the full meaning behind their words is not being valued.

Avoiding Danger

What are the reasons we so often shy from examining relationships and emotion both in research and classroom practice? Alice Brand suggests that emotions, which "make their bed in social psychology," are often perceived as needing to be "corrected" or "cured," which sullies their reputation. She also believes that social models of psychology and literacy may not recognize them because "they are experienced internally and individually" (1991, 400–401).

I speculate that there are two other reasons. First, affect, by almost all measures, is still considered a slippery, nebulous concept, notoriously indefinable—or at least still not completely defined. We do not have stage or process models of the inner-workings of emotion the way we have cognitive models of writing processes (Flower and Hayes 1981, for example). We have not yet quantified or conceptualized emotional dimensions to our satisfaction. We view them as less known and less knowable. And what is less known and knowable is more threatening.

Second, both politically and psychically, acknowledging affect in the context of our classroom teaching makes us extraordinarily vulnerable. It is *dangerous* to discuss emotions and feelings, both our students' and our own. It opens us to others' charges that we are playing amateur psychologists. It flies in the face of our cultural definition of professionalism. It reveals that our teaching cannot be as efficient as a cognitive model or a chart demonstrating *the* writing process portrays it. It opens us up to charges of subjectivity. It forces us to confront our subjectivity and biases that are, in fact, *there*: our weaknesses, our pettiness, our powerlessness when dealing with people we don't particularly like. It forces us to acknowledge the impossibility of having one hundred ten happy, productive relationships with one hundred ten students. If we share our own work—that which is most important to *us*—we run the risk of disdain from our students. All of these dangers wreak havoc on our self-perception of our own competence, something we try desperately to preserve (Goffman 1959). In short, recognizing the complexity of interpersonal relationships in classrooms highlights the impossibility of being the invulnerable super-teachers we secretly desire to be—and may believe we have to portray to the critics outside our classroom walls.

Confronting Fears, Welcoming Diversity

But we can't have it both ways. We cannot invite students' lives into the classroom and then ignore the personal and emotional dimensions they bring with them. We must address our fears and confront both our students' and our own emotions, attitudes, beliefs, and biases head-on in the same way we expect students to do when they read, write, and converse. It is never easy, but it is essential. As Lad Tobin writes:

> Traditionally we have considered the quality of the relationship in a writing classroom to be an effect of a student's success or failure as a writer; I think that it is often the other way around, that writing students succeed when teachers establish productive relationships with and between their students. It makes sense, then, for a writing teacher to focus as much on questions of authority and resistance as on invention heuristics and revision strategies, as much on competition and cooperation as on grammar and usage. (1993, p. 10)

Undeniably, the teaching and learning of literacy occur within the context of the interpersonal relationship. Ignoring the undeniable seems fruitless, so it makes sense to finally attend to the nature of the interpersonal relationship and all the emotional baggage it carries—or that carries it.

Of course, the teacher who welcomes in a more multidimensional perspective of students' lives, recognizing affect as well as intellect, faces great challenges. Each encounter with each student is original and must be approached on its own terms. Gone is a simple curriculum that easily determines the teacher's next step. In its place is a complicated chess match of moves and countermoves, each influenced by the moves that preceded it and, in turn, influencing those that follow. In conferences, each student's personality resides on a different place on the affective continuum. Some students generally navigate life and literacy from a more emotional perspective, some from a more ordered, intellectual one. In deciding how to respond to each student in conference, the teacher must consider the student's approach and alter her own approach accordingly.

This is important if we remember Erving Goffman's contention that social encounters are performances fueled by the persons' desire to appear competent to others. Any social situation is threatening when there is the possibility that we will be found incompetent or unknowledgeable. We therefore create standardized fronts for ourselves, hiding some personal traits and revealing others, depending upon how they will make us look in the eyes of others (Goffman 1959).

Classroom interactions, including writing conferences between the teacher and the student, are such social encounters. The traditional role of the teacher is as the person with the *answers,* able to pass down knowledge. Ironically, the student's idealized role is also as someone with the answers, able to meet a teacher's challenge. Tom Newkirk talks about the paradoxical position a student is put in, "needing to appear comfortable in a role, *as he or she is learning it*" (1995, 194). When a teacher is recognized as a knower but not a learner, she has an absolute advantage over a novice student in terms of appearing competent. Add to this the disadvantage the middle school adolescent faces—having to appear competent in a number of competing situations at a time when cognitive, biological, and social forces may undermine his or her ability to judge what is competent-appearing behavior and what is not.

I suggest it is *because* of these circumstances, which make competent performances more difficult, that students and teachers perform roles that are more standardized and simplified than they might be; doing so makes it easier to maintain that competent front. The result may be a classroom where teaching *is* done by formula: the class strictly adheres to a predetermined curriculum, has universal rules for student behavior, or treats all students "the same" or "equally." These formulas make the performers' roles more static and simpler to maintain. To achieve socially acceptable classroom performances we mistakenly focus less on the complex realm of individual personality and more on the simplified, formulaic script. In doing so, we abandon opportunities to bring personal creativity into the classroom.

But when we believe that good work comes from the subject matter that is most important to the individual student, we defy formula; we ask students to show their diversity—their uniqueness—at a time when everything else in their lives screams at them to conform. We ask them to drop their masks and perform new roles that are potentially dangerous to their public fronts, which try to maintain social acceptability.

Our own performances with students, then, have to make them feel safe—ensure their competence—in this new, highly risky context. We must create relationships in which the student trusts the teacher not to undermine or exploit his portrayal of competence if he reveals information potentially discrepant to his front.

But the teacher-student relationship is still unbalanced in that school is *thrust* upon most students. In most other social situations a person can opt out of, or avoid, a performance altogether. The classroom student, however, is obligated to attend this social situation despite any dangers to his or her front and despite his or her (sometimes wildly acute) misgivings.

Relationship-building is complex in a classroom like Linda Rief's because each student's now accepted unique qualities influence social interactions. A teacher cannot take an idealized role of *knower* and expect to build rapport with each student. Instead, she has to listen to discover what approach will let each reveal his or her diversity without undermining his or her sense of competence. We build rapport by adjusting our role to complement each student's role in every individual interaction. In this sense effective teacher listening means we do not commit to a performative role until we have learned what role the student takes. To take the analogy of a social interaction as a performance a bit further, we can say that a conference where the teacher focuses on predetermined subject matter or a formulaic approach is like a scripted play where the performers' roles are also predetermined. If the student, for whatever reasons, refuses to enter the performance, the script offers no compromise by which to negotiate a mutually acceptable entry. Linda Rief's conferences, on the other hand, might be considered improvisational theater. There is certainly a framework—a *general* script—with which to begin, but the performers always bring unique, often surprising, life material to each performance. At the same time they have to *react* to each other's surprises in ways that maintain a coherent plot line and move the performance logically forward. We teachers learn to improvise, to listen and react according to the situation.

The next four chapters show four different performances, which occur during writing conferences. They present four students with four very different sets of approaches, passions, problems, and needs. They illustrate not only how a good relationship, or lack thereof, helps determine the success or failure of a writing conference, but also the complexity of interpersonal interaction in a classroom built on diverse personalities and proclivities. We see what Linda listens to, how she listens, how she sometimes fails to listen, and how she succeeds in situations with these students who have unique personality types and attitudes toward language arts.

After each of the conferences within these chapters, I interviewed both Linda and the student at separate times, playing the conferences for them and asking them to respond. (The exception was Meg, whom I didn't interview because she was out ill for an extended period.) Whenever one of us found something intriguing or noteworthy, I would stop the tape of the conference and the participant would analyze and interpret what was going on. The teacher and the students began to see things they had not recognized when the conferences actually happened.

15

Meg Confers with a Trusted Friend

Linda's strong personal relationship with Meg engenders a productive academic relationship. Linda's teaching cannot be nearly as effective if Meg does not perceive her as a friendly, caring person. But because Meg does, she trusts Linda to guide her academically, seeing Linda's comments more as resources and challenges than mandates.

Linda, for her part, has to approach academic situations with one eye on how her words might affect their social relationship and Meg's confidence and motivation. She also has to allow Meg's natural exuberance its place without letting it supersede academic work. Of the four teacher-student relationships I present, this is the one that best defines the even balance and integration of social and academic concerns, which so often lead to better writing. With this integration, significant social aspects of writers' lives are more accessible fuel for the page.

Meg

Meg is friendly and exuberant in social situations with friends, speaking rapidly and excitedly about a variety of adolescent concerns: relationships, clothes, sports, schoolwork. She loves her family, the ocean, Lake George, coffee ice cream, her dog, water skiing, and miniature golf. She hates headaches, people asking stupid questions, swimming in cold water, waking up in the middle of the night, not having anything to do, bugs and snakes, and fighting with friends. She plays piano.

Tall and athletic, Meg especially loves playing ice hockey. She began to skate at eighteen months and to play hockey at age six. She plays defense on a

121

team that made it to the national championships in Minnesota, a trip she calls one of the most exciting of her life. In her final portfolio she writes, "My most important work does not have to do with school, it has to do with hockey. That is why I put in some of the best things I have done in hockey."

As outgoing as Meg is with friends, she is somewhat shy in academic settings. She rarely volunteers her ideas or opinions in whole-class discussions. In her year-end Self-Evaluation she writes, "What I would like to do better as a speaker is not to be afraid when I go in front of the class to talk." In early days she seems somewhat hesitant in class.

But in one of her first conferences with Linda, where she tells Linda she is a hockey player, Meg learns Linda's acceptance of social conversation and personal concerns in academic situations. Sonja, overhearing the conference, tells Linda that she, too, plays hockey. Two other girls at the table figure skate, and excitement rises as the group discusses skating. Linda, who contributes to the conversation with questions, comments, and stories of her own, finally laughs, "Wait a minute, I'm losing this conference here!" But a social rapport has formed between Meg and Linda, which enables Meg to talk easily in subsequent conferences.

Meg's View of Herself

While it may not be her "most important work," Meg enjoys language arts. She considers herself to be a writer and reader:

> When I was in first grade our teacher had us write a lot, and she would read through these little books where we'd write about something and she'd bind them as books. I wrote a lot of those little books when I was in first and second grade. And she always had us do vocabulary words, so that always helped with my writing, and I just liked to read a lot. I couldn't go to sleep unless I read a book and so I'd stay up 'til past midnight reading a book and then I'd finally fall asleep. . . . I did some writing during third, fourth, fifth grade. I read a lot of books in fourth grade. I remember that. Once I got to middle school, I didn't read that many books because we had more homework.

At the beginning of the year she lists "poems and stories" as her favorite writing genres and feels that she does her best writing in "research papers and sometimes poems."

Meg worries about her writing, though, feeling that she is not a very good speller and doesn't have a large vocabulary. She also says,

I always have these great ideas for writing, but they never seem to come out right. I am very surprised when one of my pieces of writing comes out well. It is always hard for me to think of good ideas of what to write.

Meg's Performance

Meg's reading and writing topics arise from what is personally important to her. For instance, she chooses Robert Louis Stevenson for her author study because as a young child her father read Stevenson's poems to her every night, and they evoke wonderful, nostalgic memories. She notes, "All of his poems are based on dreams and having fun" and "The poems he writes are always about happy and wonderful things." Her own early writing echoes many of these themes: carefree days, bucolic settings, fun, dreams, and warm moments. As the year progresses, though, her writing and portfolio reveal more troubled thoughts about struggles for popularity, boys, and the phoniness she perceives in some of her classmates. "I am lost in a sea of tears, not knowing what to do," she writes in a later journal entry as she searches for a lead to a new piece.

In language arts, Meg writes mostly poetry, but her portfolio includes a variety of genres: a cartoon, a book review, a series of short observational essays, a fantasy story, and research papers from other classes.

The sophistication of Meg's journal writing increases greatly over the course of the year. Her early responses are short and somewhat superficial:

> The one thing that gets really annoying is when you have already read the book that your reading. I read *Treasure Island* in 6th grade, but I'm reading it again because I love the way Robert Louis Stevenson writes.

But a few months later, Meg supplies much more analysis, much richer detail, and more personal connections with books. In response to *Walk Two Moons* (Creech 1996) she writes,

> . . . It made me laugh and cry. Throughout the whole book it was really funny to read about Phoebe and her so-called lunatic. She really worried a lot. At the end of the book Sal found out that her mother died in a bus crash. The only living person was Mrs. Cadaver. Mrs. Cadaver was sitting next to Sal's mom on the bus ride. Mrs. Cadaver lived and Sal's mom died. Sal's father never told her this because he though Sal would hate Mrs. Cadaver. . . .
>
> If my mother died and the person sitting next to her lived I would probably be mad. I wouldn't be mad at the person, but mad that she lived and my mother died. I wouldn't be mad forever, probably for awhile though.

At the end of the story I figured out what "Don't judge a man until you've walked two moons in his moccasins" meant. It meant that Sal's dad wanted her to go through the same trip that her mother went through, like visiting all those different landmarks.

She uses her journal in the way Linda hopes students will. When she finds a striking quote or passage in a book she marks it with a pencil, then returns to it to respond in her journal. New writing ideas often come out of her journal responses:

I was reading in Anne Frank and I found this really neat paragraph, and so I put it in there. And later, when I read [another author] it gave me an idea for that art square you had to do—it gave me an idea what I was going to draw. Reading *The Cage* [Sender 1988], I went back and read the poems that she wrote about how it was living in the ghetto. I wrote two poems about that, so it does help to write down things about books because you get ideas.

Her draft writing also changes markedly. During the second-quarter author study she drafts some sketches of characters for a story she wants to write:

Hey, Waz up? My name is Steve. Howz it going? I'm Steve and I live in downtown New York City. It's pretty cool there. Central Park is real close to where I live. My friends Sue and Tim are really cool. We go down to Central Park every weekend and play roller hockey.

Compare this with the sophisticated description from a fourth-quarter essay she submits in her final portfolio:

He stands there leaning against the wall, hands in his pockets and left foot up against the wall, making it so his knee bends at a 90 degree angle. When the girls see him they start to walk fast and when they have passed him they start to giggle. How shallow. He looks at them and grins, showing his white teeth that sparkle in the light. If he sees a girl he likes he'll take her by the arm and tell her to meet him at 7 for a movie. Just like that he gets a date. He thinks he is god's gift to the world. His smooth black hair shines from the grease he uses, just like his black leather jacket shines in the light. Every day underneath that jacket is a crisp, white tee-shirt that is stiff from ironing. And every day in one of his jacket pockets is a mustard color comb that by the end of the day has black strands of hair in it. If you ask me, the grease is making his hair fall out.

Clearly, Meg's writing in Linda's class greatly improves over the year.

Meg's View of Language Arts Class

Meg really likes language arts class:

> I like it because there's no spelling tests. It's fun, it's different from any of the other ones I've had, because you have more choice of what you want to do. And it's just fun to be in. . . .
>
> In sixth grade we were restricted to write certain things, and some things I can't write. I'm not that good at writing stories, so it was hard. But here in this class you can write anything you want and [Mrs. Rief] doesn't really assign you to read any book, she just tells you what books are good to read or not. And in her classroom she has a lot of choices for books.

Meg wishes she had more one-on-one time with Linda. She feels peer feedback is helpful, but some of her friends "are too afraid to say if something's wrong because they don't want to hurt your feelings." She says she often responds to her own friends with disingenuous praise in order to preserve friendships.

Meg however, does benefit from some classroom talk among friends. "When I read what I'm writing to the person who's sitting next to me, or we talk about ideas, it helps a lot." She says, "We talk about stuff and they're like, 'Oh, that's a good idea,' and they start writing about it. So, that works."

Meg feels the work and goals of this class are very different than those of her previous language arts classes. She says of Linda, "She wants you to write, but she doesn't tell you what you have to write about," and she perceives Linda as expecting students to write about "experiences or dreams or something like that." It had been different in sixth grade, which she had not enjoyed. Then, the teacher had assigned her topics:

> We had to pick an author and we had to read one of his books and we had to write a newspaper about what was happening. She had us write a newspaper. Every week we had to write a book review about the book we read, and we had to read nine books in four weeks, or something like that. We had to write about the book. I guess she would assign them, so she'd give us a choice of books that we had to read, and she'd have you write about the book, and there'd be this little visual project thing. So we didn't do much writing in sixth grade.

She considers this assignment to have been very different from the author study she does in Linda's class. In sixth grade, "It wasn't really a study," but a summary. She says, "It was like events that happened in the book, in the newspaper way, so we didn't really study how the author wrote." But in

Mrs. Rief's class, "We had to look for techniques, how they described character or characters, or made plots, and, if you were doing poems, how they set up the poem, or how they used their words." Though the assignments appear similar, Meg sees Linda's assignment as being built on a much richer analysis of technique, character, structure, and word usage.

Meg's View of Linda

Meg praises almost all aspects of Linda's teaching. "She discusses what she wants you to write and so it's easier for you to think about it." Her other teachers didn't discuss their assignments in class, which made it "harder to think about things that would relate to that topic." Meg also appreciates that Linda reads and writes along with students. "It's good to see the teacher doing work in class, too. It's kind of different," she says.

> It keeps the class in what they're doing because they see the teacher doing it. . . . She reads a lot of books. She gives you some ideas sometimes, when she writes quick-writes. And it's really interesting to see what the teacher writes.

But Meg focuses most intently on her relationship with Linda. She likes the way Linda interacts with students. She says, "At lunch time she's really friendly to everybody who's there. She's really fun to talk to." Meg sees this friendliness in the classroom, as well. For Meg, Linda's friendliness drives her success. "She's really nice to the students and she helps you if you have trouble with ideas or what you want to write, and she's easy to talk to about your writing. So, that's good." Linda is different than the other teachers she has had, says Meg:

> She's a lot nicer. The teachers I've had were really strict and kind of mean, and they don't really care about what you're writing about. . . . I know in sixth grade our teacher, everybody was afraid of her because they thought she was really mean, and so it's important for a teacher to be nice because then the students don't feel threatened or afraid to talk.

For Meg, friendliness does not just offer social comfort but supports academic endeavors, as well. Meg's view that she might be "threatened or afraid to talk" without Linda's display of care for her work, and without the sense of comfort it fosters, cuts to the core of the importance of rapport in bridging the social and the academic.

Meg thinks Linda is an excellent listener.

She listens like she cares about what you're writing, and some of the other teachers just listen to you because they have to. It's their job. Yeah, she listens differently. She actually cares about what you're writing, and so it's a lot easier to read your writing to her.

She compares her to a previous teacher:

We'd sit down and she'd just be listening to me, holding her pen, just turning it around. And it seems like she'd be dozing off sometimes. And then, when you ask her what she says, she always complements you and everything and doesn't really correct it that much.

Meg associates care with listening. When Linda listens because she cares, Meg responds differently than she does to the teacher who listens because she has to. Linda's caring makes Meg receptive to a more directive teaching approach. Suggestions and directives are no longer orders but signs that the teacher has, in fact, listened carefully. They become valued as truly important advice. Meg appreciates Linda's corrections as well as her praise.

She sits down and she listens to you, and after [she listens] she tells you things that you did good, but she also tells you what needs working on and she helps you with that sometimes: what needs to be changed. . . . She corrects the spelling and punctuation for you. And, if you're writing your poems, she helps you add things in or set it up differently, so it's a lot easier.

Meg says she doesn't feel obligated to use Linda's suggestions, "She's just trying to help you, but you don't have to use them." However, she considers them carefully. After one of Linda's suggestions to combine two poems, Meg resisted. She says, "I thought the poem was perfect the way it was, but then I kept on reading it over and over again with that part, and it sounded good, so I decided to use it."

Meg loves Linda's conferring style. "She listens and really helps you. If you have a problem, she can help you with it. . . . She's just really friendly and helpful during conferences." Meg says there is nothing she would change to make conferences better.

The Conference

This conference occurs late in October during the first quarter. Meg has just read one poem about apple picking to Linda, which begins:

How 'bout this tree

or

> maybe that one,
> which I can't decide.
>> I want to pick the best red
>> apples anybody can ever find.

> How 'bout this tree
>> or
> maybe that one,
> which I can't decide.
>> This one over there has 1 big apple,
>> but the other one has 9. . . .

Linda gives her first response, a praise.

Linda: I like the repetition, too, Meg. "How 'bout this tree, or maybe that one. Which, I can't decide." What I love about it is that's how I always feel like.

Meg: I know!

Linda: Because every time you look over you see another tree that's got bigger apples on it.

Meg: [Excitedly] We went apple picking a while ago, and we got the biggest bags you can get. We got two of them for my brother and I, and we were having a contest to see who could find the biggest apple and everything. And we could never find one that . . . we found this tree at the very end; our bags were almost full, and the tree had apples way up high, so I had to climb the tree, get the apples; it almost fell on my head, I remember that, and like went, "Foom!" and it bounced right off!

Linda: [Laughs]

A Personal *Response*

This exchange has a *personal* quality. Instead of beginning with text analysis, Linda responds emotionally to the poem, empathizing with the feeling of searching for the perfect apple. Meg responds with an enthusiastic "I know!" and an uninhibited story, which reveals the personal, nonacademic inspiration behind the poem. Linda laughs appreciatively. It is her initial aesthetic reaction here that fuels Meg's enthusiasm. It sets the tone for the rest of the conference, establishing a good, healthy chat that I suggest enables Meg, ultimately, to change her subsequent draft radically. In this type of comfortable, informal conversation, "the sights, the sounds, the smells" that personalize and transform writing arise more frequently.

Meg feels her first poem is good and has read it only for Linda's quick confirmation. She next produces another poem draft, "Dreams and Nightmares," which was inspired by a collection of Stephen King short stories she had read, titled *Nightmares and Dreamscapes* (1994). Meg likes the idea, but she thinks it needs a lot of work:

> As the sun sets behind the mountains, the sky turns a jet black
> The children close there eyes.
> The stars come out and the moon shines down through the
>   windows of the children
>   letting them dream happy dreams
>
> But when the sun sets behind the mountains, and the sky turns
>   jet black the children's
>   eyes close. And the stars and moon don't come out, the
>   children cry. They cry
>   in their dreams, no longer is there a dream, but a
>   nightmare.
>
> But the moon will come out and the stars will come out and will
>   shine on the children and happy dreams will start.

Linda: What do you think you did well in this? What are the places that you like?

I ask Linda what she was looking for from her question to Meg. She responds,

> I want her to tell me first what she sees as the strengths, because I don't want to dive in. I want her to be the first one to tell me what's working, so that I can get a sense of, "Does she already know this?" If I *confirm* it am I going to destroy her or help her recognize that she already knows this? Because she's got a couple of good lines in it, but it's pretty weak. I mean, you can even hear it in her voice that it's kind of boring for her to read it.

Linda's first concern after she sees weakness in the piece is to maintain a social connection, finding an approach that will not "destroy" Meg and compromise her ability or desire to move the piece forward. Although Meg has already stated that she sees the piece as weak, Linda treads lightly when it comes to constructive criticism.

I play Meg's answer:

Meg: I liked how I describe like the sun setting behind them and the jet-black sky. I like that.

Linda: Yeah.

Meg: The ending's good, but the middle's kind of weird, I think.

Meg's answer tells Linda a lot.

It tells me that she can already identify the strongest line. That *is* the strongest line. And she already knows that, so my hope is that she'll figure out "What do I do with this line," and *abandon* a lot of the rest, or start to really revise the rest. But at least she's got a thread to hold on to.

Meg's statement that, "The ending's good, but the middle's kind of weird, I think," also allows Linda to *agree* with her, softening any subsequent constructive criticism and helping preserve the social integrity of the performance. Linda can then launch into a series of questions and suggestions that provoke Meg to create ideas for revision:

Linda: Yeah, I noticed even as you were reading it, you were having a hard time reading it seriously. [Meg laughs] I think I agree with you. I like this part best, too. What do *you* think about the . . . if you just cover up this part, and you read this part to yourself, and this part, about the sunset and the jet-black sky. What do you *love* about the sun setting or the night sky?

Meg: It's just really pretty, like at the sunset, they're trying to . . . like, there's purples and pinks and peaches and stuff. I think it's really pretty, and then all of the sudden it's just jet black. And it's just really neat, and really pretty.

Linda: Just the way you just said "Pinks and purples and peaches." Those are beautiful images, and you've also got the p's, the p's, the p's: "the pinks, the purples, the peaches." And then all of the sudden it turns *jet* black. If you can somehow get that surprise in there. Just see if you're doing this: [Reads] "As the sun sets behind the mountains and the sky . . ." Where are those colors that you just told me? Have you got them in?

Meg: No, I didn't. I was gonna put them in there, but then I just didn't.

Linda: All right, maybe that's what you do. What made you decide not to put them in there?

Meg: I don't know. I guess I was just in a rush to get out, because in the morning I'm usually late.

Linda: As the sun sets behind the mountains—pinks, purples, peaches—and the sky suddenly turns *jet* black . . . What do you wonder? Or what do you think?

Meg: Well, it's like really pretty and all of the sudden it just turns dark, kind of. It's like with the pinks and peaches you think like it's really like *happy* hour, but then with the jet black.

Linda: But does that jet black scare you?

Meg: Not really. Well, kind of. If they were like little kids it would.

Linda: But *you*. Talking about *you*.

Meg: No.

Linda: It wouldn't scare you. You like that jet black.

Meg: Yeah.

Linda: If you just keep those two images, and then there are all different directions you could go in with this. You're talking about night. It might even be getting ready for bed. I know, probably there's nothing I like better than on a cold night that you're falling into flannel sheets, and reading an incredibly good book. So maybe that's the direction you head in. What's happening during this jet black night? Where do you see other directions you can head with this? I mean, even just with a sentence or two.

Meg: Well I remember when I was, like, with my friends, we'd always go underneath the covers and get a flashlight and just like draw or read, or something.

Linda: You know what, Meg? That's a great ending for that. You've got the images of the night, it's jet black, and my friends and I grab flashlights, crawl under the sheets, and color . . . peaches and purples and pinks. It's a *beautiful* poem. Doesn't that sound much stronger?

Meg: Yeah.

Meg's Spark

This is the seminal exchange of the conference. Linda gives her reaction to it:

> First I'm trying to get her to get the images in there. She's got this wonderful line about the sunset, and when *she* can describe it—when she describes it orally with these purples and pinks and peaches—I am trying to get her to see the *sound* of those words and that it *does* create an image in your head. She doesn't quite have yet that poetry creates images. So that's the first thing I'm trying to do.
>
> The second thing I was trying to do with her is . . . *I* think good poetry gives you a surprise in the end, or makes you see something in a fresh way that no one else would describe. She's got the *image* but, now, what does that image mean? That's where I'm trying to get her to describe what's *happening* on this night: here's the night. Okay, so what? When she suddenly says to me about crawling underneath the covers with a flashlight to draw or read, that's really exciting to me.
>
> I feel really good about this conference. I had things to grab hold of. She had some good starts, but I could help her find some things that she already knew. And *she* had the pinks the peaches and the purples. If I can get her to do that without saying, "Do this," then I know that she's beginning to get a grasp or an understanding of what poetry should do.

I don't know what she did, because I haven't seen the final piece. If she doesn't get it from that, then she's not ready to get it yet, but *that's* what I was trying to do. I was trying to get her to see that for herself. I mean, it *is* a beautiful poem. It's very short and tight, and my repetition of it back to her is hoping that she will take it on for herself now, because they're *her* words that I'm just repeating back.

This exchange typifies how Linda uses students' own oral words as a springboard for text revision. The two critical junctures of the exchange come with Linda's recognition of the value of Meg's spoken words—her beautiful, spontaneous alliteration, "purples and pinks and peaches," and her comforting imagery of lying under the covers with a flashlight and a friend, drawing and reading. Again, Linda listens for the *spark* in Meg's responses—the places where she spontaneously and enthusiastically reveals images and memories important to her. From there Linda's simply repeats, and perhaps shapes a bit, what Meg herself has said. "I could help her find some things that she already knew," notes Linda.

Meg's ease in creating oral language and imagery of this quality and literary usefulness illustrates the importance of the personal rapport between the two. Her perception that Linda listens and cares establishes a trust that allows Meg to converse colloquially, without constraint. Students in this class create more beautiful imagery when engaged in easy social talk than they do when engaged in drier academic discourse. Rapport encourages oral poetry, which Linda then presents back to the speaker.

Linda is very pleased. She says, "I think this conference worked really well, because when I asked her questions she knew *answers* for them. She didn't say, "I don't know." She loves that Meg has evaluated her writing before the conference:

> I think she does exactly what I would like kids to do: have a volume of writing in front of them and to be able to look at that and *already* be able to judge one piece is better than another piece. I think that worked really well. What I liked was that she was able to grasp hold of suggestions that I gave to her because they were *her* language. That's why I think this whole conference worked well. I thought the whole thing worked *very* well.

For Linda, then, success is partially guaranteed before the conference even begins because Meg is prepared to articulate her visions, and is willing to receive Linda's response. Linda's responses during the conference help sustain the rapport that leads to Meg's easy articulation and motivation.

At the time of our interview, Linda has not yet seen Meg's final draft of "Dreams and Nightmares." I show it to her. Meg has retitled it "Under the Covers":

As the sun sets behind the mountains
  The sky turns jet black

  My friends and I grab the flashlights
And duck under the covers

  There we grab the markers and start coloring
Pinks, peaches, and purples

  As the sky gets darker,
  The colors get brighter

Linda reads it and exclaims,

Oh yeah! Wow! What a difference! To me, then, the conference really worked because she took some of the images and she made them her own. She moved stuff around. It's different from the way I read it back to her, but she's got all the same images in there, and I *love* her last line, "As the sky gets darker the colors get brighter." And she's got wonderful verbs in here now: "grab," "duck" . . .

She also looks at Meg's Case History of the poem, which says,

In my journal I wrote a poem about nightmares and dreams. The two different subjects didn't really fit together. So, I took some of the descriptive words I used, and I put them in the beginning of my poem. I got the idea of the new poem from when my friend and I used to pull all the covers over our heads and use a flashlight to color or read. I took that and put the descriptive words in front and came up with a short poem.

Meg in Control

Linda remarks, "She has taken control, and I am *totally* out of it. She doesn't even talk about the conference." This is the sign of a successful co-construction of text. Meg has adopted and internalized Linda's ideas as her own because they make sense and fit into her own vision for the piece. She is in charge of the images and thinking independently about how to use them. Linda responds that it embarrasses her when students say that she made them put something into their pieces. "And even though there's a piece of me that says, 'Well doesn't Meg remember that we had this long conference?' she's doing exactly what we want them doing."

Meg includes "Under the Covers" in her final portfolio in June, and comments on it in her year-end Self-Evaluation. She reveals the personal relevance of the topic when she writes, "This poem represents me personally, what I was like when I was little. From writing this poem I learned that I could write poems the way I pictured them in my mind." She writes of the lessons she learned from writing the poem:

> I learned that you could write something that you think is good, but still really needs work on it. I also learned that when you write a rough draft you can just like a sentence that you wrote and continue on from that.
>
> . . . When I compare [my first draft to my final draft] I can tell that the first poem I wrote was choppy and that I didn't really know what I was trying to write. But with "Under the Covers" I made it flow and I knew what I was trying to say and what I was really writing about.

Again, there is no mention of Linda's help, but there is a clear self-awareness of her ability and growth. The lessons she learned were not lessons she discussed in her conference with Linda. Linda had not said that "Dreams and Nightmares" was choppy or that she suspected Meg didn't know what she was trying to write, and Meg created her final stanza, "As the sky gets darker/the colors get brighter," unassisted, after the conference. Meg has been *thinking:* analyzing and evaluating her own work carefully and using what she learns to evolve her text progressively. Undoubtedly, Linda influences the final shape of the poem, but it is equally true that Meg has the ultimate control of her work. She makes the final decisions and her decisions are motivated primarily by her care for the poem, not slavish adherence to outside forces. Linda facilitates Meg's sense of ownership by establishing a relationship built on responses that reveal her as an interested, empathic, caring audience, not as a teacher. She balances Meg's social facility with the academic purposes of the conference. In doing so she engenders trust and encourages talk that promotes deeper student thought and motivation.

16

Jason Confers with Someone He Doesn't Trust

L inda's conferences with Jason show a relationship where the rapport necessary for academic collaboration does not fully develop. Jason's academic history and his negative view of himself as a writer and reader contribute to his unwillingness to trust the teacher. Linda's love of writing and reading also makes it difficult to establish rapport with Jason as easily as she does with students who like language arts. Her frustration grows.

Jason

Intelligent and possessing a wicked sense of humor, Jason often exploits his talents at times that aren't appreciated by Linda and classmates. He is engaging, funny, and at times remarkably sensitive to others. He is also conspicuous, calling attention to himself in front of the whole class. He is the one who shouts while others work silently, who responds to questions with sarcastic jokes, who covers his arms with tape during class, who escapes to the bathroom. Says Linda, "I take a deep sigh and wonder what will it take to get him to care about language arts."

Jason writes about himself, "I usually start to get fidgety and then I'll start to talk with my friends and I won't pay attention to what's going on. I don't pay attention to anyone, really." But this isn't entirely true. In situations where he feels comfortable, Jason attends *very* well. He contributes perceptively to many class discussions.

Despite his sometimes disruptive acts, Jason is generally well-liked in class. His peers gently tolerate his outbursts, which are hardly ever angry. He has a solid group of friends with whom he spends most of his time in class talking, joking, and avoiding writing.

Outside of class Jason likes to hang out downtown or go bike riding. He is passionate about sports; he plays soccer and basketball competitively. He loves his family, movies, birthdays, TV, music, and video games. His self-proclaimed "hates" include anything to do with school and studying, bad presents, and being stuck inside. These topics are consistent themes in his journal.

This is the side of Jason that everyone in class recognizes. But a more hidden side, one deeply reflective, serious, and quieter, presents itself in a list Linda asks students to write in their journal one day—a list of "wonderings." Jason wonders, "Who made us, who made Adam and Eve, what molecules look like, what's going to happen in the future, when I'll die, what I'll do when I grow up, what's going to happen to me, will I have a lot of money, how will I die, are there genies, will I get AIDS, will I be married . . . ?" He notes his hidden side in his year-end Self-Evaluation.

> I want [people] to know that I am a lot different at home. I am more soft-spoken and I like to reflect on what I have done wrong during the day. . . . The only other thing that I want to say is that I am a quiet person who likes to read and I love to cook and play basketball.

Despite his frequent condemnations of it, there are aspects of school that Jason loves. He deeply values his friends. He can't wait for school dances, field trips, and the environmental camp the class attends. He enjoys the play-school program where eighth graders take care of toddlers for half a day.

Jason also likes math. His teacher, Michelle, is his advocate. She likes him and his humor very much. She said he is a fine math student.

Jason's View of Himself

But Jason does not consider himself to be a writer and reader. "I've always rebelled against it," he says. He had once enjoyed reading and writing, in first grade. "It was fun because we just did coloring and just drew. It wasn't really for a grade." But now, school "kind of rushes you to write." He says he dislikes writing more than anything in school. When asked, "Why do you and other people read?" he responds, "Because we're forced to," but he clearly enjoys at least some reading. During the year he transcribes several poems—short, rhyming, humorous—into his portfolio. Shel Silverstein is his favorite.

Jason identifies a good writer as someone who spells well and has a good imagination. His spelling concerns him a great deal, and becoming a better speller is one of his goals every quarter. His own best pieces, he believes, flow well and have better spelling and punctuation than usual.

Jason's Performance

While Meg generally writes autobiographically, pulling topics from her own life and writing in the first person, Jason usually writes short fiction in the third person. But his final portfolio also includes two poems, a cartoon, a myth he wrote in seventh grade, and an illustrated journal entry about his love of tall buildings.

In general Jason uses his journal to write "what I did in the day, what I read in the book," but most responses are perfunctory. He often responds vaguely to books with simple adjectives like "pretty cool" or "awesome." Early on he focuses on plot summary rather than analysis or interpretation:

> Today I read Jurassic Park for half an hour. It's a wicked good book. So far I'm at the chapter Malcom. The plot so far is that a person is making a park on a island in Costa Rica that has real living dinosaurs. They're on there way to the island right now.

Many entries appear to have been written quickly for the sake of getting the daily assignment done. His final draft writing, too, seems rushed. In his year-end Self-Evaluation Jason writes, "My writing process really has not changed. I still will write one draft and then revise it and make it a final."

However, some journal entries also produce nice imagery:

> I see a green plant that looks very good. It looks really green and looks like it's in good shape. It looks like rivers of colors joining together. I imagine that it's a plant that eats people.

> I've been trying to look for a quiet spot to read, but I haven't been able to find one. Well today I found the spot but I think it's a little too quiet. I hear the silence sound, like birds chirping, the house creaking. I hope the spot tomorrow is a little bit quieter.

"Like rivers of colors joining together" and "the silence sound" are the types of phrases that Linda asks students to consider for their draft writing. But Jason does not carry his entries into his drafts. He says, "I just *think* of something to write up. I don't usually take from my journal and then write it."

Jason's journal writing improves in the third quarter. He begins to write every day and his entries get progressively longer. A response to *The Giver* shows a new willingness to explore issues and present opinions on paper:

> I think that living in a world with no memories, no love, no color . . . is not something I think is worth giving up just so there's no poverty, disorder, or pain because I think that every person needs to once in their life feel or see

the pain or poverty. If there wasn't ever the feeling of pain [or] the thrill of doing something new or feelings, you would never feel love or caring or hate for another person. Because of not feeling these things I believe that you're not a full human being. Why would you want to give up the things that make you feel good or feel pain just so you don't have to face poverty or crime? I think that is not a way to live. Living a perfect life that has no ups and downs is boring and is too plain. It's just black and white.

A third-quarter letter he writes to Miep Gies, the woman who hid Anne Frank from the Nazis, shows a more personal and thoughtful topic selection and tone in his final drafts. It is clear and honest, states a pertinent viewpoint, and asks legitimate questions:

I believe you are a very brave individual for what you did with the Franks and other people. I think I would have been so afraid to hide people from the Nazis, especially after you know what they would do if they found out. I admire you for how long you helped the Franks and the other guests that were staying there, because you helped to keep the people alive a little bit longer with people they cared about and who they loved.

What made you so brave? How could you live with the agony of keeping them safe? What thoughts do you have for whoever told the Nazis you were hiding the Franks? And how did you work past your fears?

Much of Jason's best and hardest work, in fact, comes during the third-quarter unit on human rights and the Holocaust. The subject matter intrigues him and he loves the books he reads, especially *Night* (Wiesel 1982) and *Diary of a Young Girl* (Frank 1996). The structure of the unit fits his tastes and talents better than any other. Linda shows several movies, one of Jason's areas of expertise. There are also more whole-class discussions, which appeal to him enormously. When the class discusses the movie *Schindler's List,* Jason is one of the two primary responders. His confidence in the medium and the subject matter reveal a previously hidden talent for oral communication. Linda is impressed:

It was phenomenal listening to him. He was more with me and more with the discussion than most anybody in the class. He really watched that movie! He was able to articulate what he saw, what he thought. He was able to think what some of those things meant. He was listening harder and he was reformulating ideas. I could see it in his eyes, and I was really impressed with that. I value him for his ability to do that, and don't worry so much about the writing. [I can't] be so possessed or obsessive about him making that writing better and better and better. It's adequate and so maybe I just have to accept adequate in that way.

It feels very comfortable for him. He's more interested in talking out his ideas and thinking them out, so it's just offering all those different opportunities for kids to show what they can do with language in many different ways. I hope he got the message from me, subtly, that I was really impressed with what he was saying, the thinking that he was doing. It's almost like a conference, but it's in a whole class. You're nodding and saying, "Yeah, tell me more. Wow, yeah, that's really interesting, I really like what you said there."

But, when conversations turn to his own writing, Jason does not expound. His perfunctory responses in conferences and his reluctance to reveal personal thoughts limit his writing options all year long.

Jason's View of Language Arts Class

Jason does not view language arts class enthusiastically:

> Sometimes it's boring because sometimes there's nothing to do . . . like when you're just not in the mood to read or write, or you've done your story and today is like the last day to write and there's nothing to do if you don't feel like reading. So, you just sit around and that's boring.

He says the worst thing about language arts is "reading every day for half an hour and having to write in your journal," but some activities do appeal to him: "Watching the movies about the famous plays and playwriters." He also liked reading books out loud, together as a class. His suggestions for making the class better show his penchant for visual learning:

> I guess there weren't a lot of field trips to places. I guess [I would] show them visually what it would look like. I don't know if we could do anything about what happened with the Jewish and the Nazi people, because we can't go anywhere, really, that's close around here. . . .
>
> [Mrs. Rief] always talks about these people drawing and stuff, like these second graders and stuff. Maybe we should go to some places and look at the pictures and see what they look like . . . maybe do a Museum of Fine Arts or something like that—show people what the things are like.

Jason liked last year's class better. Whereas last year he had assignments that were due every two weeks or so, this year he has to read and respond in his journal half an hour every night. He liked the creative activities he did last year. "We'd do posters and stuff, and then we did the newspaper. That was fun," he said.

Jason also still perceives a lack of structure in Linda's writing expectations. He liked his seventh grade teachers' more directive approaches, saying, "They come down and tell you what you need to write, so it was easier that way." Then, he says, he knew exactly what to do.

Jason's View of Linda

Jason is more critical of Linda's teaching than most students. He likes her writing but says, "She likes people to write like she does. Like the way she has it":

> I guess it's kind of a bad thing because not everybody's going to be able to write like [she does]. She'll tell us to do one thing and then she'll want us to do it like the way she has the writing, and then it's harder because some people can't write like her. Like, I'm not that great a writer because, I don't know, I just don't *enjoy* it. So, I'll try to write something and then she won't like it, or something, and then I'll have to fix it. I'll have to fix it like five times before she likes it.

Though Jason wishes Linda would take more control over what he is supposed to write in class, if she directs him to improve the writing he has done, he has to analyze again. These apparently contrasting complaints both come from the same motivation to avoid writing.

Jason does like one aspect of Linda's teaching in comparison to previous teachers':

> She lets us do more free stuff. Like, we'll be open just to do whatever we want. In the other classes . . . the teacher will be in front of the class and talk to us a lot. We don't usually have those days; every day you can just go around and talk. That's what's good about the class. That's fun.

He also says that Linda's conferences and individual help are the best things about her teaching. They give him ideas for what to write. But, again, his view of teacher help is ambivalent. When Linda offers just one or two suggestions that he can easily perform, he feels she helps. But if she pushes him to make extensive changes and engage in the writing as a thinking process, he resists. He views big revision suggestions as a form of criticism. Good teacher response, he says, entails, "not telling them the story's bad, but saying that, 'It's good. Just maybe take out one or two things to make it better.' So you never really be negative, always be positive about it." He thinks Mrs. Rief only does "so-so" in this respect.

> Sometimes she'll be like, "Oh, I don't like this piece of writing. Try harder on it." Then that makes the person feel bad and then they get mad, or some-

thing. Then they don't want to do it. But if you always be positive to 'em, I guess, then it makes 'em feel better. Just say, "The piece is awesome and just take out one thing and it'll be even better."

Jason, unlike Meg, perceives much criticism in Linda's response to his writing. Where Meg sees Linda offering helpful information, Jason sees her condemning the writing. I cannot document one instance of Linda telling a student she doesn't like a piece of writing, but Jason's perception is important. *He* believes it and it affects his relationship with her, making him reticent to open up to her, reveal any concerns about his work, self-evaluate, or revise. He gives as an example of her negativity Linda's response to his letter to Miep Gies:

> I guess she kept saying the story was not that great, yeah. So she kept telling me to fix it. So then I didn't even want to do it, but then the quarter was ending so I had to finish it. . . . And then I wrote it up again and then she said she didn't like it, so I wrote it up again and she said she didn't like it, so then I just like put it in my binder and I just forgot about it until like the last day of the quarter. And then I typed it up and brought it in to school.

Ironically, Jason is expressing what Linda has told the class about herself time and again, that negative comments stop her writing and that praise keeps her going. She has vowed to put all students' writing in a positive light, even while suggesting major changes. But Jason still perceives her commentary as negative. Jason defines a good listener as someone able to "respect the child that she's listening to." He may perceive Linda's challenges as a lack of respect, which inhibits their rapport-building.

Jason says that he almost always uses Linda's conference suggestions. Where Meg sees Linda's suggestions as possibilities, Jason sees them as orders and chooses to follow them (as we shall see) as perfunctorily as possible.

In general, Jason wants from Linda a relationship where she offers praise and gives some simple, direct advice on how to improve his work, but does so without igniting his considerable insecurities about writing. His are not unreasonable expectations. Someone who does not think he is a writer will obviously put up a much larger performative mask to hide his self-perceived failings in order to preserve his aura of competence. Jason reveals little because he does not trust his writing skills and does not trust Linda.

In a strange way, then, Linda and Jason's relationship is purely *academic.* Jason only attends to Linda's straightforward academic suggestions, which limit his need to reveal too much. However, it is in the interaction of a more comfortable, social relationship that the stories that make academic work special most often reveal themselves.

Two Conferences

The first conference occurs in October. Jason initiates the conference by putting his name on the board because Linda has told everyone that they must confer with her within a few days. The conference begins with Linda's standard opening, "Okay, how can I help you?" Jason says he wants to read her one of two drafts, but he can't decide which one.

Linda: All right, which one do you think is going better?

Jason: Well, everybody says this "Farewell" is really good, so . . . I'll read it to you?

Linda: Okay. And how can I best help you with it?

Jason: Um, maybe revise it a little bit. Maybe you can say, "Oh, you can go on a little bit more with this," so maybe it can go a little longer.

Jason wants a conference that will give him a little information to add without forcing him to revise extensively. He picks "The Farewell" to read for the pragmatic reason that it will be easier to finish: "We needed [a piece] due for the end of the week," he says later, "I wanted to get something that people say is good, that would be close to final draft work." He doesn't see a need to revise: "I thought it was really good as it was. I didn't really think it needed anything." His primary objective is to make it a little longer so that he can hand it in as one of the major pieces that Linda has required. He wants quick material he can implement easily.

Linda's motivation is different. She asks Jason to tell her which piece is better because she wants him to analyze his writing, and use the conference for deep thinking. "I want kids to start evaluating from the moment that conference starts, even *before* the conference starts, all the writing that they're doing," she says, "but I think they already know what they need to do to it to make it better." When they *do* know, she can become the "sounding board" off of which they can hear their own thoughts and begin to analyze. But at this point, neither Jason nor Linda knows the other's motive. Their different goals will lead to subsequent conflict.

The conference continues. Jason reads his piece, which he had written when a visiting author assigned everyone to write a story that included a pie:

> Dear Journal,
>
> Today is August 7, 1986. Today me and my family are leaving this house we have lived in all our lives. My mother is making a pie for us for our farewell. We are going to eat it outside on the picnic table in the backyard. Good night journal. Have a safe trip. Then Johnney put his journal into a box marked Johnney's things. Then Johnney grabbed the box and went down the stairs through the living room, through the kitchen, and finally

out the door where a white and orange truck was marked *Uhaul*. He put the box in the truck and then the driver closed the back door and said "that's it!" Johnney went back in and he saw his family running around looking for things. Then he turned his head to the left and saw the pie on the table outside. He went through the kitchen and out the back door. He walked over to the table and took a piece of the pie. Then he heard his dad yell from the car "come on Johnney it's time to go!" Then Johnney ran to the door and went through the house into the car. The car drove off and the pie sat out in the backyard waiting for somebody to take it inside.

Listening to the conference, Linda notes Jason's reading fluency, and she likes the inflections in his voice. "He clearly enjoys what he's written. Part of the reading aloud is giving me some clue that he *likes* this, just from the way he reads it."

Linda: Okay, you know what I like?

Jason: No.

Linda: I like that he's writing in the journal about leaving, also the description of the U-Haul truck and the driver who slams it shut and says, "That's it." You do a nice job with that. And, also, I'm really curious about this pie. Now, why are they leaving the house?

Jason: Because they're moving. It's, like, too much for them to keep the house.

Linda: Okay, the house is too big or something?

Jason: Yeah, maybe it's too expensive. I don't now, I never thought I had to get into the house. But, they're moving.

Linda: Well, I mean, I am curious as to why they're leaving.

Jason: It's too expensive?

Linda: All right, that could be built on. What makes this pie special?

Jason: It's like a piece of the house. They're taking the house, like they're taking a piece of it with them. Like, he takes the piece of the pie . . .

Linda: Oh, so *he* takes . . .

Jason: Yeah, he takes a piece of the pie and he goes into the car with it. And it's like he's bringing part of the house with him.

Linda: What does he love about this house?

Jason: I don't know, he's grown up into it all his life.

Linda: And so how is this pie like taking a piece of the house with him?

Jason: 'Cause like the pie's the house and, like, and he takes a piece of it. It goes off with him.

Linda: Okay, in what way is the pie a piece of the house?

Jason: All the good times they've had? I don't know.

Linda: Because, does he love pie? Is that . . .

Jason: I don't know, he just . . . they made a pie, like to eat, because they're gonna leave.

Linda: What kind of pie?

Jason: It's probably a pumpkin pie [Laughs].

Her questions are ones to which Linda really wants to know the answer. "I am asking questions if I think, as a *listener,* there are gaps in information. And those are the things I wanted to know more about." These questions nudge Jason to search for what the pie represents. Linda is sick of pie writing, since every student had written a draft during the author workshop, and she remembers why she never assigns students a blanket topic. She had begun to tell kids that the pie had simply been "an exercise to help them *find* a piece of writing, and that the piece of writing may not be residing in the pie." But she continues the conference with Jason because:

> He seemed to like it from the way he read it to me, and he seemed to understand metaphor even though he couldn't quite say that. The pie was something that he really liked, and he didn't want to leave his house, and so the pie was kind of a metaphor for a piece of the house. I don't know if he *truly* understood metaphor, but he understood a *piece* of something, so I was trying to get him to clearly explain that metaphor a little bit better: what did that pie represent? I wasn't quite sure because I don't know Jason that well to know if he could do that. . . .

But Linda is also concerned about the length of the conference. "I should be able to just give him a question or two," she says. "I didn't feel like I was having an awful lot of success with the line of questioning that I *had,* and I guess I was still searching for directions to go on."

Linda Takes Charge

What is missing from their exchange is the easy, free-flowing enthusiasm of a good healthy chat, so evident in Meg's conference. Linda's many questions indicate she isn't satisfied with Jason's answers. And Jason's answers, while straightforward, are much shorter, more tentative, and less self-evaluative than Meg's. But, while Linda begins to feel frustration, Jason is meeting his own objective of obtaining more information to lengthen his piece: "She put more quotes into what would I miss if I had left my house today. And so then I just put that into my story." Linda, though, is "still searching for directions to go on," and continues to question.

Linda: So what makes this pumpkin pie so much a part of his memories of this house?

Jason: Mmm, maybe they had pumpkin pie once, and . . . I don't know! I don't know why this should be such a big thing for him. You just told me to put pumpkin pie in it, so I did it that way.

Linda: Well, what do you like about this piece of writing?

Jason: Well, one . . . I don't . . .

Linda: It is fluent. I mean, it follows really well, Jason. You read it very well, it's very easy to listen to, and very easy to read. You need to think about, though, what makes you like what it has to say. For instance, think about your own house. If you had to leave your own house, what would you really miss about it?

Jason clearly does not want to explore the metaphor of the pie. Linda still pushes, searching for what in the piece matters to him. She is not sure anything does.

I don't know what his *tie* to this is, and I'm searching for something that I can get him to tell me about himself. I listen to this pie thing and I don't know a single thing about him. I am searching for *him.*

But Linda is less patient with Jason than she was with Meg. She quickly cuts him off when he cannot formulate an immediate answer to her question "what do you like about this piece of writing?" which effectively interrupts his thought (Johnson 1993).

Linda realizes her questions have not worked. "I should have said *immediately,* 'What do you like about this piece of writing?'" But she likes her last question, "If you had to leave your own house, what would you miss about it?" She says, "That's a key question for me, and I wish I could have gotten to that a lot sooner."

It is, in fact, fruitful. Jason replies:

Jason: Umm . . . my backyard. All my friends.

Linda: All right. What's special about your backyard, friends . . .

Jason: It's big, we play football all the time in it.

Linda: And what's special about your friends?

Jason: I don't know, I'd miss 'em, I guess, because we always do stuff together.

Linda: Like what?

Jason: We always went to, like, Deerfield Fair. We'd always go to fairs together. It's like everybody on our street would always call up somebody else if they're going somewhere. Everybody's like always together. We'd always play football games together, basketball, stuff like that.

Linda: Okay, and a lot of these things like football, for instance, and Deerfield Fair, all these things take place in the fall, which might have something to do with this pumpkin pie. Maybe this boy bought the pumpkin at the Deerfield Fair, and that's what makes this pumpkin pie really special. Would that make sense, that you could say something about that? Because somehow in a piece of writing, Jason, you've got to figure out, "What is it I want to get across to a reader in this piece of writing?" It's not just the pie; there's got to be a reason for this particular kind of pie, and how it's a piece of the house.

Jason: Uh-huh.

Linda feels Jason's "uh-huh" at the end is a brush-off. But it is nevertheless a significant and potentially positive series of exchanges because Jason *does,* for the first time, reveal what he truly values: his backyard, playing with his friends, and football. His description of going to the Deerfield Fair with his friends is his longest turn of the entire conference. It is the first time he talks about his own life, and the first time he has a conversational, enthusiastic tone of voice. He offers Linda the personally relevant.

Linda recognizes the significance of Jason's comments about his friends and the Deerfield Fair, just as she had recognized the significance of Meg's oral alliteration and under-the-covers imagery. But her response here is much more specific, directive, and focused more on creating product than exploring ideas. Linda pointed out to Meg the beauty of her language, gave general suggestions pertaining to what Meg had already written, and shared an empathic personal account of herself "falling into flannel sheets and reading an incredibly good book." With Jason, Linda laments, "I'm trying to put suggestions into his head." She points out that she has begun to write for him when she says, "Maybe this boy bought the pumpkin at the Deerfield Fair, and that's what makes this pumpkin pie really special," and then tells Jason, "There's got to be a reason for this particular kind of pie, and how it's a piece of the house." She prods much harder than she did with Meg. Linda says, "He's not even listening to me any more because *I'm* doing all the talking." Jason has little chance to elaborate about his friends and his fun at the Deerfield Fair.

For Jason, these autobiographical events do not connect emotionally enough to commit him to thoughtful revision. His detachment from any real purpose for the piece is evident: "I don't really think there *was* a point to get across. Oh, I guess how people feel when they're moving," he says after hearing the transcript.

The conference continues.

Linda: So, you've got a device, though, already set up for telling us some of this. Do you know what that might be?

Jason: Mmm, by how they're moving and the journal part . . .

Linda: Absolutely!

Jason: It gets into it.

Linda: Terrific! I mean, you could even . . .

Jason: I could just go on with the journal, saying, like, "I bought this pie that my mom is gonna bake at the Deerfield Fair . . . "

Linda: Yeah! I mean, you could say something in this journal entry . . .

Jason: And I could just put it in there, "Well, we're gonna eat it out in the back-yard . . . "

Linda: Yeah.

Jason: Just add that in.

Here, Jason picks up on Linda's suggestions and takes initiative for creating new ideas for the first time ("I could just go on with the journal . . . ") because it helps him to meet his own goal. He is getting the short, simple, neat information that he wants. Now he can "just add on that stuff. . . . Get it done." But Linda is not so happy with herself. She says, "I can *hear* myself talking in the conference, and I know I want to shut up because there's only so much he can take in."

When Jason avoids deeper conversation to protect himself from writing it hinders Linda from formulating an approach that might make him feel more comfortable writing. But here he *has* offered her some openings. Linda, however, does not exploit Jason's comment about having fun with friends by becoming a sounding board for him, nor does she seem to recognize that he had begun to offer his own writing suggestions. Instead, she continues to write for him.

Linda: And maybe that would be where . . . you got it at the Deerfield Fair. These are all the things that you're going to miss. And you might even just list all the things that you're going to miss so much. And your mom forgets about the pie, everybody else forgets about the pie and they leave it outside, but you want to take a piece of that pie with you. And now it's got some significance to it—that it's part of all the friends, the fall, the football . . . and you've already got it set up for yourself. It's that journal entry, and maybe all you have to do to add to this is put an actual journal entry about Deerfield Fair, football, friends, as if, "This is what I'm gonna miss." And you might say it as simply as that. "This is what I'm gonna miss." And tell us, if you had to leave your house, what you would miss. Is that possible for you to do?

Jason: Mm-hm.

Linda responds,

I *hate* it! All I should have said is, "If you had to leave your own house what would you miss," and left it *right* there. This should not have been there! . . . I've wasted a ton of time. I said way too much. *I'm* writing the piece for him, and that's ridiculous. I should have said, "Leave the pie on the table!"

Linda: Okay. So what if you use a journal entry to tell us about what *you* would miss. I mean, this is fiction, but you're going to think about what would you miss, and that becomes part of this fiction piece. [Writing on Jason's Conference Sheet] So, it would be fall, Deerfield Fair . . .

Jason: Friends.

Linda: . . . friends, what else? Football.

Jason: Sports?

Linda: Sports. I'll let you . . . you want to be as specific as you can. And, the important thing is, when you think of a pumpkin pie, what do you think of? I mean, do you like pumpkin pie?

Jason: [Shakes his head, no]

Linda: Oh, you don't like pumpkin pie? Oh, so this is really fiction! Um, think about . . .

Jason: I like apple pie.

Linda: Okay, let's make this . . . how about an apple pie instead? Because you've got the apples. And what do you love about apple pie? Let's do this apple pie, because that would be easier for you. What do you love about apple pie?

Jason: It's good [Laughs].

Linda: What's good about it?

Jason: Umm, I like how the apples are sweet.

Linda: Okay, you've got sweet . . .

Jason: They're juicy.

Linda: What's it smell like? [Writes] "Sweet, juicy . . . "

Jason: Umm, smells good. Smells like apples.

Linda: Mmm, I mean, just the aroma of cooked apples . . . [Writes] Okay, all the things that are in that pie are all the things that you want to try and remember, that you put in this journal entry. So you want to set this journal entry up like you were really leaving home. And now you've got a reason. Now the reader can think about, "Wow, what would it be like if I left home?" And that apple pie has got some significance to it. Okay? All right, does that make sense to do?

Jason: Yeah!

Linda: All right. If you get lost, you can just look through some of these comments.

Jason: Okay. So I just change a little bit of it, put like football and . . .

Linda: Yeah!

Jason: . . . apple pie instead of pumpkin pie.

Linda: Yeah! And do you know how to add something to this without rewriting the whole thing?

Jason: Yeah, I can just, like, add on in little spots, like, put a line to where it should be.

Linda: Yep. Or, you could put a little sign. I mean, you might put a star and then write. This would be your journal entry, and you could put the star over here, and this would be the whole journal entry; you'd write about the sights, the sounds, the smells. . . . So you want to think about that. [Writes] "Sights, sounds, smells, of fall . . . , of apples . . . , and friends." I mean, it might even be things that if you had to leave, what do friends say to each other, what do you play with each other, all of that. Okay?

Jason: Yeah.

Linda: All right, so you want to work on that.

Jason: Yep!

Linda: All right. Good job.

Listening to this last passage, Linda mocks herself derisively, groaning, "That was the worst conference I ever heard!" Not only has she overpowered Jason, the conference is also outlandishly long. That her suggestions came from her recognition of what was important to Jason offers her little consolation. She has forced the issue and has not seen him internalize a vision for exploiting his own interests. There has been no collaboration, no co-construction. She wishes fervently she had stopped the conference the minute he had mentioned the Deerfield Fair; asked him to jot down everything he could about his friends, the fair, football games, and his street, and then moved on.

This doesn't feel good to me at all. I would think that the conferences that work the best are where the kids are talking twice as much as the teacher is, and all you're doing is really confirming what they say. I'm not being a mirror to Jason at all. I'm *feeding* him. He doesn't pick up, and when I see he doesn't pick up, then I should stop the conference! It's not a *conference* anymore. It's me searching for things to give him to possibly write about, and I could do that a lot easier in a lot quicker time. I think I'm searching so hard I'm not hearing what he's saying.

Linda concludes:

You know what I think? He read the piece, he liked it. He wanted me to say it was a great piece; it was *finished.* And he could've turned it in for a grade and then thrown it away. . . . I guess in conferences I don't want kids to write writing they're going to throw away! I think that's why I keep talking to them, which is really kind of stupid because if I don't figure out a way to get them talking *sooner,* it's not a valuable conference. . . . Unless he's connected to it he's going to write it and throw it away anyway.

Jason Follows Orders

She then predicts, "He'll probably change the pumpkin to apple and then still have some kid leaving the house. I'm going to be really curious to see what he's done with this now, after this conference. No *wonder* teachers have trouble conferencing!"

She is right. Jason adds exactly two sentences to the story, both derived from Linda's explicit suggestions. His final draft is identical to his first except that he separates Johnney's journal entry into its own paragraph, gives it a different font from the rest of the piece, and adds the two sentences (highlighted below in italics).

> Dear Journal,
>
>   Today is August 7, 1986. Today me and my family are leaving this house we have lived in all are lives. *I am going to miss playing football, basketball, and soccer in this neighborhood.* My mother is making a pie for us for our farewell. *She is using apples I won at the Deerfield Fair.* We are going to eat it outside on the picnic table in the backyard. Good night journal. Have a safe trip.

Although perfunctorily, he has met his goal to add without extensive revision *and* obeys what he sees as Linda's directives. Jason includes the piece in his portfolio. His Case History says,

This writing came to be when we had that day of all the writers in and we stayed with them the whole day. Well, I had the writer who was in Mr. Nichol's room. Well, one of the things she told us to write was to write a story about why a pumpkin pie was out on the picnic table out in the back yard for a long time. I wrote the story in her class, then me and you had a conference and then we fixed some stuff and then I typed it on my computer. The decisions I made were to add things I would miss if I were moving. That's how I felt when I moved from Hampton here to Lee.

Note the stark contrast between this Case History and Meg's. While Meg wrested ownership of all conference ideas and discussed her own extensive thought and writing processes, Jason focuses more on his teacher's. He explains his idea came from the visiting writer and fully acknowledges Linda's role in shaping the piece. He focuses on plot rather than thought; he is less self-evaluative. He does not portray himself as the one in control the way Meg does.

Conflict

Two weeks later another conference occurs during the time that students have begun to put together their quarterly portfolios. Jason includes two pieces that Linda hasn't yet seen. One is a myth, "Why Does Rain Fall from the Sky," which he actually wrote in seventh grade. He is not worried that it has no accompanying drafts. "She won't know," he says, "I'll type in a couple of mistakes and make a rough draft."

Unfortunately for him, Linda comes over to confer with him and he is found out. Knowing that she will find his seventh grade paper, and trying to head off trouble, he says to her, "A teacher looked this over last year."

"Last year!" exclaims Linda.

"She said it was fine," protests Jason.

"Then have *her* grade you!" What ensues is an initially contentious conference, with a visibly grumbly Jason resisting every step of the way:

Jason: I don't want to read it.

Linda: All right, then we're going to . . . um, what do you like about this piece of writing?

Jason: It's . . . good.

Linda: What's good about it?

Jason: I like it. I like how it flows.

Linda: What flows? What works well about it?

Jason: What?

Linda: What is the plot? Can you describe the plot to me?

Jason: Why rain falls from the sky.

Linda: Oh. Why does rain fall from the sky?

Jason: You gotta read the story!

Linda: I did read it. I want you to summarize it for me.

Jason: Why does it?

Linda: Jason, can you put your knees down and sit up, please?

Jason: Uh … Uh … A kid from a long time ago, he went up to the person of rain and thunder and he got him to rain.

Linda: All right, why does he go up there to represent the tribe?

Jason: Because … he wanted to. [Long pause]

Linda: But what's the reason that he wants to? Why would he be the one selected to do that?

Jason: Because he's the main character. [Pause]

Linda: Okay. What's this guy's name? Diokles? Why is he not willing to give them rain?

Jason: Because he's a mean old man.

Linda: All right, where do you say that in here?

Jason: You know he's mean because he doesn't do [unclear].

Linda: Well, I'm not sure … I'm not … [Long pause]. You've got to tell us right here, you've got to tell us what kind of man he is.

Jason: Why?

Linda: You said he's a mean old man. Why is he a mean old man?

Jason: Why is that important?

Linda: It's important because there's got to be a reason that he won't let them have any rain.

Jason: There doesn't have to be.

Linda: Yes there does! That's what this story does.

Jason: He could be tired.

Linda: All right, he's tired. What's he tired from?

Jason: Air sickness. I don't know!

Linda: Maybe he's sick of making it rain. Because nobody thanks him for the rain. Maybe nobody thanks him for the rain. Okay. Jason. You do have to add that to it.

Jason: Why!? It's like …

Linda: Jason. All right. You know what? I'm going to tell you, you can't even hand this in to me. Either you talk to me about this and you let me tell you something that can be done to this, or you can just put this away and you're going to have to write two new pieces.

Jason: I already have two.

Linda: You need *five* pieces.

Jason: You said four.

Linda: Five. Five has been there all along.

Jason: No, it hasn't. You said four to five.

Linda: I think Jason . . . I'm not going to argue. Either we fix this or you don't hand it in at all. So, would you get a pen so you can start fixing it?

A vicious cycle has begun in which both participants become more and more unwilling to listen to each other. There is a complete lack of rapport. Linda notes, "I can't hold on to this piece yet so my tone or stance feels not real *receptive* to him." Her lack of connection with Jason leads her to assume a role she does not embrace:

> I can tell in my tone of voice that I'm kind of being a stinker with him. I'm being a *teacher*. I'm in charge, and he's going to do what I want—that's what I mean by being a stinker. I'm putting my back up, and I am saying, "Hey, *I'll* tell you what you need to do. *You're* not gonna put this in here and get away with it." I'm being too teacherly, aggressive, and obnoxious.
>
> I'm *already* becoming frustrated with Jason. I'm already thinking in my head, "Oh, great! Here's another kid I'm going to spend the *whole* year trying to get to move. He's going to take *most* of my time and he is not going to move."

Linda Falls Back to Mechanics

With her frustration comes an unwillingness to listen to Jason carefully. She becomes more insistent and demanding, causing Jason to close himself off from her. As a result, Linda then adopts what she perceives to be the fallback role of writing instruction: teaching subject matter that is not open to interpretation and thus requires much less thought:

Linda: [Reading Jason's myth] All right. This is really good! You've got a really good beginning here. This is the god of rain and thunder. [Reads] "He climbed the sacred stairs." Can you fix that? This should not be a capital, it'd be a small *t:* " . . . the god of Rain and Thunder." So you put an *of* there.

In the conference, Linda continues to read out loud, interjecting, "So you're missing a *y* there . . . all right, capital *W* . . . comma . . . " She concludes by saying, "All right. Good. You just need those minor corrections."

Listening to the tape, Linda reacts:

> He's got me resorting to mechanics. I want to move him with the content and what I've resorted to is the mechanics because I think that's the only

thing he can grasp hold of, and that annoys me. I don't even know why I ask him to fix it. It should just be in there. Leave it as it is. It bores me to even listen to it. I guess I was trying to retrieve the conference by saying, "Okay, maybe I never told him what *was* good about it. I need to tell him this is a *really* good beginning."

The result of this conference is almost identical to that of the first conference. Jason adds exactly one line to his piece: "He was a mean old man, and sick of making it rain," which corresponds with a brief note Linda wrote on his draft as he explained who Diokles was.

The Problem

As a student who doesn't like writing or reading, Jason is reluctant to trust Linda or develop a relationship with her that will lead to conversation about them. Linda says, "The more I talked the more he was sitting sideways. He wasn't really looking at me." Listening to "The Farewell" conference, Linda remarks, "It's the kids like Jason, in trying to find what really matters to them, that make conferencing so hard, because I can't seem to make it happen *quickly*." As frustration breeds impatience, Linda begins to do what she cannot get Jason to do:

> Talking and writing are thinking. *I'm* doing the writing for him, *I'm* doing the thinking for him. *I'm* doing all the *wondering* and he's not. He's being the receiver. And he's not even receiving any more. You shut it off when it's not you doing the thinking.

It isn't until she listens to the tape of the conference that Linda understands the implications of her more forceful approach:

> I didn't quite get the connection that the more I talked the more I was pushing him away, because I think I was giving him *way* too much to consider. I was trying to get him back into the conversation, but I was still doing all of the thinking. I should have been phrasing things like, "Well, tell me about. . . ." And I wasn't. I gave him no *option*. I just kept giving him options of saying, "Uh-huh," because, the way I phrased everything, that's all he *could* answer. I wasn't phrasing it so *he* could do the talking.

I ask Linda, "Why do you think teachers do that?" She replies,

> I think I do it because I feel this *guilt* that I see something that holds potential in the writing, and if the kid doesn't get it right away I feel like I'm not teaching unless I cover all bases and tell them what it is I see. I do that at the

beginning of the year all the time. . . . You see all the names that are on the board and you know that you've got to get to twenty other conferences, and you go, "All right, I can't just sit here and just smile at him and say, 'Tell me more about this,' when he doesn't say anything!" So I jump in after *two* seconds of silence with, "What if . . . " or "Have you thought about. . . ." I think I do it in the name of speed, in the name of guilt, and in the name of wanting them to . . . do better in the writing. Even if they may not be ready for it yet. I think that's why I do it, and maybe that's why other teachers do it, too.

One reason she continues the first conference when she should have stopped it has to do with building a productive relationship with a student whom she does not yet know:

Certainly part of it is establishing some kind of rapport with him. I don't want to have him read the piece to me and immediately go, "So! You talked about this, this, and this. If you had to talk about the one thing, what might it be?" and just dive in. I think he would be able to sense in my voice immediately that I didn't like what he had written. So I was trying to focus on what he *had* written, just to establish some kind of rapport with him so that he knew that I liked what he had down the first time. I don't know if he's never written a sentence before and this is the first time he's written two full pages. But his voice and his face seemed to tell me he really liked this piece of writing, so I certainly couldn't tell him, "What the heck? Is this another pie piece? So what's with the pie, because I didn't quite understand it." So, part of it was getting him comfortable with me, and really trying to find something that I could hold on to, to get him to talk more about.

But note that if Linda is trying to develop rapport in this early conference, she does so by focusing on *writing,* the one thing Jason dislikes most. Here her agenda—her enthusiasm for writing—dominates his. She does not know him well:

I don't even know what his history as a writer is. I don't know if that's the first piece he's ever written. I don't know if that's the *most* he's ever written. I'm not sure if he's *hated* writing before and he's so proud of this because he got all these words down on paper.

Moreover, Linda does not appear to listen to Jason as carefully as she does with almost all other students to find out more about him. This year, Jason is one of those students whom she likes, but, because of his disdain for language arts, she can't get close to. With Jason, who puts Linda in an attitudinal limbo between personal regard and professional frustration, her responses become forced:

> I *did* like him, which is probably why I worked harder with him than I should have. I was way too patient with him in the conferences. I should have known in the conferences that they weren't going anywhere and just let the writing go. I became possessed, or obsessed, with wanting his writing to get better, and he wasn't *ready* to make the writing better. I should have just accepted the fact that he wrote something in the first place despite the fact he hated writing.

Linda *is* patient with Jason in regard to time spent; her conferences with him all year are usually longer than with others. But in reading the above transcripts Linda surmises she has not been patient in trying to learn about him and his interests outside the context of literacy instruction. Her ambivalent feelings about him—her detachment created by his aversion to her passions—may have discouraged her from trying to listen harder to him. She admits, "I knew nothing and *still* know nothing about Jason personally, other than the way he behaved in class." But only through knowing students well, she says, does she develop more patience and understanding for them.

The Possible Solution

When working with students who are not committed to the academic agenda, helping them move forward academically is the ultimate goal, but Jason's conferences suggest it may not be the *immediate* one. While Linda tries to sustain a productive conference performance with Jason, its script still revolves around academic writing. Jason, feeling ill-suited to his role, usually remains unresponsive. So how might Linda help Jason fit into his role as a language arts student?

She might take a longer-term view of Jason's situation and also recognize his desire for respect outside the domain of his academic performance. Just as she spends two months at the beginning of the year teaching students how to organize, she might spend time preparing Jason—and herself—to interact with one another inquisitively and respectfully in a social venue *before* his acceptance of the academic can take hold. With Linda's style of teaching, her interpersonal relationship with students seems as important as the academic instruction—perhaps *more so* with reluctant readers and writers. That she is more emotionally ambivalent about students like Jason simply means that she has to make her rapport-building more conscious: she has to search more deliberately for what she can value about them and their interests.

Her responsibility in their relationship is to learn to appreciate Jason, no matter how difficult. She says,

> Even if I knew *nothing* about him outside of school, [I should have said] to him constantly, "Jason, you have incredible energy and I wish I had half the energy you do," so that he began to see, "Yeah, okay, that's all right. She's not going to yell at me because I'm bouncing around."

The work of this rapport-building is front-loaded and it may not show results until much later in the year, but once it occurs learning may be exponentially greater.

In "The Farewell" and other pieces he writes, Jason's revisions all come from those brief conference moments where Jason opens up and shares his interests. If Linda consciously addresses her ambivalent attitude toward Jason, abandons her fervent pushes to immediately improve the piece, tries harder to engage him in "a good healthy chat," and only focuses on his flashes of empathy and enthusiasm (as she does with the already receptive Meg), she may distill, highlight, and better exploit the shorter academic lessons Jason is willing to receive. His performance in the long run may benefit; he may be more willing to accept Linda's nudges eventually. The texts he begins to revise may demonstrate a more earnest commitment to his life and writing growth.

17

Ted Confers with a Writing Expert

Linda's conference with Ted depicts a relationship built primarily on academics—on the cognitive end of the affective continuum. Ted's confidence in his abilities and his commitment to his work allows Linda and him to attend to his text almost exclusively. He views Linda's role narrowly, as purely academic; he is ready to discuss writing without necessarily developing a social relationship. The academic trust and respect the two share show that if the student's and teacher's academic goals are compatible and the student is confident in his own abilities to meet those goals, more emotional connections can be peripheral: while they are important for *most* students, they are not for all. Ted's attitude also ensures that Linda can make some tactical mistakes that might inhibit a less confident student like Jason.

Ted

While Jason is an ever-present force in the class, Ted's is less obtrusive. He goes about his business quietly, efficiently, and well. He is an excellent student and has learned how to balance his many extracurriculars with his schoolwork.

Ted considers himself somewhat shy in larger groups, but he has an air of self-confidence about him. He is extremely polite and self-effacing. One classmate remarks that he is the only person in class she can't imagine swearing. He is popular with his classmates—one of those students who doesn't seem to hang out with a particular clique but rather is looked upon by all groups as a friendly, fun, and decent person. He is also a star athlete: one of the best cross-country runners in the school and recognized for his soccer skills.

Ted loves his family, sports, and doing well in school, but he also loves many of life's smaller pleasures, including "hitting the snooze button on the alarm clock," and "waking to the smell of pancakes." He dislikes "rounding the last curve in a race (only it's not the last curve)," "not getting the grades you feel you deserve," and his (self-perceived) "absent-mindedness." He also shows a whimsical side. He hates "finding coconut inside a good looking Halloween candy." His major science experiment for the year is finding the effect of milk on different cereals' sogginess.

Ted's View of Himself

Ted has one love, in particular:

> Quite simply, I love to read; no ifs, ands, or buts. I can read anytime, anywhere as long as I have a good book. I can also read fast and still get a good grasp of the story unless I'm reading a textbook. My fast style bombs, however, when applied to textbooks and I'll need to work on becoming more proficient as a textbook reader.
>
> However, disregard textbooks and reading is perfect. Not only is reading exciting, it has helped me tremendously.

Ted estimates he has read over seventy books during the school year and says he likes books with plot twists and surprise endings. He describes himself as a reader and writer:

> I like to write letters to friends, pieces to express what I feel, or things [about] how I'm thinking on a certain point. When we read outside of school, I read basically to pass time. I like fantasy books, mostly medieval times, and I read for fun. And I find out by reading and writing [that] your basic use of the English language is increased.

More than either Meg or Jason, at the beginning of the year Ted has an acute awareness of the influence of his reading on his writing. "Many, many of my ideas are spawned from books," he writes; "This year in particular I've noticed more description in what I read and what I write." He says he picks out authors' styles and tries them in his own writing.

Ted believes a good writer is good at revision and says, "I like to read my piece and make changes 'til I like it." In the first quarter he describes two things to which a writer has to attend to be good:

> The first is the content. Does the story affect you? Is the writer arranging the words with meaning? What do you get out of the story? If any of these are

positive or intentionally negative, the writer is doing good. The second is mechanics. Can you read the story easily and understand it?

Ted seems to have more of a sophisticated sense of the technical qualities of good writing than do Meg or Jason. He also has a clear concept of what he needs to do to improve, saying, "I have to write what I want to write. I start writing and then bend it to fit the requirements. If I write any other way it just doesn't sound like I mean it; my writing feels corny." In June he gives a reflective review of his year-long work, saying, "Developing plots, characters and working on the emotions are all growing strengths in my writing. However, I can't write whole stories without weak 'joining' scenes." He also writes, "Over-describing is probably my main weakness, though. In several pieces I confused the reader by over-describing something better left to a few description words."

Most of his writing ideas, "just sorta hit me when I think and brainstorm," but he also writes, "I have a harder time with making [journal entries], just things to write. Writing is hard for me unless I have an idea and begin to write. . . ."

Ted's Performance

Ted focuses serious attention on the academic tasks of language arts. Where both Meg's and Jason's portfolios include many family pictures and artifacts devoted to their out-of-school lives, Ted's final portfolio is almost exclusively writing and schoolwork. He does examine his social life in his journal, but his portfolio reveals that his school life is an integral part of his overall self-view. He enjoys school and takes it seriously.

Ted does not use his journal writing as a direct source of draft material, but rather as a place for reflecting about human nature, analyzing the books that strongly affect him, and practicing good description. The books he reads influence his writing topics and style more than the personal accounts evoked through his quick-writes; none of his portfolio pieces are autobiographical. Most of his pieces contain characters who clearly are on one end or the other of the moral spectrum. The battle between good and evil, a common theme in his fantasy and science fiction reading, dominates his writing. His journal writing does, however, reflect the *tone* and *message* of his final pieces. It depicts his interest in the moral choices of man. The third-quarter unit on human rights and the Holocaust is a perfect venue for him to ponder these issues. Responding to Elie Wiesel's *Night* he writes,

> I can't even begin to describe some of the horror that filled me when reading this. What, why, and how could these things happen? Sons BEATING

their fathers to death for a fistful of bread? And people on the outside throwing in more bread because they enjoy it? What have we come to? Sons leaving their fathers behind because "They were too much bother." Too much bother?! This book connects where we can visualize, too much so. Can any of us visualize beating our father to death for a handful of bread? I find myself horrified as Elie desperately clings to his father, saving him from certain doom time after time, and then, so close to the end his father dies.

Through the heroes and villains he creates in his own writing, Ted seems to try to come to terms with human nature—looking for neat categories for good and evil actions. An excerpt from his fantasy story, "Hobo," illustrates two characters in typical moral conflict:

It was always this way with his magic.

It all started when he was a boy. He and his cousin Rand. Only them. They were the only ones with it and Rand didn't like that. Rand was always the popular one, using his skills to impress friends and always for his own benefit, he never realized the drawback and now it was too late for him. The magic had converted his mind and amplified what he used his magic for, creating the new creature. Bob had known it from the start, as he too tried to develop the skill that had been infused in him at birth and felt when the magic took advantage of his hatred, his anger. He experimented further and found the joy, the light, the flying excitement of using the magic for help-ing, to strengthen, and as he did so his will to do so increased, making him all the stronger, and causing problems.

As Bob grew in strength and stature, Rand sunk into jealousy, people grew afraid of the cold cloak that covered him, his magic had overcome him, infusing him with an unquenchable thirst for power and a deadly ha-tred for his cousin, Bob Hobokin.

While Ted meets one of his goals to write in genres other than fan-tasy, most of his pieces still have some sort of moral struggle between the characters.

Ted's View of Language Arts Class

Ted says of language arts class, "I like it. We don't seem to focus on *proper* English. More, we get to practice and learn for ourselves, which I think helps because practice makes perfect." By "proper" English, Ted means, "Just learn-ing the right use of verbs, when to use this, when to use that, how you should structure your sentences."

In describing what he likes most about the class, he recognizes one of the things Jason likes *least* about it.

> I really like the free choice. You get to do what you want and when you're doing something that you like to do and want to do it's a lot better piece of writing, because it's what *you* think, what you want to write about.

He can't quite understand how students could be stymied by free choice:

> Well, if you really don't like reading and writing, I suppose there's not a lot you can do in this class because basically we read and write, which could lead to talking or not doing the assignments. But there's got to be *some* book somewhere or *something* you want to write about. It's just so broad of a world. . . .

Ted's independence, confidence, and self-motivation invite the freedom Jason does not want.

Ted feels the class can be improved through more formal discussions about books, which would allow students to get in touch with others in the class who have similar tastes in books. He sees some benefit from the student talk that occurs at tables, but he draws a sharper distinction than do most of his classmates between social and academic talk.

> There's helpful talking and non-helpful talking. When you read your pieces and you talk to each other about your piece or recommend ideas, there are a lot of helpful things that you can get, or just plain *discussing* books some-times gives you an idea on more things to write. But if you're, say, discussing last night's football game and who's going to win, there are probably more productive things you could be doing. . . . Say somebody was describing something they did, like an embarrassing moment or something. You think of an embarrassing moment for yourself. You write about that. You have a piece. But probably the majority of the time, if it's not focused on your writ-ing, you're not going to just come up with a brainstorm. You'll be more en-grossed in the conversation than the writing aspect of it.

Ted doesn't see social conversation as a major problem, though, because "we spend most of our time reading, writing: doing what we're supposed to." What students are "*supposed* to" do—read and write—is clear and separate from social talk in Ted's mind. Social exchanges, if handled carefully, might inform academic work, but more often than not they divert attention from the real work at hand. This view influences his conference approach with Linda.

Ted's View of Linda

Ted likes Linda's style:

> She seems to give you a lot more freedom and stuff than some teachers do. We haven't had any tests or anything—quizzes type of thing—which we've had in other LA classes. She's got a lot of books. She seems to have us respond a lot more than she telling us what to do.

In contrast to Meg's emphasis on the importance of Linda's friendliness to her work, Ted doesn't mention the importance of the personal aspects of their relationship. He focuses on academics:

> She's good at conferences. [They] really help as a good experience in telling you where you can go and what to do. . . . Basically, you read the piece to her and she tells you what she thinks could be better, and you decide if you like it or not. You change it.

Conferences give Ted access to Linda's *academic* insight. But, as with other confident writers, he also feels comfortable rejecting her suggestions if they contradict his own visions:

> I feel it's still your piece of writing. She's making suggestions about what she thinks would be good, and if you don't think it's good [you] see if you can maybe incorporate it a different way. . . .
>
> I kind of think it's basically the way she talks to you. It's not like, "Oh, you should do this," or, "It'd be better if you did this." It's just like [a] "What if you tried this?" type of thing. Then you respond to her, saying, "No, I don't think that'll work," and she says, "Okay, don't do it."

His only criticism of Linda's conferences is a familiar one: she simply doesn't have the time to respond personally to every student as much as each would like.

Ted's view of Linda as a listener is not cluttered with the complexities of social relationship building; instead, listening is a simple tool for getting academic needs met.

> How do you describe a listener? You listen to what the person says and you offer your input into what they say, maybe your opinions and stuff. She doesn't seem to be discourteous or anything. She listens to you while you get across what you need to get across.

To Ted, listening is not necessarily a strategy where the teacher *provides* something new to the student. Instead, he sees Linda the way she wants to be seen: as a sounding board where students can express and listen to themselves. Ted wants more to express himself with the aid of Linda rather than being told what to do. He is more concerned with crafting his own ideas than he was with her literal response. When Linda does respond with her own opinions, he sees her as thoughtful and full of unique ideas, someone who offers him new perspectives but does not force them upon him.

> I'm not sure if she's trying to *teach* you something, but sometimes she comes up with different things than you were looking for. Like, if you were trying to see what was wrong with this, she might say she likes this and find something wrong with this that you thought was fine. But she doesn't really seem to have an agenda like, "Oh, I want him to have better description," and then, no matter what you say, she says, "Oh, you need better description."
>
> You might just kind of write something in because it's fun to write, but it might not really go well with the story. It may be nice on its own, but it might not fit into the story, and she'll tell you that. And, [when I] re-read it, I usually do pick up what she's saying, actually.

Ted's confidence in his writing and his view of Linda's role makes it easy for Linda. His implicit message to her is, "Help me examine my own writing for myself in a fresh way and let me go to work." He simply wants thoughtful input.

Ted also values Linda's sharing of her own writing:

> It basically seems informative so you get an idea. Sometimes the questions seem sort of vague, like, "Write what this makes you feel." Then she gives you an example. And it's always easier to have something to kind of *spring*-board off of—to have some place you're trying to *get* to so you know how to get there instead of just kind of bushwhacking.

As we shall see, a good conference relationship is easy to maintain because Ted values Linda as an academic source of new and important ideas for his texts.

The Conference

This conference occurs in March. Many students are working on pieces that are influenced by their readings and discussions of the Holocaust. Linda has also given the whole class an assignment to create an "art square" that depicts some sort of message they have learned from their Holocaust reading. Ted requests a conference. As Linda approaches him I follow behind, and she begins by making a joke about my presence.

Linda: We come in pairs.

Ted: Teachers in general or . . .

Linda: [Laughs] Well, we need supportive help. Pretty scary, you know, teaching eighth graders.

Ted: Just read it?

Ted's response to Linda's playful social introduction exemplifies his academic focus. He wants to dive right into the work and responds to her banter with an anticipatory, "Just read it?" Linda immediately refocuses and begins the conference in earnest.

Linda: Yeah, why don't you just read it to me. How can I help you with it, though? What are some things that . . .

Ted: Well, I decided to write to the Gestapo instead of to the other [unclear] and I'm basically wondering if I've covered what I need to cover to make my point. Because I don't want to overdo the point.

Linda: Yeah.

Ted, comfortable with conferring, articulates clear and specific concerns. Linda identifies two issues: "He's 'wondering if I've covered what I need to cover'—is there enough here?—and also, 'I don't want to over*do* the point.' So, those are two opposite things: 'enough or too much?' "

Linda has listened well. In a separate interview, Ted states that that was his point. He was looking for suggestions about the balance between too much and too little.

In the conference, Ted reads his draft to Linda:

TO THE GESTAPO

I've got a few questions I'd like to ask you. And I'd really like to know, why? And I really want to know if you can answer that.

So why did you start the Holocaust anyway? To create the "Master Race" you said. What made you the master race anyway? The fact you can stomach kicking helpless old men. The fact you enjoy gunning down innocent children, or maybe it was how efficient you were. How efficiently you could deprive Jews of everything they stood for. You said they were less than human, well I suppose they were after you deprived them of food, making them weak and dependent, deprived them of hope, making them unwilling to resist you, and deprived them of family, of love and support. Who could be human with these conditions?

Yes you truly had "Mastered" the art of abusing people. Oh, I'm forgetting, how did you say this helped to create your "Master Race"? You claim the Jews were unsuperior and couldn't fit in, yet you still treated other groups this way. All of this so only the "Master Race" would survive, some master race. We all can't wait to be part of this, so we too can throw people from their homes, separate families and boost our ego by hitting the hand that feeds us. Can you tell me what people saw in you, why people were proud of you, and why this was necessary? Did you really believe that you could solve the world's problems like this?

Ted: And I sign it . . .

Linda: Good. Wow. I love everything you've got so far. I mean, it should make somebody feel pretty guilty and pretty rotten.

Listening to the tape, Linda says she had been confused about how to respond to Ted's stated need. She did not know if he had too much or too little. "I think I was still groping when I started to talk to him about what was it I should say to him," she says. However, her response has already helped Ted. Her initial praise was important to him: "When you write like a piece like that, you're not really sure about it at first. You want to have some positive reaction to know that it was okay." He now also knows that his writing has achieved one of its purposes. He notes,

> She liked it. And she told me *why* she liked it—what I had accomplished in this piece—and basically in my *next* line I'm responding that, yes, that was a goal and I did accomplish one of the things I was thinking:

Ted: I think that was a goal.

Linda: [Pause as she reviews text] The one thing . . . I feel like I'm still standing on the edge of a cliff, though, with it, and I don't know how you want to tie it together.

Ted: Yeah.

Linda: What are you thinking might . . .

Ted: That was one of my problems; I wasn't really sure how I could, like, bring it to a close. I like what I've got, but I'm not really sure how I'm going to tie it all together.

Linda: I love the repetition that you used because it just strengthens what they did over and over again. It makes me hurt, listening to what you've said they did. I'm wondering if somehow you could tie it together by asking them questions as if they may still be around? There are people still . . . not really hiding. I mean, people know they're former Nazis. They may be living in Canada. They may be living in the U.S. I wonder if you can tie it together by asking those older people some questions on, "Where are you now? How comfortable are you in your bed at night? Do you sleep well?"

Ted: "How do you live with it?"

Linda: Right. "Do you sleep well with the lights out?" And tie it together by bringing it to the present. You might just try that. And just leave it with those questions, because nobody can answer them. And the only people who could would be somebody who did that.

David: [Sitting at Ted's table] But most of them are dead.

Ted Gains Power Through Confidence

This is an important set of turns for a couple of reasons. First, Ted had given a specific request to Linda to look for overkill, but Linda finds a different problem with the piece: it is somehow not resolved or "tied together." Her response to Ted suggests that she has found something vaguely ludicrous about writing a letter to the Gestapo, something too disassociated from the here and now. To Linda's ear it makes the piece sound more like an exercise, and her suggestion tries to make the purpose of the letter more realistic—perhaps Ted can address it to someone who is still alive. In our interview she comments,

> We know historically this is such a horrific time, and I want the kids to write something that has meaning for *them*, but if you're writing to somebody who doesn't exist any more it's almost like what's the point? It's like saying, "Dear Hitler."

But, in listening to herself talk during the conference, Linda finds an area for potential examination:

> "It should make somebody feel pretty guilty and pretty rotten." I think when I first said that, that's where it popped into my head that there are some people who are still alive, who no one has found. They've been in hiding themselves in a way, hiding their histories. I think that's what I was trying to get Ted to see: "What if you wrote to somebody that. . . ." His writing could leave an impression on somebody. I'm trying to help him find who that somebody is, that it's still *today*.

Offering a suggestion not directly related to Ted's initial concern might be a risky move. Linda notes it is "more what *I* perceived as the problem, not what *he* perceived." But his confidence and sense of ownership of his writing appear to help him recognize its value. In fact, he comments that he has recognized that same problem. Linda redirects the focus of the text analysis, but Ted's response indicates they are still operating in syncopation. In reference to her concern, Ted says,

> That makes sense. I'd agree with that. It ends. I mean, it ends like, "All right, that's not going anywhere." But she helps me keep it flowing. The way it

ends it just kind of trails off instead of actually coming to a close. I'd agree with her on that, that it does sort of trail off.

Linda's specific advice is unsolicited, but Ted, intent primarily on improving his piece, welcomes the insight. He says, "It's a possibility that I could have picked it up if I re-read it several times, but she definitely helped make sure that I noticed that so I know what I'm supposed to do." This is one conference relationship where the student wants to hear exactly what the teacher thinks. Ted gets what he expects from Linda. He considers her suggestions as vital to his thought process:

> She recommended bringing it to the present, which at the time I wasn't ready to do. I'd have a hard time just bringing it to the present if she said, "Oh, bring it to the present," and went off and *walked*. I mean, "Present? What do you mean present?" By elaborating on what they did, how people fled to Canada, how they are living in the U.S., and how some of them are still alive, then I know what I'm trying to do. I'm trying to almost aim it at them—their life up until now, and how they live. . . .
>
> Originally I wasn't sure if I liked that suggestion. I kind of liked how the piece ended: "Did you really believe you could solve the world's problems like that?" But I *tried* writing it, because there was some time left in the period and it was kind of dull. I liked how it was sounding so I finished it up, and then I thought it sounded better than before, so I kept it.

This is the same type of collaboration that occurs in Meg's conference. Linda influences the text, but Ted controls which decisions to make. His ownership of the text depends upon his attitude and his current ability to evaluate Linda's suggestions before using or rejecting them. Other students, like Jason, may not yet be ready to do this. Linda must listen carefully to see how far she can take her suggestions.

Talk to Think, but Not Too Much

This passage is also important because it reveals Linda's thinking process during the conference. Initially unsure of how to respond to Ted's text, she begins to talk as a way to *think*. Only by talking out loud about someone feeling guilty does she discover what she knows, the same way that a writer writes to discover what it is he knows. She orally composes a subsequent response by first listening to her *initial* response.

The conference continues. Linda responds to Ted's table-mate, David, who has said that most Nazis are dead.

Linda: Well, most of them are, but there are a lot of people living. Matter of fact, on the news two or three weeks ago they discovered a man in Canada who was one of the heads of the Gestapo, and he's living in a complex with Jews who survived the concentration camps! Matter of fact, I've got the video-tape. I probably should show it to you guys. Somebody videotaped out of the news for me. But maybe end with those questions so that we know that these people are all not dead. What you've done is great, so far, Ted. But it just needs something to . . .

Ted: . . . to bring it to an end.

Linda: . . . to bring it to a close.

Ted: Okay.

Linda: And I don't mean that it is brought to a close, because it may never be brought to a close, but it's at least brought to the present, which would bring it to a close.

Note that that as Linda says, "But it just needs something to . . ." Ted cuts her off. He says, "Well, I was kind of ready to do something, you know. I had an idea and I wanted to work on it before I lost the idea!" Ted wants Linda to leave. Laughing, he responds, "I knew what I was going to do, yeah."

Yet, surprisingly, Linda continues on.

Linda: How about your art square?

Ted: It's coming. Um . . .

Linda: Yeah, that's a really good piece.

Ted: Yeah.

Linda: All right, let's see what . . . [Pause as she looks at his art square draft]

Ted: I had a hard time drawing. I know what I want to draw, but I'm having a hard time drawing it. Lately I've been trying to . . .

Linda: What do you want to draw?

Ted: Well, I wanted to have, like, basically the prison walls being made up of prejudice that was against the Jews. Our prejudice was what was really . . .

Linda: Yeah. You mean . . .

Ted: . . . against them instead of . . .

Linda: . . . made up of the words "prejudice"?

Ted: Yeah. Well, not the words "prejudice," but, like, the thoughts, the sayings, the . . .

Linda: Oh! And have the walls have all those squares—have all those things on them. Yep. That would work really well.

Ted has *much* less command of his art square than he does his letter. He has not chosen to confer with Linda about it, and his explanation of his needs are much more vague. Linda's response strategy is different, too, and it shows how a student's attitude and preparedness affect the tone and structure of the conference. At the beginning of the first conference Ted conveys clearly what he is trying to do, so Linda can launch right into suggestions. Here, Ted *can't*, so Linda must ask questions like "What do you want to draw?" to orient herself and make him think. These types of questions often indicate that a student has not yet conceptualized his or her writing needs.

Ted, for his part, recognizes that the piece is not what he wants it to be and, in fact, is not something on which he particularly wants to work:

> I was really frustrated with the art square. I have a better time writing what I want to than *drawing* what I want to say. I mean, I *had* the idea; it just wasn't really coming on. I was having fun working on the other piece, and the art square is just kind of like an assignment I was trying to fulfill. It wasn't coming out right, so I was kind of, "Oh, yeah. The art square."

The conference continues, with Ted countering Linda's comment that his drawing concept would work really well by saying he was "having trouble" with it.

Ted: 'Cause I want to portray the fact that they were holding the people in. I also was trying to have, like, some of, like, Allies, like, almost opening the prison and, like, through the wall of prejudice to . . .

Linda: Right. Well, how about if you build big, almost like cinderblock squares? And, if in every single block square there were just different sentences of things that were done against them. I mean, that's gonna take some time, but instead of bricks, make it bigger, but it looks like cinder blocks. Maybe that would work. And . . . [Pause] you know what? It doesn't even have to be the real thing. What if it looked like the walls were made up of gravestones? You know how they used Jews' gravestones to build roads, and they walked on them. It was just the ultimate insult . . .

Ted: Yeah.

Linda: . . . in the camps. But maybe these bricks resemble gravestones, and you have different things that were done, different quotes that you pull from places, on those gravestones. I don't know. That might . . .

At this point Linda begins to offer suggestions in much the same way she offered them to Jason—she has formulated an idea that is interesting to *her*, and now begins to dominate the conversation by explaining it in detail. Listening to the tape, Linda says,

> This conference is going badly. I'm doing more talking that he is and he is just going, "Mm, yeah, mm." And when they do that, that's a hint: get the heck out of there! Let them either abandon or redo it or figure something out, because I'm not helping him.

The pattern indicated by this exchange and Jason's conferences is that when Linda senses students are unsure of what to do next, she sometimes pushes too hard and begins to take over the writing for them. However, the attitude behind Ted's "yeah" is *much* different than that behind Jason's "yeah's." Ted is still invested in his piece on some level, whereas Jason had not been. Ted's "yeah" is a response of noncommitment while he carefully ponders the implications of Linda's suggestion. It gives him time to continue thinking:

> I was acknowledging what she said, but it's kind of hard to draw a gravestone as a floor piece. I mean, I picture gravestones as just a circular hunk of granite or whatever rock they use, with the "RIP" written across the top and stuff about them. I was having a hard time picturing how I was going to stick that into my picture. . . . I was having a hard enough time drawing my original idea. I wanted to make sure I had something okay at first, before then.

Ted Takes Charge

The conference *is* going badly in that Linda's suggestions arise more from her agenda than from Ted's, but this conference demonstrates that the attitude of the student sometimes makes conferences almost foolproof. Ted's confidence means Linda *can* go somewhat overboard with her suggestions without swaying his intentions. We can imagine Jason hearing these suggestions, saying "Yeah," and immediately adding a couple of gravestones to his drawing. Ted, on the other hand, gently rejects Linda's suggestion.

Ted: Interesting drawing, but . . .

Ted's "*but*" is a badge of autonomy:

> I was trying to picture how I was going to fit it in. I was not overly enthusiastic about the idea, but like I said, in the last [conference] I wasn't sure how [her suggestion] was going to work out and it worked out good, so I was just trying to picture if it might come out good or not.

Ted says he listened very carefully to Linda's suggestions but, at the same time, "I wanted it to be a piece that *I* wrote."

But Linda's exuberance still gets the best of her. She apparently hears the "interesting drawing" part of Ted's response, but not his "but." In the conference she responds,

Linda: Yeah. Or, even, you can make the doors bigger so you've got less space . . .
Ted: . . . to fill up?

Linda: . . . to fill up. I mean, that might be better, too. You could also make this so big that there is no space to fill up, and it could be the gravestones as the path walking into this door, in some . . .

Listening to the tape, Linda does not like her response. She says, "I should be turning it back to him, saying, 'How could you do that?' . . . and just *sit* there." If she sat there long enough, Ted would think and create his own answers (Rowe 1974). But, she admits she has trouble waiting out uncomfortable pauses. "I have to learn how to do that better because I'm doing the thinking for him."

But Ted is still doing his *own* thinking. In the conference he next offers a thoughtful argument against her suggestion. Though he has trouble drawing his concept, he knows what he wants his piece to represent and isn't afraid to tell Linda that her suggestion undermines his intent:

Ted: I sort of . . . it's walking into the door, kind of. I mean, the door's supposed to be like opening through them.

Linda: The door's the freedom. Okay.

Ted: Yeah. And it just doesn't . . .

Linda: And that doesn't work, then. Okay. [Pause] I don't know. I'd just keep playing with what you're doing. I don't know how it will turn out, but I think I like the idea. You just might make this bigger so you don't have to put any of those in there. What have you got for a quote?

Ted: I'm not sure yet.

Linda responds to this passage, "See, he's still doing the thinking, which is good. I mean, he's getting a little irritated with me."

In his interview, Ted laughs, "I don't think we were connecting":

I understood that she wanted to have a *door,* but, like I said, my picture is not very easy to comprehend, and I think she was picturing something else. And I'm picturing what I have, as I see it, and that something else wasn't really fitting into it.

In the conference, Linda finally abandons the art square, asking Ted, "What books did you read?" Ted tells her.

Linda: Okay. So you've probably got plenty of ideas. All right. Okay, you're fine. All right, you don't have to give me anything, Ted. Just keep working on it this weekend.

Ted: All right.

"Ah, *dumb* way to end it!" Linda exclaims. She has not brought Ted back to his own ideas. She says she had no idea what would have helped him, so her fallback strategy should have been to ask, "What do you think you are going to do next?" She says, "I *have* to leave them being the active thinkers. . . . He's not having success, so it's not making him think, 'All right, what *could* I do?' Just posing the question might help have him think what he could do."

Linda is ambivalent about the conference. She likes the discussion about the "Gestapo" piece.

> I felt like I gave him a suggestion and that he finally got to the point where *he* could identify what it was that was weak in the piece, and that together we reached some conclusions about what some possible solutions were. I think that was a good conference.

The other discussion, she says, "was just dumb."

> That's a good thing to wonder about: what are the percentages of dumb conferences that I have? . . . I should never do *two* pieces of writing with the same kid one right after the other, because clearly one has more potential than the other and they're going to read the one with more potential to me. I watered down the first conference by talking about the *second* possible thing, and he could have gone right off to doing that.
>
> Clearly I want to leave them with something really concrete that they're going to start working on and thinking about and doing, and the *minute* I move to the next piece of writing, I've moved him off thinking about his first piece of writing. It's good for me to listen to these because I can see things that really stop the kids from writing—or stop the kids from doing something. The conference should keep the kids writing right at that moment when you leave.

Students need to use flashes of insight while they are still fresh. With hindsight, Linda reads Ted's sentiments perfectly. He *had,* in fact, wanted to go right on to his "Gestapo" piece and she had held him back. Ted says,

> With the Gestapo piece I had something I was proud of, something I was ready for comment on. I had a need of comment. The art square I hadn't actually gone to the conference for. It was kind of brought up and I'm like, "Ooohhh, yeah! The art square!" and I showed her what I had, which was not coming along so well at the time.
>
> I wanted to conference about the Gestapo piece, and she was there to help me conference. I hadn't really thought about my art square. She brought it up because it was a piece I think other people had conferenced on. She wanted to give input on that to help me if I needed help on that, and I just wasn't very enthusiastic about the piece in general. It wasn't really going how I wanted it to, so I was more concerned about making the piece

look how I wanted it to originally instead of adding a whole bunch of new things into it.

I don't think the art square was at a point where it was ready to be revised. You don't write one paragraph and then bring it to her to revise. You write a page—several pages—until you really need revision. The art square was not ready to revise.

Ted then suggests three elements he feels are essential for a successful conference. First, the teacher and the student should be on the same wavelength, where "there's some agreement between the teacher and the person on what they're deciding about what is helpful." Second, the writer has to *want* to confer about the piece: "It's not an arbitrary thing where she just kind of says, 'What do you have for writing?' and then starts talking about it. If I didn't need help, then help's not necessarily helpful." Third, the teacher has to know when to stop the conference: "I thought it would have been helpful if I could have gone back and written [the Gestapo piece] right away." He has a clear conception of his needs. He is in charge.

Stability

This conference does significantly influence Ted's final draft of "To the Gestapo." He does *not* forget the idea he had come up with. After making several minor changes to his original three paragraphs, primarily to tighten the language, he adds a two-paragraph ending that "tied everything together":

> So how did you escape? On a boat to Canada? Or maybe on foot to South Africa, I bet that didn't sit right, the "Master Race" walking. Who did you leave behind to pick up your mess, to try and explain your actions? What did you tell the customs officers to get yourself in? What have you done in the last couple of years? Do you still go out in public, proudly declaring your relationship to Hitler? How does it feel to live in hiding as you made so many live?
>
> What do you think when you meet a Jew in a store? Do you still consider them inferior? Have 50 years been enough to see you're wrong? Can you really sleep with yourself at night? If a little child asks you, "Why were the Gestapo so mean?" what would you say? Can you answer these? Please, try, explain what happened to loved ones, why you were justified in your actions. What's wrong, doubting your actions? I would.

He considers the piece one of his best and includes it in his portfolio. He writes in his Case History:

The writing originated after learning about the Holocaust. One is flooded with so many questions, so much disbelief and so much anger. A good way to get it out is on paper. I had all my ideas but I did have a little problem in expressing them in a complete piece. Through several conferences I got enough input on how I wanted to put my thoughts down and soon did so.

Ted clearly recognizes the contributions of the different people with whom he has conferred, but note how he again retains ownership, stating, "I got enough input on how I wanted to put *my* thoughts down. . . ." Others, again, are not primarily there to feed him ideas, but to help him clarify and enhance his own.

Ted pays little attention to his art square. He hands in a final draft, as is required, but doesn't include it in his portfolio and doesn't mention it again in any of his evaluations. He does not value it.

This conference represents stability. A productive, academically-based relationship flourishes because Ted knows what he needs and can listen to Linda's suggestions thoughtfully, making informed decisions as to their merit. His conference indicates that with some students one may attend primarily to academics because that is what the student values, expects, and needs.

Yet Linda has an admonition. After the year ends she speculates that Ted, certainly a wonderful writer, might have gone even further if she had helped him tap more into his less academically-oriented moods and feelings with the same vigor she nudged more social students to explore the academic. But gender differences again appear to influence her instruction. She feels she had not developed a more emotionally oriented rapport with Ted because "I'm a female teacher." She had watched Ted work with a male teacher one day. "It was a totally different relationship. He really opened up to him, and he was fascinated with his writing. We really need models where we can see ourselves in the model."

When looking at the four students I present here, Linda's greater difficulties in the two conferences with males are not in themselves generalizable. However, her difficulties do fit into a larger pattern we had both recognized throughout the year. Gender issues should be something to which we attend more consciously when establishing working relationships with students. Linda feels her challenge is to do what she always tries to do: listen carefully to what is important to boys before responding to them, knowing that sometimes she might not be the perfect model. At the same time, she tries to introduce her students to a variety of authors who might serve as better immediate models. But, Linda says, she also wants to help students like Ted find and exploit a wider array of personal attributes they might not otherwise recognize, thus expanding the field of potential models within which they *can* see themselves.

The next conference shows a student on the other end of the affective continuum from Ted. This conference, which immediately follows Ted's on this day in March, demonstrates the complexity of Linda's job—the wildly different approaches she must adopt with different students, often within a span of seconds. Elena wants something very different from Linda than does Ted.

18

Elena Confers with
Someone Who Loves and Cares

E lena's conference is a meeting where a student finds emotional sustenance and acceptance at a period in her life when things seem bleak.
More than any other student in class, Elena views Linda as a loving
friend. Conferences for her are times to reconfirm and strengthen their social,
emotional bond. Elena, a committed, prolific writer on her own, rarely accepts academic feedback from Linda. Instead, she uses Linda as an audience
in thrall: a listener from whom only responses of amazement and approval are
acceptable. She needs someone to hear her and to help her laugh; her laughter keeps her writing.

Elena

Elena is not timid. Exuberant, talkative, and sometimes brazen, everyone in
class knows at least part of her story. Born in India, her parents had separated
and she came to the States last year to live with relatives. She knows how to
speak Italian, French, English, German, and several Indian dialects fluently;
she loves music and dancing and joking and teasing; and she constantly falls
in love. She is a born storyteller.

In fact, telling stories is what Elena most wants to do. She searches out
the people willing to listen to her and regales them with intricate and fas-
cinating accounts of her life. She goes to great lengths to confer with Linda,
either blatantly praising Linda's beauty in the hope Linda will cut another
conference short or sneaking her name to the top of the conference waiting

list. When she gets her audience she does everything in her power to hold it. Linda recounts one conference:

> Yesterday she grabbed me by the wrist and said, "No, you're going to listen to the *whole* thing," and before I went over to conference with her, I watched her mouth *every* word of the seven pages. She had *memorized.* I think what she was doing was, if she could maintain eye contact with me then I couldn't leave her. . . . It forced me to stay right beside her and listen. She wants someone just listening to her.

Two years ago, Elena was in an automobile accident. When she awoke from a three-month coma she had to overcome permanent major injuries to her brain and body. Formerly an excellent athlete, she now walks with a slight limp, her right hand sometimes shakes, and she suffers from blurred vision and slow speech. She has also lost a substantial portion of her short-term memory. Her recovery has been remarkable, but at this point therapists don't know how much more she will improve. In a country she does not know well, living far from her parents, struggling mightily to overcome the ravages of her accident, Elena often feels overwhelmed and lonely. Her self-described "best" experiences document milestones in her recovery after the accident— waking from her coma; standing, swimming, and talking again for the first time; remembering things she thought she had forgotten. Her "worst" experiences revolve around nightmares she had during her coma, fears about never again living with her little brother, and incidents stemming from her parents' separation.

Seventh grade had been enormously difficult for her. Still recovering from her injuries and unschooled in American culture, Elena had not found acceptance with many students. This year her classmates have come around but are still a little puzzled by what seems to them to be her exotic behavior. She has grown up in a variety of cultures and traveled the world, is articulate beyond her years, uses the English language better than many native speakers, is deeply philosophical, knows how to monopolize classroom conversations, and speaks extremely personally about her accident. Her words sound like languorous poetry—slow, rich, melodic, and flowing. She communicates more easily with adults than adolescents. Fortunately, she does have one close classmate, Diane, who is loyal, thoughtful, and caring—a true friend who understands and respects her.

Elena's other true friend is Linda. They developed a close relationship at the very beginning of the year. Elena had come into Linda's room while her aide went to get her lunch in the cafeteria. Linda asked her why she had no lunch and Elena replied, with a grave look on her face, that it was a special holiday in her country and she was fasting. Seeing Linda's serious acceptance of her response, Elena burst out laughing. The joke continued the next day as Linda watched Elena devour a candy bar. "Hmm, Elena," Linda remarked, dryly, "I see you're still fasting." Elena thought this was hysterical and for the rest of the year pointed out her continued "fast" as she wolfed down her lunches. Months later, Elena writes in her journal, "Mrs. Rief, you really and truly are my favorite teacher. You make me laugh so much!"

To Linda, Elena reveals her deepest thoughts: her agony over her separation from her parents and her belief that she does not live up to their expectations, her long list of those with whom she is in love, and the deep emotional effects of her accident. Unlike some students, Elena does not hide or temper deeply personal issues in Linda's presence. While almost always exuberant, flirtatious, and teasing in social situations, in private conversations and in her journal Linda is the person with whom Elena shares her despondency. She writes, "I always look happy and joyful on the outside, but on the inside no one knows how much I suffer." For Elena, Linda is much more valuable as the person who will listen while she pours out her heart than as a literacy expert. Elena means it when she says that she truly loves Linda Rief.

Elena's View of Herself

"I'd say that I was a fabulous writer if I weren't too modest," laughs Elena. She tells Linda, "You know that I write just for the joy of writing, don't you? Whenever I am sad or angry, or even happy, my journal is the best thing to help me empty my heart on." A self-described daydreamer, her writing ideas come from a different place than do Ted's. She says, "My *good* writing— which is *all* good—comes from my imagination, doesn't come from the books."

> I get the ideas for my pieces of my writing from my ideas, thoughts, experiences, dreams, nightmares (I have a lot), and most of them come from the dreams I had while I was unconscious (in coma). Till I was about three years old, my life was fabulous. Fantastic. I had a father and a mother who loved each other. After I was three, my life became horrible! My parents fought from morning till evening, I started losing friends at school . . . my own writing also comes from that.

Elena says, "I write anything. I write even inappropriate things, but I don't revise at all. I just write it down. But later on, after Mrs. Rief has checked, I read it a thousand times over." She claims that most of her stories end up "in the dustbin." For Elena, who insists that she writes perfectly the first time, revision and the final product aren't as important as the *act* of writing and the feedback it elicits.

She is ambivalent about reading. Part of her discomfort, according to aides and therapists, is that her lack of short-term memory prevents her from being able to remember things she has recently read. However, sometimes she enjoys reading very much: "I never 'like' reading. Sometimes I LOVE reading, sometimes I HATE reading. But mostly I read with my mind on some other planet." She reads almost every day, on the bus to school and before bed.

Her favorite book is *Charlie and the Chocolate Factory* (Dahl 1985), the first book she read after awaking from her coma. She credits its character, the highly active Willy Wonka, for helping her get better. "He was always jumping around and dancing while working. It wasn't exactly jealousy that I had gotten, but a craving that I had for doing what he was. I tried, tried . . . tried . . . and got to where I am now." She often describes her total absorption—being sucked into her books. In her journal, she sometimes converses with book characters. Responding to *Morning Is a Long Time Coming* (Greene 1993), she writes, "Calm down, Patty! You've already had three love affairs with: Anton, Michael, and Roger! You are only eighteen!"

For Elena, reading and writing are forms of escape. But while she has full control over her writing, her difficulty holding the context of a lengthy read makes the act less pleasurable for her.

Elena's Performance

Elena's work is intensely personal. Her journal looks more like a private diary than a public place to compile writing ideas for a class. As the year progresses, she writes letters to Linda expressing her fears and sorrows. She also uses her journal to vent her frustrations. In June, at the environmental camp that caps off the year for the eighth graders, she is placed in a separate bunk from her classmates so that her aide can help her more. In her journal she writes,

> How do you think I feel DOWN HERE while my room-mates are all UP THERE?! DON'T YOU FREAKIN' UNDERSTAND!?!! The only way that I can become NORMAL again is by being treated like a normal kid. I don't need MORE help than other kids do! I don't freakin' want an aide! I thank you for all you're doing for me, but I don't want more than other kids! Obviously if I have an aide, I'll take advantage of her—But how did I manage at the beginning of last year?

Later, sorry for her anger, she responds,

> Mrs. Rief—Please try to understand why I treated you like I did in my log. I am a girl who always fought/fights to get what she wanted/wants. Please tell the other teachers not to tell me that I'll never become normal—I mean: like I was before. I believe that I will, even though I know that I won't. It is

difficult to explain. It's like encouraging myself by believing that I will. If someone breaks that belief of mine, everything will go down the drain. Please tell that to all the other teachers.

Elena has a good grasp of dramatic conflict; her autobiographical essays clearly reflect her personal conflicts.

MY RIGHT HAND

I cannot bear it any more! My right hand is controlled by the brain, the brain thinks, and I am telling myself: "Don't shake right hand . . . DON'T!". . . But still, it shakes! How is it possible?! Do I have two brains? . . . One is thinking, "Shake, right hand. You will get more attention from everyone," and the other is thinking, "Don't shake, right hand. You will be considered more normal."

And who is the judge? Who makes the decision of which brain is correct? Do I have a third brain? The judge brain? And how does it make the decision? Do you believe in miracles? You better, after you read this story! Because this is one big miracle. And that too, is a true one!

The doctors I have seen say they can't say whether the tremors will stop, or not.

From this vignette one can already get a sense of her writing style. It is different from any other writer in the class. She always seems to be having a passionate discussion with someone imbedded in the page. Her writing is conversational but intense, and it always refers to things awe inspiring or other-worldly. She infuses her writing with words like "dream," "fantasy," and "mysterious."

Her lack of substantial revision makes it more difficult to gauge any evolution in her writing process, but throughout the year her writing remains consistently unique, mystical, mesmerizing, and touching. Her most frequent genres are poetry, essays about the nature of life and the world, accounts of her experiences, and wild fantasy stories. Elena writes for reasons that supersede academic requirements. She has a more personal and emotional purpose, exploring her fears, fantasies, and desires. In a poem to her brother she writes,

ARJUNA—LOVE

I have the craving—for living with you again
Like brother and sister
What have we been made for?
For living separated?
I love you, puppy mine

> And I want for that day
> Where we will be together again

During the second semester, Elena's studies the work of poet Naomi Shihab Nye, a choice that she feels fits beautifully with her own writing. "She describes my life somehow. Because of the atmosphere in her poems." She writes Nye a letter describing the connection between Nye's poetry and her life. Her coma dreams, she says, were similar to Nye's poems. Nye's concern with poor people and with nature are also Elena's topics. Elena uses her schoolwork to connect to a personal life both beautiful and harsh, a life with which she is trying to come to terms.

Elena's View of Language Arts Class

Elena adores language arts. "I think it's wonderful," she says. "There is a lively spirit in the class, I don't know. Kids are always bashing on each other!" She laughs. She feels there is nothing Linda can do to make the class better. "Nothing. I like her that much that I don't have anything to say."

Elena's View of Linda

But the best thing about language arts is Mrs. Rief. Mrs. Rief *is* language arts class. "I believe that she is my favorite teacher," says Elena.

Elena's relationship with her teacher is intensely personal. Describing Linda as a teacher, she avoids academics completely. Instead, she offers Linda's social and personal qualities, and the emotional sustenance she provides.

> She is very funny, very. She has lots of humor with me, and we joke a lot. I talk to her about my problems. I feel very close to her. I just tell her everything. . . . I just feel very safe with her. I think she acts very simply, she dresses very simply, and she's beautiful.

Linda's value in conferences has little to do with improving Elena's writing. Elena says, "Since we joke a lot—we joke tremendously—that's what helps me the most. Nothing else. I always was a good writer. Nothing else helps me besides the humor." Elena simply wants to laugh with Linda about her writing ideas, and she insists that Linda's friendship is much more helpful to her than Linda's duties as a teacher.

But this emotional relationship may still influence Elena's academic success. When asked if Mrs. Rief would be more helpful if she offered more academic direction and specific assignments, Elena adamantly replies, "No. Not at all. Totally the opposite, maybe." A more analytical approach may halt Elena's creative flow. This view influences the shape of Elena's conferences.

She firmly resists suggestions from Linda, insisting instead that her stories be heard for what they are: "When she gives any suggestions of how to improve the story, I will start arguing then. So, it's more like for me to read it to her." The only academic value of the conference comes in the form of writing ideas that pop up when Linda makes a suggestion. Elena says, "Well, I try to think of it. Then I totally go into another story and start writing another story, so the thing keeps multiplying itself."

Elena thinks Linda is a wonderful listener, again lauding her for bringing humor to their relationship. She says, "She comments on stuff, then I say something funny, then we both start laughing, then we make a joke out of the comment that she has given me. That's the type of teaching that I like." Unlike other teachers, she says, Linda listens to her in an authentic way.

> I know she listens to me because I *feel.* I have a feeling that she is very interested in me and that she likes me a lot, and that she wants to know more because I have so many adventures to tell, out of which three-quarters of them are not true!

To Elena, the teacher's reactions to the student are the most important thing. "I think that some of their reactions encourage. Mrs. Rief's reactions encourage me tremendously. . . . It encourages me to work harder in class."

Elena always notices Mrs. Rief writing and reading with the class and notes that none of her other teachers have ever done that. When I ask her if Linda's reading and writing affects her in any way, she straightens her shoulders and gives me a serious stare. "I feel very proud because I obviously know that she's going to write something *wonderful,* absolutely *wonderful,* the most *wonderful* thing about me. And crap about everyone else."

She begins to laugh uncontrollably.

The Conference

Elena has written her name on the board and eagerly awaits Linda's arrival. Linda leaves her conference with Ted, walks across the room, and sits down with her. At this point in the year Linda has a substantial history with her students, and she knows what to expect from Elena as they begin.

> I know that I need a lot of time for her, that no matter what this conference is about, she's going to direct it. She's got her own agenda. I have to be prepared in a kind way to say I have to move on or somehow get right to the point. . . . *Lately* I expect to hear a lot about swearing and obsessions with whom she loves latest. . . . And I have to respond to it somehow.

"I Want Her to Listen to My Voice"

As the conference begins, Elena cannot remember her exact reason for calling Linda over. However, she now has Linda's attention and is determined to keep it.

Elena: I, yesterday, finished a piece of writing with you. So, I did that and I forgot what I wanted to tell you.

Linda: Okay, this one is all done, right? And that's a great job. You did a wonderful job. All right.

Elena: And I wrote a quote from the book.

Linda: Yep. Excellent.

Elena: And I wrote this story, which is true.

The autobiographical story is entitled "The Mischief I Did." It begins with an account of her father and her eating together. She has included several footnotes in her draft.

> My father and I had just finished dinner at a restaurant named Aristo.
>
> I had eaten Palak Panir (a cheesy sauce) with rice, and my father mutton curry (sauce with goat meat) and naan (kind of pancake).
>
> After my father paid the bill for the food, we decide to go to Pondichery (Pondicherry in English, the French colony I live near to) 's beach and enjoy an ice-cream. My father bought his favorite ice-cream and said:
>
> "I scream
> You scream
> We all scream
> For ice-cream.
>
> Hmm . . . this 'gelato'* is good. What ice-cream did you get, Elena?"
>
> —I got butterscotch Papa.
>
> —Do you know what ice-cream I am eating?
>
> —No wonder you married an Italian woman. You hoped she would make Tutti Frutti for you every day.
>
> —Aah. What a smart daughterino** I have. Assai. Ghello coribu***. How did you guess that it is Tutti Frutti?
>
> —You get it every time.
>
> Then I jump into his arms, and he squeezes me tightly.
>
> After we finish our ice-cream, we jump on the motorcycle and go home. It is about half an hour on the bike. We reach home and my father asks me: "Tonight there is a full moon. Do you want to go for a swim in the sea? The water is very warm at night."
>
> —Yes. And let us take Poncho**** with us.

* Ice-cream in Italia
** What my father calls me. Actually, it stands for daughter.
*** Come. Let me give you a kiss.
**** Our handicapped dog.

Unfortunately for Elena, Linda is already familiar with this piece.

Linda: Okay. Now, wait a minute. You . . . now wait a minute. Is this the one I remember? Okay, you read part of this, yes . . .

Elena: No, I, I, no!

Linda: Yeah, I've read this, about the ice cream. You read part of this to me.

Elena: I did?

Linda: Yeah. Okay, which . . .

Elena: I don't think it's possible.

Listening to the tape, Linda laughs at Elena's adamant argument. "She just likes reading it again. That's all." Elena confirms: "I wanted her to listen to my voice again!"

But there is relief for Elena. Linda has only heard the first half of the piece.

Linda: Yes, because I remember you reading, "Do you want to go for a swim in the sea?" Okay. [Reads] All right, this part you *didn't* read to me. Why don't you read this page to me?

Elena: Okay.

Linda: I've heard all the rest.

Elena: [Reads] "So, I go up to my room and put my light blue swimming suit on. While we are swimming in the ocean, my father and I are having a nice chat. 'Elena, do you remember . . .'" he has kind of an accent, "' . . . do you remember when you learned how to swim?' 'Yes, Papa, you were working as a tourist guide and you took me for this tour. One day you took the people whom you were working with to see the different [Indian] things, and you left me in the care of the hotel manager. I was about five years old then. We were staying at a five-star hotel with a swimming pool.'"

Linda: Whoa!

Elena: "'So, I . . . so I stripped . . . and jumped [Laughs] . . .'"

Linda: Yeees? Okay.

Elena: "' . . . and jumped into the pool . . . into the . . .'" Where am I?

Linda: [Reads] "'So I stripped . . . and jumped in the fifteen-feet-deep . . .'"

Elena: I think, since it was twenty meters high.

Linda: Fifteen feet. That's pretty deep. Whoa! Okay.

Elena: No, it was ten meters high.

Linda: Okay.

Elena: So that must be roughly about fifteen feet.

Linda: Well, a meter is about three feet, so it would . . .

Elena: Oh, whoa!

Linda: [Laughs]

Elena: So ten multiplied . . . so thirty feet deep!

Linda: [Laughs] Whoa, that would be pretty deep.

Laughter

What strikes Linda most about this exchange is the humor (which Elena has said all year is Linda's greatest value to her):

> Just laughing with her, knowing that she's going to ad-lib between every sentence she reads — that she has something more to say but I can't seem to get her to say it in writing. *Every* sentence she reads, she looks up and tells me something about it. I would like to get her to put it in writing, because I think that's an incredible voice. But, she doesn't do that, yet. . . . I didn't tell her this, but I love the way she speaks like her father. "Elenaaa." She really accents it. She has an incredible voice. And it's probably because she speaks eight languages.

The conference continues. Elena reads again, and again orally footnotes with elaborations, as she does in every conference.

Elena: [Reads] "'So I jumped in the fifteen . . . thirty feet . . .'"

Linda: [Laughs]

Elena: "' . . . deep pool, so I had to learn how to swim. And I learned how to *swim!* Since I was so proud of myself, I ordered so much stuff for myself . . .'"—which is repeated, the word, in the same sentence, which is wrong!—"' . . . from the hotel manager, food and drinks.'" Food, ooh!

Linda: [Laughs]

Elena: [Reads] "'When you got back from work, the manager gave you a bill of five-hundred rupees.'" That's about thirteen dollars, I think. But that's nothing for here. For India, it is like half a thousand rupees. It's a lot. You can buy two bicycles or two bicycles and a tricycle with . . .

Linda: [Laughs] Maybe you want to say that there.

Elena: No.

Linda: Okay.

Elena's elaboration has sparked Linda's interest, and Linda suggests she add it to the piece. It is the *only* direct suggestion Linda will make during the entire conference. Linda speculates as to why Elena refuses to add.

> I think she's *impatient.* I think that this injury has slowed her down and I think she's impatient to just get everything down and do it well. And also, she believes she's a perfectionist, and she doesn't like to mess up the *page.* She was pretty shocked at the beginning of the year that I would even ask her to mess up the page. . . . I don't know if it's cultural as much as what she's learned through her previous teaching. Because she's been in schools where they've been pretty severe and pretty strict. People have *not* been kind to her. I think there's a *very* different kind of school. And that could be part of the culture. She's trying to get it perfect the first time.

In the conference, Elena continues her aside about her illicit lunch:

Elena: But it is sooo much for India. [Reads] " 'You were furious, so were coming to beat me. But I stood up just in time and said, "Papa, you cannot beat me, I learned how to swim!" So you didn't! Then we both cracked up. After the swim we went back home and slept.' The end."

Linda: [Laughs] You mean, when you cracked up you fell apart?

Elena: [Pause] Um . . . oh, but don't worry, I brought a tube of glue with me!

Linda offers no academic question, no suggestion, no explanations—just a laugh and a corny joke. Listening to the tape, Elena smiles. "I would like to tell her how much I like her. Maybe today, if there is time."

Linda: Oh, good! [Laughs] So everybody got put back together again. *Good!* Okay, so, what you're trying to tell us is . . .

Elena: This is my finished piece of writing for today.

Linda: Really.

Elena: Yes.

Linda: What if you have to do something to it?

Elena: [Pause] Umm, uhhh. . . .

Linda: [Laughs] No, no. It's fine. It's fine. I like the story of your dad, and he wouldn't really have beaten you, would he have? What do you mean "beat me"?

Elena: I was beaten by my parents like my whole life.

Nudges

Here Linda gives a joking probe to test again Elena's willingness to revise: "What if you have to do something to it?" It exemplifies how, despite the one-sided social nature of some conferences, Linda continues to look for tiny cracks—areas where she might still bring Elena's wonderful talk into the writing without destroying subsequent talk. Linda says, "I guess I was just trying to nudge her to see if she would add some stuff to it. I sort of know she won't, but I'm still trying to nudge."

Secrets

But another notable aspect of this exchange is one that some teachers have noted as problematic when they begin to welcome students' total lives into the classroom (Hall, Crawford, and Robinson 1997; Hawkins 1995): they begin to hear highly personal stories that they may not be equipped or permitted to address alone. Elena is telling a life story with serious implications. Linda says,

> I can't let a kid write, "He would beat me," and not ask her what that means. I don't know what that means in her culture. I don't know if it means he would spank her. I don't know if it means he would just say, "You were naughty." I can't just let that *pass*. And it could lead me to do something else. I can't project what would happen. If she told me some pretty graphic horrendous things in a great deal of detail I would definitely have to go to somebody.

In the conference, Elena describes being spanked and "thrashed" as a child for being mischievous, a practice she later claims is perfectly culturally acceptable in India. She describes her mischief.

Elena: This thing that I'm saying is because I was a very active kid, so I broke lots of plates and all that stuff and, let's say this, let's admit this—I trust teachers and I don't think that they'll think anything bad of me—I used to steal, too.

Linda: What? What would you steal?

Elena: All sorts of stuff: money . . .

Linda: From your parents?

Elena: Money and food. No, not from my . . .

Linda: From other people.

Elena: From . . . our land is on the beach and we have three huts that are for renting.

Elena, as she does in almost every conference, begins to reveal intimate aspects of her life to Linda. She says later, "I've told her, actually, every single secret of mine." She can't do this with other teachers. "I don't feel comfortable with them," she sighs.

Linda: So you would steal from people renting sometimes?

Elena: Rarely. No, from people renting it was mostly their food.

Linda: Yeah.

Elena: The kitchen was in the open. I used to go sneak in when they were not there. They were in the city or something.

Linda: But you know you would not do that now.

Elena: I positively know that.

Linda contemplates Elena's many elaborate tales evoked by this single piece of writing.

> These are her *stories.* I don't know sometimes if she's telling me stories. She will look you straight in the eye and say something just to *shock* you, and then she'll burst out laughing. I never know if what she's telling me is the truth or not. So, if she's not being hurt, if she's not hurting anyone else, I have to accept these as stories. Maybe it is about her. And it probably *is* about her. But I'm just listening. I know she has *never* added anything back into her writing. I also don't want to say to her every time she tells me something, "Why don't you write about it?" I *hate* that! . . . I just want her to talk, and maybe she'll find the stories for herself. And if she gets a reaction from people—they either laugh or they're shocked or they want to hear more—maybe she'll figure out for herself, "Hm, maybe that's a good story to write down."

Patience

Linda doesn't know if Elena's stories will someday translate into writing, but she speculates that this conferences serves another important purpose: "I'm letting her take pleasure in the fact that somebody's listening to her and learning about her without probing deeply."

> I'm letting her go off on some tangents sometimes, but also knowing when I have to pull back. I really was enjoying listening to her, and I think some of that rubs off on kids, too. They know that somebody really listened to them. Maybe that sense of the relationship that's *forming* there becomes part of when they bring the story back up again some other time.

Linda exhibits a patience with Elena she does *not* have with Jason. Yet she also continues to search for openings in the discussion where she might nudge Elena to revise. When Elena says, "I positively know that," Linda finds a place of closure from where she can redirect the conversation. She suspects Elena will not write about being spanked or stealing and says, "I feel in my ethical way that I've tied that little piece of the conference up, so let's go back to the piece of writing."

Linda: Yeah. Yeah. One question I would ask you about this piece, Elena: when you jumped in, what did you do to learn to swim? I mean, you said you jumped in this, so what do you remember doing?

Linda says, "I'm still trying to think of ways to get her into thinking about revising the writing, because there is going to be some time when adding information to it could make it a better piece."

Elena: I remember jumping in and, well, I hardly remember, but I guess that I jumped in and was forced to learn how to swim if I didn't want to drown.

Linda: Did you go to the bottom and come back up?

Elena: No.

Linda: Did you start moving your arms and legs?

Elena: Yes. Yes. But I still don't know how to swim properly. I still swim like a doggie, like a monkey, like a . . .

Linda: [Laughs]

Elena: . . . like a whatever. I mean, I could do this, but now that I've had the accident I have some problems with my left arm.

Linda: Would that strengthen your arm, though, starting to do that?

Elena: Very much. Swimming is, in fact, one of the best yogas.

Linda: Do you do that?

Elena: No opportunity.

Linda: Oh. That's too bad.

Linda's questions elicit new stories from Elena, which open up new potential topic avenues about her accident, her therapy, and her lack of opportunity to exercise. But Elena still will not connect her talk to *revision*. She wants to use this piece only as a starting point for the new stories that keep Linda *listening* to her.

The conference continues with another of Elena's stories, inspired by her statement that she has no opportunity to exercise. It caricatures some people she knows. I promised Elena I wouldn't repeat it. Suffice it to say, the story is wickedly accurate, it is rude, and it ends in profanity. It is also wildly funny.

Linda: [Laughing uncontrollably] Elena!

Elena: [Laughs uncontrollably]

Linda: Okay, I'm sorry, I was not laughing. Okay, I was not laughing.

Listening to the tape, Linda laughs again. "See, now she knows! She's got this incredible audience and she's going with it!" The conference has turned into a showcase performance.

At this point in the conference a couple of students come over to have Linda look at their work as Elena continues to laugh hysterically. Linda answers their questions and looks at their work, still somewhat flustered by Elena's brazen punch line. Later, Linda recognizes a problem: "I think the kids are coming in because I've been sitting here so long with Elena that they're getting a little bit bent out of shape, and *that's* the problem with dealing with her." But Linda sticks with her, she says, because she is enjoying the talk so much. Elena now also has confirmation that she has a great sense of humor. Linda says,

> I don't know if she'll ever write that stuff down. But I think writing and telling stories are to make people laugh or cry or feel differently, and she made me feel good about being in the classroom that day. She made me laugh, and a lot of kids don't make me laugh. And that's the *fun* of it.

As Linda begins to address students' questions and look over their work, Elena attempts to connect with her one last time:

Elena: I definitely am your favorite student.

Linda: Yes, you are. You are my favorite student. Absolutely. Definitely. I don't want to be called biased.

Linda laughs and says, "Well, what do you say? 'Of *course!*'"

Connection

Elena does not end up revising her piece. Her primary goal in the conference, she reiterates later, is to maintain her personal relationship with Linda: "I would like her to know more about my life and maybe [get her to] feel closer to me like I feel close to her." Despite the fact that it does not lead to further work, Linda sees the conference as successful: "I consider it a good conference because she got to tell a story. She got a *reaction* from people, which I think is what good writing does. *I learned a lot about her.*" Importantly, she says, Elena left feeling good about herself.

> She left laughing, and that kid doesn't have an awful lot to laugh about. I don't think she was thinking about her writing. I don't think it even *occurred* to her by the time she left. She wanted to confirm what other kids want to confirm: "Am I your favorite student?" They don't *ask* it, but if you're not listening to them then they think that you don't care about them. If you *are* listening to them then I think deep inside they feel, "I must be her favorite student because she took the time to listen to me and shut everybody else out around me." If that's what she left with, then that's perfectly okay. I would hope that that's okay for other kids, too. It's just giving them, "You exist, you're special in whatever way you have to be special." I'm sure she left laughing, and in a very assertive, proud way.

The conference, then, may still be considered "educative" if we define the word the way John Dewey does, as an experience that leads to new experiences. Linda's listening, I speculate, promotes in Elena a state of mind that *keeps* her writing, day after day, when other personal circumstances might well overwhelm her literary attempts. This relationship influences the student in ways that extend well beyond the realm of the text, or of language arts directly, but are nonetheless vital to the student's emotional and academic well-being and growth. The conference serves as an outlet of emotion—a point of connection between friends. It keeps the student happier and mentally healthier. Linda sees many students needing this emotional connection.

> With a lot of kids, several of the conferences are really not about the piece of writing. The kids just want someone to tell what they're doing. It really is a social conference: "Here's what I'm doing. What do you think? I just want you to know that I'm doing some writing or this is what I'm thinking." It really *isn't* specific; it's just not like Ted's all the time.
>
> I don't know if it *is* important to their writing. It's important to their *being.* It's important to their learning. It's important to the relationship between us that I care enough to listen.

"Sometimes there is no agenda," she says, and the conference must evolve from a caring, listening attitude. "I think kids only really work when they really care about what they're doing. And a lot of times that relationship between the teacher and the kid helps drive whether they do their work or not."

These conferences, more personal than academic, set up the proper atmosphere and attitude for future, more effective instances of actual instruction. Linda says, "*Very* few people talk about that. I think it *really* matters. If I can't get to kids personally, it's really hard to get that stuff out of them." The point is crucial. Research has focused on how conference responses address the *text,* but few (Tobin 1993) have contemplated how teacher responses set up the right relationship that can *then* lead to a more quality look at the text. Linda says,

> I think for young kids who are just emerging as better writers, maybe you spend more time with the social aspect of it, saying to them, "Yes, you're heard. Yes, your ideas are important." We may not have gotten to the ideas yet, but they may be just testing the waters to see if you care about what they have to say. Even if they're not really saying much at all, it's, "I want somebody to listen to me."

But, in reviewing the transcripts, Linda is also astounded at the complexity of her job. How do you care for so many students with such different needs?

> I look at the difference between Ted's conference and Elena's conference. Until I can look at them again, I don't even think about the *wildly* different ways they approach a piece of writing, and how you have to shift gears. . . . I know the minute the kid starts to talk there are probably a million things going on in my head about how I have to approach the kid. And when they're not going on in my head I usually have a bad conference because I'm not really listening or calling up all those things I know about that child. You have to shift gears *so* quickly. There is no *time.* I mean, it's like *nano*seconds.

The complexity, of course, also occurs in recognizing our own sometimes subconscious attitudes toward students. Linda feels an affinity with Elena because of the student's exuberance, receptiveness, and shared passion for writing. It is therefore easier to determine what she needs, even on the spur of the moment. Listening to *other* students often requires a more conscious, diligent effort.

19

How Will You Value Students' Voices?

How do we value students' voices? For many teachers it is the most important question, but finding a place to begin to answer it often seems like a daunting task. Here, then, I offer you some possible starting points, intended to help you reflect upon your teaching and learning for the explicit purpose of evolving your practice.

Answers From the Teacher

After I completed the manuscript for this book, Linda Rief read it. The experience, as you might now expect, pushed her toward deep self-reflection; she began to ponder what she had done well and where she felt she might improve. She said that reading her own story as presented through the lens of an outsider allowed her to see her teaching and learning in a new light.

Intrigued to learn what *she* had learned by having me in her class and by reading my manuscript, I interviewed her one more time. The answers Linda gave are a far better summary to this book than anything I could have written, because they come from a reader intent on using the research to improve her practice. Here is a list of some of Linda's important lessons.

1. Understand that Conferences Are More Complicated Than We Thought. "I have to know the student, know what kind of information helps her, know how far to push her, know if I *can* push her, know what her relationship is with the kids around her, know how much of a relationship I've built with her. . . . With this research I was hoping that the findings could be

195

succinctly stated. Perhaps even a *list*. I wanted to be able to say, 'This is all you have to do in a conference,' but that's not the way it is. And I knew that!"

2. Listen to and Learn from Students. "It's the only way I'll ever learn what to teach and how to teach it. I have to *think*—really focus on the child every time I go into a conference, and be able to shut out the rest of the class-room. And *that* is really hard.

"I was surprised to realize that students even watch my body language in a conference. I tend not to look directly at them as they read their writing, so that I can really focus on listening. Many students said this told them they had to use *words* to get across their meaning. They couldn't use facial expressions or body language to express their intentions.

"I have a harder time listening to kids who are resistant to writing. I have to learn to be more open and listen more patiently to find that spark of inter-est. I have to pay attention to gender, too. It is sometimes more difficult for me to relate to some of the writing that boys tend to do. I don't really under-stand the pieces with violence and gore. I have to understand the reasons why some boys write this way. I also learned that when conferring I often have to change my whole way of listening and thinking in a matter of a split second. Each student's need is so different; one way of hearing won't work. Finally, I learned that students understand why a conference was helpful or not helpful to them. Things that I had to think about they knew right away. If we ask them we can learn how to confer better."

3. Base Conferences on the Wants and Needs of the Student. "No mat-ter how much I want a student to do something, if he doesn't already see it for himself, he's not going to move forward with the information I give him. If he *does* use the information or suggestion, without knowing why or wanting it for himself, then he's just giving me the piece of writing he thinks I want from him. It isn't his writing anymore. I also learned, if a student says to me, 'I re-ally need help with this lead,' then I shouldn't tell her about the *ending*. When I stick to what I know works, which is the question, 'How can I help you?' then I succeed. Let students lead."

4. Understand that Students' Needs Are as Idiosyncratic as They Are. "Every student comes to a conference with a different want or need. I have to listen carefully to address each unique need on an individual basis. There is no list of set questions or suggestions that works for all writers."

5. Let Students Know that We Value Them as Individuals. "There are some kids for whom the conference is most important only because they need someone with whom they can talk. Other kids, who are not comfortable with themselves academically, see me only as a writer-reader and feel *more* un-comfortable. I need to build rapport with them to let them know that I value what they have to say, also. They need to know someone is just listening. Letting them know that may be an essential first step toward anything academic that comes later."

6. Shorter Conferences Are More Productive. "This really surprised me. The most important things are said in the first minute or two. If a student doesn't understand the questions or suggestions at the very beginning, and can't tell me what she needs from me, then the conference is not very helpful. More is not necessarily better in conferences. Kids are usually only enthused about one piece or willing to cope with one problem at a time. Once I've given them information that they can really use, then I have to leave and let them use it."

7. Dominate the Conversation Less and Have More Happen When We Leave. "The conference works best when I step out of the way of the students. I am *always* contributing information, experience, suggestions, and encouragement, but things work best when kids can say, 'I did this myself.' My job is to act as a sounding board to their own words, giving comments and suggestions that turn the decisions and thinking back to them."

8. Have Students Who Share Similar Interests Sit Together for Richer Conversations and Writing. "I don't think it works really well when I mix students up *too* heterogeneously. If they are interested in mountain biking or science fiction or Emily Dickinson, when they get together they seem to get more out of the conversation and support one another's writing in more productive ways. I want to group kids who feel comfortable with one another together at tables. But that comfort must still be academically driven. When this happens, conversations become more informal, but I learned that this talk leads directly to more effective work."

9. When Giving Students Suggestions, Give Them Examples of What We Mean. "If say, 'Why don't you use a question for your ending,' or, 'Why don't you try the present tense,' I can't just walk away. I have to show them an example. Even the most academically confident kids really like seeing models and specific examples."

10. We Have to Read and Write with Our Students. "The more I share my own writing—the false starts, the problems I run into, the techniques or strategies I use to try to clarify my ideas, the topics that are most meaningful to me—the more kids trust my comments to them in conferences."

Questions for You

I began this book with Linda Rief, introducing her as a teacher who values her students' voices. I end this book with you. When I first began pondering this last chapter, one of the readers of my manuscript asked me if I would consider ending the book with a brief appendix or checklist that listed the essential ingredients of successful classroom conversations and conferences. I thought a summation of this sort would be a fine idea with one important caveat—the appendix could not be viewed as a step-by-step process of how one creates the successful classroom. After all, this book shows how formulas of this type are the antithesis of what we need! Instead, I decided to focus on how you or I might work to create the conditions that promote effective communication. How might we create a classroom atmosphere where other concerns don't get in the way of fluid conversation, where students learn to use freedom responsibly, where they feel comfortable talking with their teacher and classmates, where they willingly listen to other people and know how to exploit feedback to further their work? This book shows you how one teacher gets to this point and works hard to stay there, and I think her practices serve as a model to us all.

But every one of us is different. We all take different paths to where we need to be. We need to find our own answers. What this chapter *can* do is ask you some critical questions you might try to answer in order to lead yourself toward a classroom that values voices. Your answers may lead to actions you can take to improve your classroom.

Identify Your Philosophy and Goals

- What are your goals for your students? Write a list of what you want them to leave with at the end of the year.
- What roles do you believe students should assume? Write them down, including metaphors that describe the roles (e.g., the student is an explorer).
- What roles do you believe teachers should assume? Write them down, including metaphors that describe the roles (e.g., the teacher is an explorer's guide).

Build a Communication Classroom

As you answer these questions, always consider how your answers match your philosophy and goals.

- How does your classroom layout promote or inhibit good conversation and independent work? Draw a map of your classroom to analyze the question. Draw a new map that shows how you might improve the classroom.
- How much of your students' work is displayed in their classroom? Make a list of new ways to display student work.
- How many books do you have in the class and what kinds are they? Survey students to find out what new books to get.

- Are your books displayed in ways that (1) invite students to pick them up and (2) allow students to access them easily? Write down how you might improve book display and access.

- What is your book checkout procedure? Create a system that helps everyone keep track of who has what books and makes book access easier.

- What type of furniture do you have in your class? Write down a list of how your furniture promotes easy conversation and allows students to work, read, and write quietly and comfortably. Make a separate list of improvement suggestions.

Build a Communication Curriculum

- What outlets of communication do you have so that students can reveal their interests and talents as readers, writers, and learners? Make a list of possible projects students can do at the beginning of the year to reveal these interests and talents.

- Are your curriculum themes ones in which students have at least a little prior knowledge upon which to build? Write down ideas for how students can help to create and shape a curriculum that offers time for independent research and extended reading, writing, and conversation.

- Do you have an integrated curriculum? Get together with teachers from other subject areas to see how your classes might inform one another.

- Do you have alternative literacy outlets (art, music, drama, etc.) for students who are reluctant readers and writers? Work with students to devise ideas for introducing alternative communication formats.

Organize for Student Independence

- Do students navigate the room efficiently and independently of your direction? Spend time watching and recording how they maneuver around the room to discover problems.

- How well do your students handle freedom of time and choice? With students, create a list of procedures that will give direction to their freedom.

- Do your current rules promote or inhibit student movement? With students, create a list of rules that will promote and channel their motion.

- Have your students internalized classroom organization, rules, and procedures so that following them has become second nature? Front-load your teaching of organization and procedures, focusing intensively on them at the beginning of the year.

- Are student writing, portfolios, journals, books, etc. organized and stored in ways that students can access them without your help? Create systems that allow independent student access.

- Are you diligent and consistent in requiring students to keep the room organized for easy flow? Make a plan for maintaining organization, rules, and procedures throughout the year.

- What outlets do you have for students to document and present their work efficiently to others? Create a list of outlets for expression, including portfolios and journal sharing.

Read, Write, and Share Good Work—Including Your Own

- How often do you share students', and your own, good work with the class? Schedule a time every day when you share.

- How often do you share students', and your own, writing processes? Schedule a time every day when you share.

- How often do you read and write with your students? Schedule at least one day a week where you read and write with them.

- Do you live the life of a student? Do student assignments in order to learn which ones are effective.

- What lessons do you give that show how good writers always write about personally relevant topics? Create a list of possible mini-lessons.

- What lessons do you give that show how good writers give details and relevant specifics in their writing? Create a list of possible mini-lessons.

- What lessons do you give that show the importance of writing a lot and revising in order to craft a piece? Create a list of possible mini-lessons.

- Do you take risks with your teaching, knowing that some of your attempts might fail (thus prompting excellent learning opportunities)? Make a list of how you might take more risks and share more of your failures, using them as modeling lessons.

- What current practices will you give up so that you can replace them with more authentic reading, writing, and sharing? Make a list.

- Do you allow students to abandon reading books or writing pieces if they have no interest in them? Allow them to.

Promote Student Talk that Inspires New Writing and Reading

- How easily do students talk in your class? Write down a list of steps you can take to promote ease of talk.

- During a lesson, how much time do you spend talking? Write ideas for lessons where students talk more than you do.

- Does the work you present and share with students inspire students to connect it to aspects of their own lives? Record and analyze any connections between your presentation and their talk and work in order to create a plan for improvement.

- Do you identify and promote students' social talk and stories as places from which good writing comes? Record instances when it does, then use them in a mini-lesson.

- Do the students initiate topics in your class that you discuss? Write a list of obstacles to student initiation and try to eliminate them.

- Do students use music, drama, art, etc. in language arts class? Create mini-lessons that offer these options.

Reflect on How You Confer

To answer these questions, you will need to tape-record several conferences with your students and analyze them.

- What do your conferences with students generally look, sound, and feel like? Analyze your recordings for patterns.

- Do you move away from your general procedures when you see that a student needs something different?

- Who usually initiates conferences in your class, you or the students?

- Do your conferences encourage students to evaluate their reading and writing?

- Do students share control of the conference, defining the agenda and talking more than you do?

- Do your conferences encourage gaps of information in students' writing?

- Do you find yourself putting suggestions from your *own* agenda into students' heads?

- Do students talk about things that are truly important to them in conferences?

- What do you do more: ask questions, give suggestions, or give explanations?

- Do you talk more about ideas or conventions in conferences?
- Do your questions inspire students to keep talking?
- Do your suggestions come from what the student has told you?
- Do your questions relay back to the student what he or she has just said?
- Do students draw, act, or sing during conferences in order to explain to you what they mean?
- Does students' oral talk in conferences help them eliminate writer's block? Analyze your recordings for instances when students say, "Wait! I have an idea!"
- In conferences, do students usually discover their own solutions to their dilemmas?
- Do you stop a conference the minute a student has an idea to move forward independently?
- Do you focus on one primary concern per conference?
- How long are your conferences? Time your recorded conferences.
- When talking with students do you allow thoughtful silences that give them time to think? Time the pauses in your recorded conferences.

Become a Better Listener

Your answers to the questions in the section above will give you valuable information. Use what you learn to help you become a better listener and responder.

- How do you define good listening? Write down your definition.
- How good are you at listening? Write separate lists of when you were a good listener and when you weren't.
- Would you define yourself more as a "giver of knowledge" or a "listener and responder"? Write down how your answer affects your conversations with students.
- How well do you know your students' tastes and interests? Create a list of how you might learn them.
- How and where do you sit when conferencing with students? Write down what message this sends them and decide what changes you need to make.
- When a conference begins, do you try to learn the specific need the student has? Begin to ask, "How can I help you?" consistently.

- Does the student read his or her text while you listen or do you read the text yourself? Let students read and analyze how it affects your ability to listen.

- Do you give specific praise based on what you have learned? In every conference, look for one aspect of the writing from which the student can build.

- Do you go into a conference hoping to teach a student or hoping to learn from a student? Begin to ask questions to which you really don't know the answers so that students can teach you.

- How well do you hear it when a student has excitement—a "spark in the throat"—during a conference or conversation? Consciously listen for those sparks.

Establish Relationships that Encourage Talk and Growth

- How would your students describe you and their relationships with you? Evaluate whether this is the description of someone with whom you, yourself, would feel comfortable conversing.

- How well do you deal with students you don't like or who have a different agenda than you? How might you improve your approach? Make a list of these students and, in conference, focus on learning what their interests are.

- How comfortable are your students talking one-on-one with you? List possible reasons why or why not.

- Would students say you care about them and their work? List ways in which you show you care.

- Does your care make students more willing to discuss personally relevant topics, ideas, and interests? List possible reasons why or why not.

- Does your caring result in a deeper receptivity that allows you to respond more effectively? List instances in which this happens.

- Are you willing to abandon your academic agenda in order to build social relationships that will encourage students to talk about personally relevant ideas (which might lead to academic success)? Make a list of times you have been willing to do this.

- Do you have rapport with your students? Write down which factors contribute most to this rapport or lack of rapport.

- Are your conferences enthusiastic, animated, and full of humor? List specific reasons why or why not.

- Do you feel social or intellectual camaraderie when conferencing with students? List ways in which you do.
- Are students willing to consider your writing suggestions thoughtfully? Interview them to find out how they use your suggestions.
- Are students willing to reject your suggestions for logical reasons, or do they always adopt your suggestions? Interview them to find out which ideas they reject, and why.
- Do your conferences sound more like conversations—"good healthy chats"—or more like lessons? Interview students to get their impressions.
- Are students comfortable enough with you to allow you to challenge them academically without inhibiting their motivation? Document instances in which they are.
- Do students adopt your ideas as their own without realizing it? Document instances.
- Do you treat male and female students differently in conferences? Analyze your recordings to find patterns.
- How might you need to address males and females differently? Write a list of speculations.
- How well informed are you about the effects of adolescence on students' attitudes and performance? Create a plan for learning more about adolescence.
- What are your students' histories with other language arts teachers? Learn more about their histories in order to address any previously negative relationships.
- How well do you deal with the different personalities in your class? Make a list of how you individualize your approach.
- Are you fascinated by what students are saying when you conference? If not, analyze what parts of their talk you are listening to in order to listen to other parts.
- Is your conference speaking style direct or indirect? Speculate on how it affects students' attitudes and performance.

Address Emotion

- Do you consciously address emotion as one of the influences on your students' writing and reading work? Ask yourself why or why not and consider changes you need to make.

- How might you determine whether individual students work from a more emotionally-based foundation or a more academically-based one? Interview students and use what you learn to individualize your instruction.

- Do you recognize the students who want to focus more exclusively on academic concerns during conferences? Document individual work patterns.

It takes courage to open up our professional lives to scrutiny. As teachers who value students' voices, we know this well. However, it is this scrutiny—this struggle to listen and learn and grow—that turns our practice into art.

Afterword

When Doug Kaufman called to tell me he wanted to conduct his doctoral research in my classroom, I think I shouted, "I won! I won! Thank you!" Several weeks earlier Doug had told me he was visiting a number of classrooms and teachers in his search for a place to conduct his research about *listening* with respect to a teacher of writing. When he finally chose my classroom I felt like I had won the lottery.

"You *want* someone watching and listening to you every day, the whole year?" a colleague asked, incredulous.

I did. And I am so grateful. Doug held up a professional mirror to me day after day by recording not only all that he heard, but by asking questions that constantly turned my thinking back again and again to what I had done, what the kids had done, and what those things meant. What's working? What isn't working? What *was* I thinking? In what ways were *they* thinking and growing?

Doug said it takes courage to open our professional lives to such public scrutiny. It's not courage. It's simply smart. In the same way that my best conferences and conversations with students are sounding boards for what they already know, Doug's observations, meticulous recordings and transcripts, and questions (sometimes endless) pushed my thinking so hard I could finally see and hear myself as I interacted with students. It is a privilege we are denied when we are alone in our classrooms. It is a perspective too difficult to see well by ourselves. Doug's scrutiny let me truly be a *reflective practitioner* because there was someone who listened so well I could talk, and ask and answer the questions for myself.

Doug is an intelligent, meticulous researcher because he is an astute listener. In conversations with him, I was the one always talking. The more I talked, the more I learned. It was a practice that I try to remember every time I sit down next to a student for a conference.

What is the most compelling lesson I learned from having a researcher in my classroom? There is no one right way to have a writing conference. When I enter the conversation as an interested listener, who can respond honestly, enthusiastically, and directly to the wants and needs of the student, the most profound things happen with the writing.

In the words of the little bat in *The Bat-Poet,* "The trouble isn't making poems, the trouble's finding somebody that will listen to them."

—Linda Rief

Jarrell, Randall. 1987. *The Bat-Poet.* New York: Macmillan Publishing Company.

References

Atwell, Nancie. *In the Middle: Writing, Reading, and Learning with Adolescents.* Portsmouth, NH: Boynton/Cook, 1987.

————. *Side by Side: Essays on Teaching to Learn.* Portsmouth, NH: Heinemann, 1991.

Bakhtin, M. M. *The Dialogic Imagination: Four Essays.* Austin: University of Texas Press, 1981.

Barbieri, Maureen. *Sounds from the Heart: Learning to Listen to Girls.* Portsmouth, NH: Heinemann, 1995.

Barbieri, Maureen, and Linda Rief (Eds.). *Workshop 6: The Teacher as Writer.* Portsmouth, NH: Heinemann, 1994.

Barnes, Douglas. *From Communication to Curriculum.* 2nd ed. Portsmouth, NH: Heinemann, 1992.

————. "Talking and Learning in Classrooms: An Introduction." *Primary Voices K–6.* 3.1 (1995): 2–7.

Bergeron, Bette S. "What Does the Term Whole Language Mean? Constructing a Definition from the Literature." *Journal of Reading Behavior.* 22.4 (1990): 301–329.

Brand, Alice. "The Why of Cognition: Emotion and the Writing Process." *College Composition and Communication.* 38.4 (1987): 436–443.

————. "Social Cognition, Emotions, and the Psychology of Writing." *Journal of Advanced Composition.* 11.2 (1991): 395–403.

————. "Defining Our Emotional Life: The Valuative System—A Continuum Theory." *Presence of Mind: Writing and the Domain Beyond the Cognitive.* Eds. Alice Glarden Brand and Richard L. Graves. Portsmouth, NH: Boynton/Cook, 1994a. 155–165.

————. "Defining Our Emotional Life: The Cool End (Plus Motivation)." *Presence of Mind: Writing and the Domain Beyond the Cognitive.* Eds. Alice Glarden Brand and Richard L. Graves. Portsmouth, NH: Boynton/Cook, 1994b. 167–178.

Britton, James. *Language and Learning.* 2nd ed. Portsmouth, NH: Boynton/Cook, 1993.

Brown, Karen K., Mary Jane Blasi, Danling Fu, and Bess Altwerger. "Forging New Roles and Relationships in Literature Studies." *The New Advocate.* 9.3 (1996): 209–225.

Bruffee, Kenneth. "Collaborative Learning and the 'Conversation of Mankind.'" *College English.* 46.7 (1984): 635–652.

Bruner, Jerome. *Actual Minds, Possible Worlds.* Cambridge, MA: Harvard University Press, 1986.

Carnicelli, Thomas A. "The Writing Conference: A One-to-One Conversation." *Eight Approaches to Teaching Composition.* Eds. Timothy R. Donovan and Ben W. McClelland. Urbana, IL: National Council of Teachers of English, 1980. 101–131.

Cazden, Courtney B. *Classroom Discourse: The Language of Teaching and Learning.* Portsmouth, NH: Heinemann, 1988.

Cisneros, Sandra. "Eleven." *Woman Hollering Creek.* New York: Vintage, 1992.

Coman, Carolyn. *What Jamie Saw.* Arden, NC: Front Street, 1995.

Creech, Sharon. *Walk Two Moons.* New York: HarperTrophy, 1996.

Crichton, Michael. *Jurassic Park.* New York: Ballantine, 1990.

Dahl, Roald. *Charlie and the Chocolate Factory.* New York: Knopf, 1985.

Delpit, Lisa. *Other People's Children: Cultural Conflict in the Classroom.* New York: The New Press, 1995.

Dewey, John. *Experience and Education.* New York: Collier, 1963 (First published in 1938).

Dunn, Saundra, Susan Florio-Ruane, and Christopher Clark. "The Teacher as Respondent to the High School Writer." *The Acquisition of Written Language: Response and Revision.* Ed. Sarah Warshauer Freedman. Norwood, NJ: Ablex, 1985. 33–50.

Dyson, Anne Haas. *Social Worlds of Children Learning to Write in an Urban Primary School.* New York: Teachers College Press, 1993.

Eccles, Jacquelynne S., Carol Midgely, Allan Wigfield, Christy Miller Buchanan, David Reuman, Constance Flanagan, and Douglas MacIver. "Development During Adolescence: The Impact of Stage-Environment Fit on Young Adolescents' Experiences in Schools and in Families." *American Psychologist.* 48.2 (1993): 90–101.

Edelsky, Carole, Bess Altwerger, and Barbara Flores. *Whole Language: What's the Difference?* Portsmouth, NH: Heinemann, 1991.

Erikson, Erik H. *Childhood and Society.* New York: Norton, 1950.

Fleckenstein, Kristie S. "Defining Affect in Relation to Cognition: A Response to Susan McLeod." *Journal of Advanced Composition.* 11.2 (1991): 447–453.

Fletcher, David C. "On the Issue of Authority." *Dynamics of the Writing Conference: Social and Cognitive Interaction.* Eds. Thomas King and Mary Flynn. Urbana, IL: National Council of Teachers of English, 1993. 41–50.

Floriani, Ana. "Negotiating What Counts: Roles and Relationships, Texts and Contexts, Content and Meaning." *Linguistics and Education.* 5 (1994): 241–274.

Flower, Linda. *The Construction of Negotiated Meaning: A Social Cognitive Theory of Writing.* Carbondale, IL: Southern Illinois University Press, 1994.

Flower, Linda, and John Hayes. "A Cognitive Process Theory of Writing." *College Composition and Communication.* 32 (December 1981): 365–387.

Fox, Mem. *Radical Reflections.* San Diego: Harcourt Brace Jovanovich, 1993.

———. *Wombat Divine.* San Diego: Harcourt Brace Jovanovich, 1996.

Frank, Anne. *Diary of a Young Girl: The Definitive Edition.* New York: Anchor, 1996.

Freedman, Sarah Warshauer. *Response to Student Writing* (NCTE Research Report No. 23). Urbana, IL: National Council of Teachers of English, 1987.

Gere, Anne Ruggles, and Ralph S. Stevens. "The Language of Writing Groups: How Oral Response Shapes Revision." *The Acquisition of Written Language: Response and Revision.* Ed. Sarah Warshauer Freedman. Norwood, NJ: Ablex, 1985. 85–105.

Gilligan, Carol. *In a Different Voice: Psychological Theory and Women's Development.* Cambridge: Harvard University Press, 1982.

Gilmore, Perry. "Spelling 'Mississippi': Recontextualizing a Literacy Related Speech Event." *Anthropology and Education Quarterly.* 14.4 (1983): 233–255.

———. "'Gimme Room': School Resistance, Attitude, and Access to Literacy." *Journal of Education.* 167.1 (1985): 111–128.

Goffman, Erving. *The Presentation of Self in Everyday Life.* New York: Anchor, 1959.

Graves, Donald H. *Writing: Teachers and Children at Work.* Portsmouth, NH: Heinemann, 1983.

———. *Discover Your Own Literacy.* Portsmouth, NH: Heinemann, 1990.

———. *A Fresh Look at Writing.* Portsmouth, NH: Heinemann, 1994.

———. Keynote Address. University of New Hampshire October Literacy Conference. 17 Oct. 1997.

Greene, Bette. *Morning Is a Long Time Coming.* New York: Laurel Leaf, 1993.

Haley, Alex. *Roots.* New York: Doubleday, 1976.

Hall, Nigel, Leslie Crawford, and Anne Robinson. "Writing Back: The Teacher as Respondent in Interactive Writing." *Language Arts.* 74.1 (1997): 18–25.

Hansen, Jane. *When Learners Evaluate.* Portsmouth, NH: Heinemann, 1998.

Harris, Muriel. *Teaching One to One: The Writing Conference.* Urbana, IL: National Council of Teachers of English, 1986.

Hawkins, Carol. "In the Wake of Whispers: Formulating a Response to a Student Narrative on Abortion." *NWSA Journal.* 7.3 (1995): 95–107.

Hayden, Torey. *One Child.* New York: Avon, 1995.

Heath, Shirley Brice. *Ways With Words: Language, Life, and Work in Communities and Classrooms.* New York: Cambridge University Press, 1983.

Ianni, Francis A. J. "Providing a Structure for Adolescent Development." *Phi Delta Kappan.* May (1989): 673–682.

Jacobs, Suzanne E., and Adela B. Karliner. "Helping Writers to Think: The Effect of Speech Roles in Individual Conferences on the Quality of Thought in Student Writing." *College English.* 38.5 (1977): 489–505.

Johnson, Jo Ann B. "Reevaluation of the Question as a Teaching Tool." *Dynamics of the Writing Conference: Social and Cognitive Interaction.* Eds. Thomas King and Mary Flynn. Urbana, IL: National Council of Teachers of English, 1993. 34–40.

Johnston, Peter H. *Knowing Literacy: Constructive Literacy Assessment.* York, ME: Stenhouse, 1997.

Kaufman, Douglas. "The Value of Blabbing It, or How Students Can Become Their Own *Go Yows.*" *All That Matters: What Is It We Value in School and Beyond?* Eds. Linda Rief and Maureen Barbieri. Portsmouth, NH: Heinemann, 1995.

———. *In Pursuit of "A Good Healthy Chat": The Roles of Organization and Rapport-Building in Effective Middle School Literacy Instruction.* Doctoral dissertation. University of New Hampshire. Durham, NH, 1998.

King, Stephen. *Nightmares and Dreamscapes.* New York: G.K. Hall, 1994.

Lowry, Lois. *The Giver.* New York: Houghton Mifflin, 1993.

Marcia, James. "Identity Formation in Adolescence." *Handbook of Adolescent Psychology.* Ed. J. Adelson. New York: Wiley, 1980.

McCarthey, Sarah J. "The Teacher, the Author, and the Text: Variations in Form and Content of Writing Conferences." *Journal of Reading Behavior.* 24.1 (1992): 51–82.

———. "Authors, Text and Talk: The Internalization of Dialogue from Social Interaction During Writing." *Reading Research Quarterly.* 29.3 (1994): 201–231.

McLeod, Susan. "Some Thoughts About Feelings: The Affective Domain and the Writing Process." *College Composition and Communication.* 38.4 (1987): 426–435.

———. "The Affective Domain and the Writing Process: Working Definitions." *Journal of Advanced Composition.* 11.1 (1991): 95–105.

———. "Pygmalion or Golum?: Teacher Affect and Efficacy." *College Composition and Communication.* 46.3 (1995): 369–386.

Mehan, Hugh. *Learning Lessons: Social Organization in the Classroom.* Cambridge, MA: Harvard University Press, 1979.

Murray, Donald M. *Learning by Teaching: Selected Articles on Writing and Teaching.* Portsmouth, NH: Boynton/Cook, 1982.

———. *A Writer Teaches Writing.* 2nd ed. Boston: Houghton Mifflin, 1985.

———. *Write to Learn.* 4th ed. Fort Worth: Harcourt Brace Jovanovich, 1993.

Myers, Jamie. "The Social Contexts of School and Personal Literacy." *Reading Research Quarterly.* 27.4 (1992): 297–337.

Newkirk, Thomas. "The Writing Conference as Performance." *Research in the Teaching of English.* 29.2 (1995): 193–215.

Newkirk, Thomas, and Patricia McClure. *Listening In: Children Talk About Books (and Other Things).* Portsmouth, NH: Heinemann, 1992.

Noddings, Nel. *The Challenge to Care in Schools: An Alternative Approach to Education.* New York: Teachers College Press, 1992.

Oye, Paula M. "Writing Problems Beyond the Classroom: The Confidence Problem." *Dynamics of the Writing Conference: Social and Cognitive Interaction.* Eds. Thomas King and Mary Flynn. Urbana, IL: National Council of Teachers of English, 1993. 111–119.

Rief, Linda. *Seeking Diversity: Language Arts with Adolescents.* Portsmouth, NH: Heinemann, 1992.

————. "Writing for Life: Teacher and Student." *Workshop 6: The Teacher as Writer*. Eds. Maureen Barbieri and Linda Rief. Portsmouth, NH: Heinemann, 1994. 84–101.

————. "Staying Off-Balance and Alive: Learning from My Students." *All That Matters: What Is It We Value in School and Beyond?* Eds. Linda Rief and Maureen Barbieri. Portsmouth, NH: Heinemann, 1995. 5–29.

————. *Vision and Voice: Extending the Literacy Spectrum*. Portsmouth, NH: Heinemann, 1999.

Rief, Linda, and Maureen Barbieri. *All That Matters: What Is It We Value in School and Beyond?* Portsmouth, NH: Heinemann, 1995.

Rogers, Carl R. *Client Centered Therapy: Its Current Practice, Implications, and Theory*. Boston: Houghton Mifflin, 1951.

————. *On Becoming a Person*. Boston: Houghton Mifflin, 1961.

————. *Freedom to Learn*. Columbus: Charles E. Merrill, 1969.

Rosenblatt, Louise. *The Reader, the Text, and the Poem*. Carbondale, IL: Southern Illinois University Press, 1978.

Rowe, Mary Budd. "Wait-Time and Rewards as Instructional Variables, Their Influence on Language, Logic, and Fate Control: Part One— Wait-Time." *Journal of Research in Science Teaching*. 11.2 (1974): 81–94.

Rylant, Cynthia. *When I Was Young in the Mountains*. New York: Dutton, 1992.

Sadker, Myra, and David Sadker. *Failing at Fairness: How America's Schools Cheat Girls*. New York: Scribners, 1994.

Sender, Ruth Minsky. *The Cage*. New York: Bantam, 1988.

Siegel, Janna, and Michael F. Shaughnessy. "There's a First Time for Everything: Understanding Adolescence." *Adolescence*. 30.117 (1995): 217–221.

Silverstein, Shel. *A Light in the Attic*. New York: HarperCollins, 1981.

Slattery, Patrick J. "Using Conferences to Help Students Write Multiple Source Papers." *Dynamics of the Writing Conference: Social and Cognitive Interaction*. Eds. Thomas King and Mary Flynn. Urbana, IL: National Council of Teachers of English, 1993. 80–87.

Sperling, Melanie. "I Want to Talk to Each of You: Collaboration and the Teacher-Student Writing Conference." *Research in the Teaching of English*. 24.3 (1990): 279–321.

Sperling, Melanie, and Sarah Warshauer Freedman. "A Good Girl Writes Like a Good Girl: Written Response to Student Writing." *Written Communication*. 4.4 (1987): 343–369.

Tannen, Deborah. *You Just Don't Understand: Women and Men in Conversation*. New York: Ballantine, 1990.

Taylor, David. "A Counseling Approach to Writing Conferences." *Dynamics of the Writing Conference: Social and Cognitive Interaction*. Eds. Thomas Flynn and Mary King. Urbana, IL: National Council of Teachers of English, 1993. 24–33.

Taylor, Denny. *Learning Denied*. Portsmouth, NH: Heinemann, 1991.

Thomas, Dene, and Gordon Thomas. "The Use of Rogerian Reflection in Small-Group Writing Conferences." *Writing and Response: Theory, Practice, and Response*. Ed. Chris M. Anson. Urbana, IL: National Council of Teachers of English, 1989. 114–126.

Tobin, Lad. *Writing Relationships: What Really Happens in the Composition Class*. Portsmouth, NH: Boynton/Cook, 1993.

Vygotsky, Lev. *Mind in Society: The Development of Higher Psychological Processes*. Cambridge: Harvard University Press, 1978.

———. *Thought and Language*. Cambridge: MIT Press, 1986.

Walker, Carolyn P., and David Elias. "Writing Conference Talk: Factors Associated with High- and Low-Rated Writing Conferences." *Research in the Teaching of English*. 21.3 (1987): 266–285.

Weaver, Constance. *Reading Process and Practice: From Socio-Psycholinguistics to Whole Language*. 2nd Ed. Portsmouth, NH: Heinemann, 1994.

Wells, Gordon. *The Meaning Makers: Children Learning Language and Using Language to Learn*. Portsmouth, NH: Heinemann, 1986.

Wiesel, Elie. *Night*. New York: Bantam, 1982.

Wigginton, Eliot. *Sometimes a Shining Moment: The Foxfire Experience*. New York: Anchor, 1985.

Williams, Margery. *The Velveteen Rabbit*. New York: Camelot, 1996.

Wright, Richard. *Black Boy*. New York: HarperPerennial, 1993.